THE EDUCATION OF AN URBAN MINORITY

THE URBAN LIFE IN AMERICA SERIES
RICHARD C. WADE, GENERAL EDITOR

THE EDUCATION OF
AN URBAN MINORITY

Catholics in Chicago, 1833-1965

JAMES W. SANDERS

NEW YORK

OXFORD UNIVERSITY PRESS

1977

To my mother

Foreword

We no longer need to be told that constant mobility is the central fact of urban life in modern America. Scholars for more than a decade have carefully described and analyzed the ceaseless movement in our cities. Not only has the population risen dramatically, but internal migration is occurring on an even larger scale. We are just beginning to assess the consequences of this continuing change on metropolitan institutions. The kinetic quality of city life has always made public policy-making difficult. Programs based on a current set of assumptions often become obsolete before implementation. Although some problems readily lend themselves to simple solutions, others are subject to unforeseen setbacks.

The building and the maintaining of an educational system have been especially difficult. The law early required schooling for all children in the elementary years. Later the requirement was extended to include secondary education and the cities had to contend with soaring increases in numbers. Urban systems never really did catch up with the increasing demand. The number of schools required for one decade was hopelessly inadequate for the next. Nor was building the only problem. There were never enough teachers or administrators. But the public educational system always had one trump card—the tax levy. Growing cities furnished a continuously expanding tax base for one of their most essential services. The financing was seldom generous, but there was enough money to keep the doors open for ever-increasing school populations.

Most of the recent scholarship in the history of education has concerned itself with this growth and the organizing ideas that informed the development of the public school system. And well it might since most Americans attended public institutions. Yet there is also another educational tradition in this country, which is comprised of private schools. Although some are simply tuition schools, others are religious. The parochial systems have had less scholarly attention despite their importance. This is especially true of the Catholic schools, which serve a significant portion of our urban population.

In *The Education of an Urban Minority*, James Sanders goes a long way toward filling that gap. The book is both a detailed description and an arresting analysis of the growth of the entire Catholic education system in Chicago from its early beginnings in the nineteenth century to 1965. In that period, Chicago developed the largest Catholic school system the world has ever seen. The author defines education very broadly, to include charitable activity, settlement houses, youth groups, and professional training, as well as more formal instruction, which encompasses everything from the primary schools to the universities. This is history on a large scale.

The choice of Chicago is a happy one. The Diocese was not only immense but encompassed an extraordinary ethnic mixture. It began as French but quickly became Irish and German. Later Southern and Eastern Europe poured in a dozen other nationalities. The handling of the inevitable conflicts by the Diocese is an important theme of the book. The competing ethnic groups were ultimately reconciled when the national parishes were replaced by territorial ones and the Cardinal insisted on a uniform curriculum with English as the primary language. The cutting-off of immigration facilitated the orderly, though not always happy, phasing out of the national parishes. Mr. Sanders is not unaware of the irony that the Catholic Church should be a more effective instrument of "Americanization" than the public schools for many immigrant children.

The welding together of national churches into a consolidated system throughout the Chicago metropolitan area was the achievement of George Cardinal Mundelein. Inheriting a maze of self-governing national churches and weak, impoverished elementary schools in 1916, he succeeded, before his death in 1939, in erecting a relatively prosperous and comprehensive structure to meet the educational needs of all his parishioners, young and old. This achievement has few analogues in the history of American education. The author was the first scholar to have access to the Mundelein papers and his use of them allows new insights into the building of this extraordinary empire.

But Mr. Sanders is too good a historian to believe that it was only the force of the Cardinal's personality that made the Chicago Catholic educational system succeed. The author places the system directly in the context of the development of Chicago to show that Mundelein would never have succeeded if he had not moved with the grain of the city's growth, with his financial base the new prosperity of Chicago's Catholics in the 1920's. The establishment of a uniform curriculum sprang from the high mobility in the area. Catholic families were no less on the move than other families and they demanded schools that served their newly acquired status. The residual anti-Catholicism in the city also promoted a cohesiveness among the faithful, while the Irish captivity of inner city politics provided protection in the public arena.

The author never lets the story break out of its urban context and become disembodied institutional history. Nor does he overlook the Church's failings and its internal differences. National churches clung to their autonomy as long as they could; bureaucratic infighting hampered the striving for classroom quality. And the grim story of segregation that greeted Black Catholics is told without restraint. Although the brief Epilogue that treats the present decline of Catholic schools across the country conveys a bleak future even at the moment of great success, the theme here is achievement not glorification.

This volume also has a comparative dimension. Although it might have been tempting to relate parochial school education in Chicago to the Catholic experience elsewhere, the author prefers to compare it to the Chicago public school system, at least on the primary and secondary levels. The Catholic schools competed, in a sense, for Chicago's immigrant children; they also competed for public approval and funds. This competition, with all its religious, political and, later, racial overtones, is another thread that runs through *The Education of an Urban Minority*. The present tranquility surrounding the parochial school issue is the result of a truce, not a surrender, by either side.

The book is convincing not only because of the skill with which Mr. Sanders presents his argument but also because of the wide range of his sources. To the considerable body of Chicago material he has added the richness of the diocesan archives with their detailed records of the schools after consolidation. Catholic newspapers and journals provide the official view of the problems, achievements and aspirations of the whole educational effort, as does the Mundelein collection. The lucid, fast-moving text is complemented by helpful tables and maps. *The Education of an Urban Minority* is what a pioneering book should be: thoroughly researched and persuasively presented.

Richard C. Wade

GENERAL EDITOR
URBAN LIFE IN AMERICA SERIES

New York
August 1976

Preface

Until very recently, historians of education in the United States paid little attention to the impact of urbanization on the nation's effort to school its children. Lawrence Cremin's groundbreaking study, *The Transformation of the School,* though not professedly an urban history, did deal extensively with those educational upheavals of the late nineteenth and early twentieth centuries that resulted from the process of urbanization. More recently, a group of younger historians has directed specific attention to the historical roots of the present malaise known as urban education.[1] For the first time we are beginning to see in well-documented detail how the growth of the American city affected the curricula, organization, and staffing of schools and the true extent to which popular myths about public education were realized in the metropolis.

But to date, all these efforts have bypassed an enterprise that must be held accountable for the education of perhaps a quarter of the urban population, at least in the great northeastern and midwestern cities. In each of these urban centers Catholic schools enrolled anywhere from 20 percent to 40 percent of all schoolchildren. Yet, we know little about them. Rather than embarking on the presently too ambitious though ultimately more necessary task of dealing with Catholic education in the cities nationwide, I have selected a single school system as a starting point. The choice of Chicago stems from no particular logic other than my personal preference at the time this study began and the fact that since the late nineteenth century the Chicago Archdiocese has boasted the largest Catholic school system in the United States. My research strongly suggests that what happened in Chicago typifies the experience of other urban dioceses in some respects, but that Catholic school systems did not result simply from papal and episcopal fiat, all stamped from an identical mold. Indeed, though the Church's official position undoubtedly set certain parameters, the book's central thesis argues that the particular social context, in this case Chicago, determined to a great extent both the scope and the nature of the effort.

Even though confined to but a single urban school system, keeping this project within reasonable bounds proved more than a little difficult. I had intended to concentrate on development of Catholic elementary and secondary schools from 1890 to 1930. But research, though confirming an original hunch that these four decades were indeed the most crucial, nevertheless led to the conclusion that some developments of this period could only be understood in their antecedents, others in their later results. Perhaps even more significant, limiting the study to elementary and secondary schools could not be justified, given the nature of my investigation. Catholics viewed their educational efforts as a much more global undertaking extending over a whole range of orphanages, settlement houses, adult and continuing education programs, colleges and universities, and the like. Therefore, while concentrating primarily on the elementary schools, which certainly constituted the system's backbone, and secondarily on the high schools, which by the 1920's had taken on crucial importance, I have included all those enterprises that contributed to the well-founded conclusion both in Catholic and non-Catholic Chicago that the Church had embarked on a truly total effort.

Further, the fact that this study began with the intention of viewing Catholic education not as an isolated phenomenon but in its many relationships to the total urban scene, led inevitably to the inclusion of much material dealing with the general social, political, and economic climate in Chicago, and more specifically with the public schools. Indeed, the evidence more than suggests that Catholic education largely originated from and fed on reaction to unfavorable aspects of the public schools and the city's other public and private institutions. Conversely, because many Catholics frequented these institutions, the Church's educational concerns extended to them as well as to its own. I have therefore deliberately not entitled this book simply "A History of Catholic Education in Chicago." It is more than that.

I have concentrated primarily on the City of Chicago proper. However, the process of suburbanization as it affected Catholics and their education seemed too important to ignore. The choice of a geographical boundary, therefore, became necessary, and posed a problem. At one time the Chicago Diocese included the entire state of Illinois. For a hundred years, the creation of new dioceses whittled away this area until since 1949 it has encompassed only Cook and Lake counties. The inclusion of the whole state in the earlier period hardly seemed in keeping with the urban nature of this study. On the other hand, the exclusion of some areas outside Cook and Lake counties after 1949 would distort the dominant trend of that period, an exodus to the suburbs. I have therefore included, in addition to the City of Chicago, the area of Cook, Lake and DuPage counties. These constitute less than the Chicago Diocese prior to 1949, and more after that date. But they encompass the suburbs most affected by Catholic mobility, and are included on those grounds.

The study's rather broad chronological, geographical, and topical scope forced the imposition of a somewhat unorthodox, though one hopes intelligible and justifiable structure upon its contents. While adhering as much as possible to chronology, the book is organized thematically, with the major themes determined by what appeared to be the most dominant social and cultural trends that influenced the development of Catholic education. Chapter 1 explains this approach somewhat more fully.

The inclusion of a time period spanning a century and a third, a geographical boundary including not only the city but its suburbs, a spectrum of educational institutions and enterprises from the settlement house to the university, plus the rooting of all this in its broader urban context, necessarily precluded detailed descriptions of particular institutions, individuals, or events. In the interest of intelligibility and readability and in the effort to convey a general sense for the sweep of trends and developments, many institutions, individuals, and even groups have been introduced to exemplify a given point, to the exclusion of others that might equally deserve mention. I hope that these latter will recognize their expected moment of glory as part of the larger enterprise that was the education of Chicago Catholics.

Finally, a word to those who might approach this book with certain value systems. Adherents of the parochial school may find in it a source of pride and justification. Opponents may read it with resentment as the account of a senseless exercise in sectarian futility. But the purpose in writing was neither to praise nor to condemn. Certainly, the fantastic expenditure of human and physical resources that went into the education of Catholics in Chicago deserves to be recounted as a significant act in the drama of urban history. More important, the sources of this monumental effort need to be understood and explained. This has been my major purpose.

Richmond College   J. W. S.
Staten Island, New York

July, 1976

Acknowledgments

This work evolved out of participation in a research project on School and Society in Chicago, funded by the United States Office of Education and co-directed by Professors Robert McCaul and Robert Havighurst of the University of Chicago, to both of whom I owe a huge debt of gratitude for a rare combination of unconditional personal support and professional criticism. Special thanks also to both Professor Richard Wade who first introduced me to the importance of urban history, helped provide much of the conceptual background for this study, and offered crucial advice at several stages of its development and to Professor Donald Erickson whose interest in American nonpublic education and criticism of an earlier version of the manuscript gave encouragement and direction.

Completion of this work would have been impossible without cooperation of those who controlled access to the sources. John Cardinal Cody allowed free use of the Archdiocesan archives, and archivists at St. Mary's of the Lake Seminary, Mundelein, Illinois, assisted in every way. Officials at the Archdiocesan Catholic School Board opened their records and files and provided office space for research. The *New World*, official Archdiocesan newspaper, generously lent a complete set of microfilms. Librarians at the University of Chicago, DePaul and Loyola universities in Chicago, and the Chicago Historical Society extended their usual courtesies.

The final revision, editing, and preparation of the manuscript was aided by a City University of New York Faculty Research Award grant. Friends, most notably Cathy Lavin, helped in typing and editing several earlier versions. In the final stages the assistance of Susan Rabiner, Carol Miller, and Alice Daggett proved invaluable. Lastly, my wife, Joan Lark Sanders, provided valuable editorial comment, but most of all exhibited exceptional patience, loyalty, and encouragement during what must have seemed an endless gestation.

Contents

THE EDUCATION OF AN URBAN MINORITY

I

A TIME
OF TRIBULATION—
THE FIRST CENTURY

1

Introduction

When, in the early spring of 1833, a little group of "almost one hundred" mostly French and French Indian Catholics residing in the newly incorporated town of Chicago petitioned the bishop of St. Louis for a resident priest, not even the most visionary among them could have suspected that on this marshy, wind-swept prairie would one day develop a city with the largest Catholic school system the world had ever seen.[1] Certainly, the several thousand destitute Irish and German Catholic immigrants who arrived during the next few years to dig the canal that promised to transform this former trading post into the commercial capital of the West did not portend such a momentous achievement for Catholic education or for the Church itself. The creation of Chicago as a separate diocese in 1843 perhaps first indicated that Catholics expected an important future in this unlikely setting. By the death of the City's first bishop, in 1848, the Catholic community already boasted a college for boys, a private academy for girls, and three parochial elementary schools. After that, unremitting expansion probably constituted the most impressive single fact about Catholic education in Chicago.

The elementary schools attached to local parishes formed the backbone of the Church's educational enterprise.[2] Every decade,

3

from the 1840's to the 1960's, saw more of these parochial schools
and, with the exception of the 1930's, expanded enrollment. By the
early 1850's, when the town's nascent Catholic newspaper first
reported educational statistics, attendance at the several elementary
schools numbered about 900 pupils.[3] In 1870, 10,000 pupils attended
the City's 15 parish schools, with another 355 in three outlying
towns. Sixty years later, in 1930, the City schools numbered 235,
with 145,000 pupils, and the suburban schools 88 with almost 24,000
pupils. Though the city and suburban enrollments declined during
the 1930's by a total of 22,000, between 1940 and 1965 Catholic
schools in the entire tricounty area more than doubled their rosters,
adding almost 160,000 pupils. The handful of schools and 900 pupils
of 1852 had mushroomed into a complex of 455 schools, with 304,000
pupils.

CATHOLIC ELEMENTARY SCHOOLS
City of Chicago
1865–1965

Year	Parishes	Schools	Parishes with Schools (%)	Enrollment
1865	17	14	82	5,770
1870	21	15	71	10,612
1880	31	29	94	16,713
1890	81	62	77	31,053
1900	114	87	76	49,638
1910	187	134	72	84,429
1920	227	196	86	112,735
1930	253	235	93	145,116
1940	259	245	95	124,692
1950	275	258	94	145,466
1960	282	270	96	182,262
1965	283	268	95	177,187

Source: *Official Catholic Directory*

CATHOLIC ELEMENTARY SCHOOLS
Suburbs
(Cook–Lake–DuPage counties)
1865–1965

Year	Parishes	Schools	Parishes with Schools (%)	Enrollment
1865	21	2	10	355
1870	28	3	11	355
1880	31	14	45	1,019
1890	37	17	46	1,571
1900	31 °	20	65	2,313
1910	57	32	56	5,349
1920	77	55	71	12,169
1930	99	88	89	23,729
1940	109	95	87	21,870
1950	130	108	83	34,916
1960	174	162	93	105,747
1965	202	187	93	127,295

° Decrease of parishes due to incorporation of suburban parishes into the City.
Source: *Official Catholic Directory*

Sketchy evidence indicates that through the nineteenth century about one-half the Catholic children of the City attended parochial schools, with a much smaller percentage in the suburbs. By 1960, a more solidly based estimate placed the proportion in both city and suburbs at closer to two-thirds.[4] In 1865, only about 16 percent of all children enrolled in public or Catholic schools attended the Church's schools in the City, with a negligible percentage in the suburbs. One hundred years later, the parochial schools accounted for 30 percent of the public–Catholic school total in the entire area. All the statistics point, if anywhere, to an ever strengthening commitment of Chicago's Catholics to the parochial school.

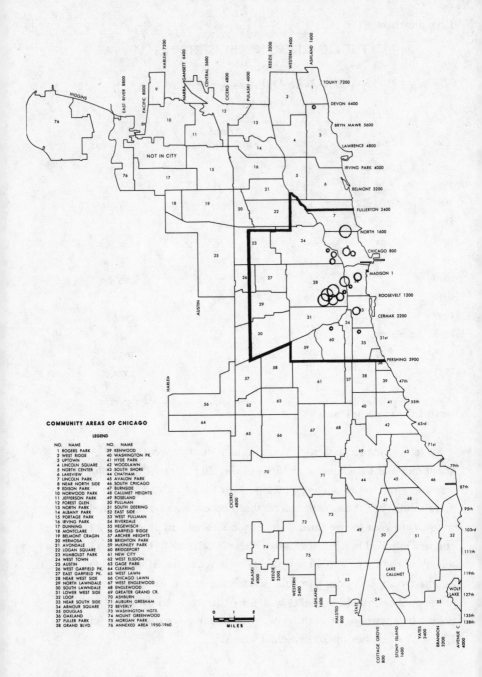

HARLEM 7200
EAST RIVER 8800
PACIFIC 8000
NARRAGANSETT 6400
CENTRAL 5600
CICERO 4800
PULASKI 4000
KEDZIE 3200
WESTERN 2400
ASHLAND 1600

TOUHY 7200

DEVON 6400

BRYN MAWR 5600

LAWRENCE 4800

IRVING PARK 4000

BELMONT 3200

FULLERTON 2400

NORTH 1600

CHICAGO 800

MADISON 1

ROOSEVELT 1200

CERMAK 2200

31st

PERSHING 3900

47th

55th

63rd

71st

79th

87th

95th

103rd

111th

119th

127th

135th

138th

NOT IN CITY

AUSTIN

HARLEM

CICERO 4800

PULASKI 4000

KEDZIE 3200

WESTERN 2400

ASHLAND 1600

HALSTED 800

STATE

COTTAGE GROVE 800

STONY ISLAND 1600

YATES 2400

BRANDON 3200

AVENUE C 4000

LAKE CALUMET

WOLF LAKE

COMMUNITY AREAS OF CHICAGO

LEGEND

NO.	NAME	NO.	NAME
1	ROGERS PARK	39	KENWOOD
2	WEST RIDGE	40	WASHINGTON PK.
3	UPTOWN	41	HYDE PARK
4	LINCOLN SQUARE	42	WOODLAWN
5	NORTH CENTER	43	SOUTH SHORE
6	LAKEVIEW	44	CHATHAM
7	LINCOLN PARK	45	AVALON PARK
8	NEAR NORTH SIDE	46	SOUTH CHICAGO
9	EDISON PARK	47	BURNSIDE
10	NORWOOD PARK	48	CALUMET HEIGHTS
11	JEFFERSON PARK	49	ROSELAND
12	FOREST GLEN	50	PULLMAN
13	NORTH PARK	51	SOUTH DEERING
14	ALBANY PARK	52	EAST SIDE
15	PORTAGE PARK	53	WEST PULLMAN
16	IRVING PARK	54	RIVERDALE
17	DUNNING	55	HEGEWISCH
18	MONTCLARE	56	GARFIELD RIDGE
19	BELMONT CRAGIN	57	ARCHER HEIGHTS
20	HERMOSA	58	BRIGHTON PARK
21	AVONDALE	59	McKINLEY PARK
22	LOGAN SQUARE	60	BRIDGEPORT
23	HUMBOLDT PARK	61	NEW CITY
24	WEST TOWN	62	WEST ELSDON
25	AUSTIN	63	GAGE PARK
26	WEST GARFIELD PK.	64	CLEARING
27	EAST GARFIELD PK.	65	WEST LAWN
28	NEAR WEST SIDE	66	CHICAGO LAWN
29	NORTH LAWNDALE	67	WEST ENGLEWOOD
30	SOUTH LAWNDALE	68	ENGLEWOOD
31	LOWER WEST SIDE	69	GREATER GRAND CR.
32	LOOP	70	ASHBURN
33	NEAR SOUTH SIDE	71	AUBURN GRESHAM
34	ARMOUR SQUARE	72	BEVERLY
35	DOUGLAS	73	WASHINGTON HGTS.
36	OAKLAND	74	MOUNT GREENWOOD
37	FULLER PARK	75	MORGAN PARK
38	GRAND BLVD.	76	ANNEXED AREA 1950-1960

0   1   2
MILES

Catholic Elementary Schools, 1870
Chicago
(Size of school indicated by area of circle.)

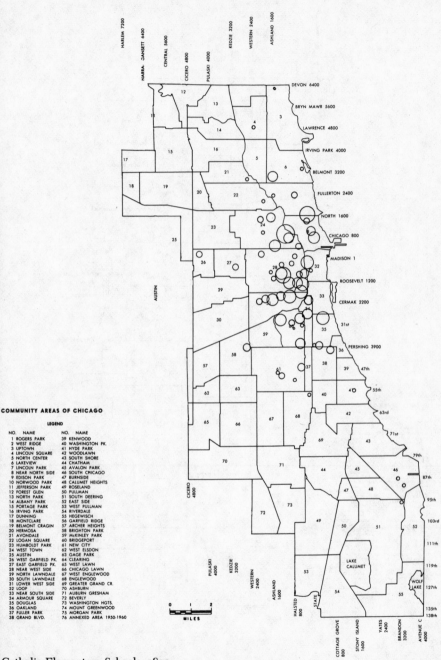

Catholic Elementary Schools, 1890

Chicago

(Size of school indicated by area of circle.)

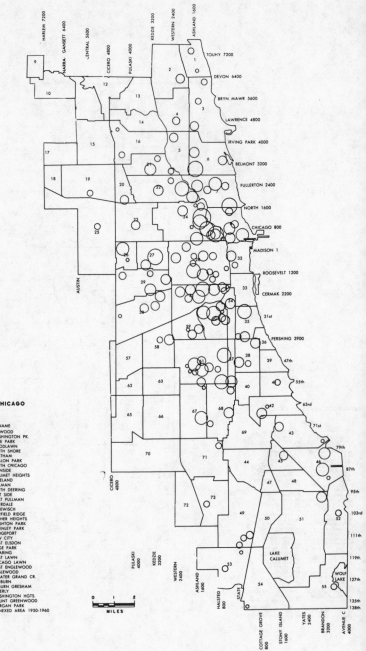

Catholic Elementary Schools, 1910
Chicago
(Size of school indicated by area of circle.)

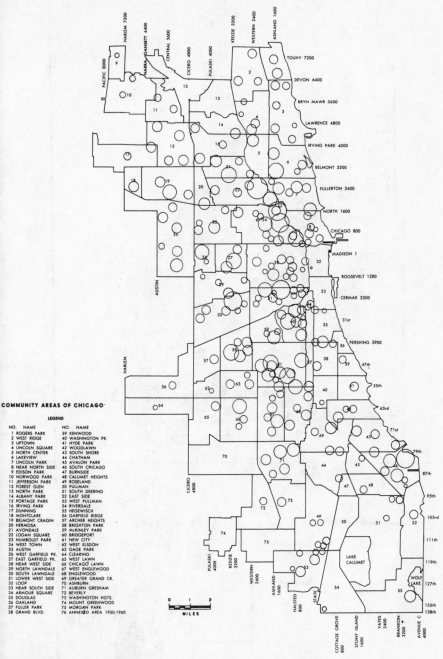

COMMUNITY AREAS OF CHICAGO

LEGEND

NO.	NAME	NO.	NAME
1	ROGERS PARK	39	KENWOOD
2	WEST RIDGE	40	WASHINGTON PK.
3	UPTOWN	41	HYDE PARK
4	LINCOLN SQUARE	42	WOODLAWN
5	NORTH CENTER	43	SOUTH SHORE
6	LAKEVIEW	44	CHATHAM
7	LINCOLN PARK	45	AVALON PARK
8	NEAR NORTH SIDE	46	SOUTH CHICAGO
9	EDISON PARK	47	BURNSIDE
10	NORWOOD PARK	48	CALUMET HEIGHTS
11	JEFFERSON PARK	49	ROSELAND
12	FOREST GLEN	50	PULLMAN
13	NORTH PARK	51	SOUTH DEERING
14	ALBANY PARK	52	EAST SIDE
15	PORTAGE PARK	53	WEST PULLMAN
16	IRVING PARK	54	RIVERDALE
17	DUNNING	55	HEGEWISCH
18	MONTCLARE	56	GARFIELD RIDGE
19	BELMONT CRAGIN	57	ARCHER HEIGHTS
20	HERMOSA	58	BRIGHTON PARK
21	AVONDALE	59	McKINLEY PARK
22	LOGAN SQUARE	60	BRIDGEPORT
23	HUMBOLDT PARK	61	NEW CITY
24	WEST TOWN	62	WEST ELSDON
25	AUSTIN	63	GAGE PARK
26	WEST GARFIELD PK.	64	CLEARING
27	EAST GARFIELD PK.	65	WEST LAWN
28	NEAR WEST SIDE	66	CHICAGO LAWN
29	NORTH LAWNDALE	67	WEST ENGLEWOOD
30	SOUTH LAWNDALE	68	ENGLEWOOD
31	LOWER WEST SIDE	69	GREATER GRAND CR.
32	LOOP	70	ASHBURN
33	NEAR SOUTH SIDE	71	AUBURN GRESHAM
34	ARMOUR SQUARE	72	BEVERLY
35	DOUGLAS	73	WASHINGTON HGTS.
36	OAKLAND	74	MOUNT GREENWOOD
37	FULLER PARK	75	MORGAN PARK
38	GRAND BLVD.	76	ANNEXED AREA 1950-1960

0   1   2   3
MILES

Catholic Elementary Schools, 1930

Chicago

(Size of school indicated by area of circle.)

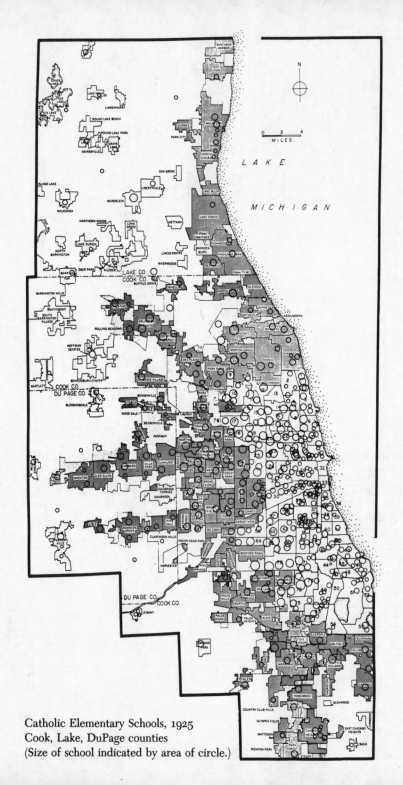

Catholic Elementary Schools, 1925
Cook, Lake, DuPage counties
(Size of school indicated by area of circle.)

Church authorities in the United States had long advocated the founding of Catholic schools. Seven times between 1829 and 1849 the bishops met in Provincial Council. Each time they issued exhortations to Catholic parents about the religious education of their children. The First Plenary Council of Baltimore in 1852 urged pastors to "encourage the establishment and support of Catholic schools; make every sacrifice which may be necessary for this object." The Second Council, in 1866, again exhorted bishops to "see that schools be established in connection with all the churches of their dioceses." In 1875, the Roman Congregation for the Propagation of the Faith, at the request of some American bishops, issued a stronger statement still. Finally, the Third Plenary Council of Baltimore in 1884, while allowing exceptions for "serious difficulties" or "sufficient reasons," passed the first definite legislation mandating parochial schools: "After full consideration of these matters, we conclude and decree: I. That near every church a parish school, where one does not yet exist, is to be built and maintained *in perpetuum* within two years of the promulgation of this council. . . .

CATHOLIC SECONDARY SCHOOLS
Enrollment
1850–1965

Year	City	Suburbs	Year	City	Suburbs
1850 °	118	0	1910 °	7,084	356
1860 °	220	0	1920 °	8,685	427
1870 °	765	0	1930	15,663	2,350
1880 °	950	65	1940	23,379	3,135
1890 °	1,283	65	1950	33,322	5,331
1900 °	3,640	69	1960	47,252	12,761
			1965	55,455	25,280

° These figures include an undetermined number of elementary school children who attended private Catholic academies that included some elementary grades.
Source: *Official Catholic Directory*

IV. That all parents are bound to send their children to the parish school." [5] This legislation continued as official Church policy in the United States.

In Chicago, the hierarchy committed itself to the parochial school from the start. One account of the first bishop stated that "his most conspicuous quality was intense devotion to Catholic education." [6] The Diocesan Synod of 1860 directed that "wherever possible a school is to be set up in each parish." [7] Archbishop Patrick A. Feehan presided as chairman of the committee on schools at the Third Plenary Council in the 1880's and afterwards vigorously promoted the Baltimore legislation in Chicago. Feehan characteristically took no part in a controversy over the possible phasing out of parochial education that agitated the Church nationally during the 1890's, apparently preferring to express his position simply by building schools.[8] When he died in 1902, the *Chicago Tribune* described his administration as one characterized by "an insistence on parochial schools." [9] Feehan's successor, James E. Quigley, roundly reaffirmed the previous legislation at the Diocesan Synod of 1906.[10] When Archbishop Quigley died in 1915, it was said that "one of the distinguishing features of his short administration over the Archdiocese of Chicago is the astounding growth of the parochial school system." [11] The policies of each succeeding bishop left no doubt about the Church's official position in Chicago.

Yet, neither simple obedience to the Church's decrees nor the pure faith on which it supposedly rested could adequately explain all that actually took place in Chicago. Religious conviction did not produce a similar flowering of Catholic education everywhere. No European country, for example, had anything comparable. Even in America, despite the universal legislation, not every diocese developed an educational program on the scale of Chicago's. And in Chicago itself, the facts belied the thesis that Catholic schools stemmed purely from obedience and faith. In fact, the history of Chicago Catholic education bore a sometimes inverse relationship to Church legislation on parochial schools.

For example, in 1880, four years prior to the Third Council of

Baltimore, 94 percent of the City parishes had schools. Yet, within six years of the Council's decree ordering a school in every parish, only 77 percent had them. By 1910, the proportion dropped to 72 percent. Also, in 1929, Pope Pius XI issued a strong encyclical enjoining religious schooling on the world's Catholics. Yet, during the following decade, Chicago's Catholic schools registered the first enrollment loss in their history. Thus, the only apparent lessening of Catholic commitment to parochial schools came immediately after the two most important pieces of legislation mandating them.

The evidence indicates not deliberate defiance of such legislation but the pressure of economic and social forces that made their fulfillment impossible at the time. The quarter-century after the Baltimore Council witnessed an immense tide of Catholic immigration to Chicago. In the years between 1880 and 1910, the City grew at a relatively stable rate of 560,000 a decade or 56,000 more inhabitants each year. A very large proportion of these new people were Catholic immigrants. The three decades after 1880 saw the creation of 156 new parishes in the City alone, a growth of 500 percent. Little wonder, then, that though only two parishes lacked schools in 1880, 53 did in 1910. Problems of construction and staffing forced many parishes to delay the opening of a school. Also, the papal encyclical of 1929 coincided with a severe economic depression and the results of a declining birth rate. Though the lower birth rate affected Catholics minimally, if at all, the depression itself clearly depleted parochial school enrollments. Catholic schools during the first years of the depression declined at every grade level. Further, they declined only in the poverty areas of the City and the industrial suburbs, an indication that extreme financial hardship forced many Catholic parents to remove their children from parochial schools.

Differences between the City and the suburbs in the development of parochial schools also support the thesis that, even assuming the great influence of religious faith and obedience to Church directives, social factors played a crucial role in determining the scope of the enterprise. For example, in 1880, when 94 percent of the City parishes had schools, only 45 percent of the outlying towns in the Cook–Lake–DuPage tricounty area had them. Not until 1930 did 90 percent of the suburban parishes support schools. The small and widely scattered character of the Catholic congregations outside Chicago accounted for the earlier differences. Only when woven into the City's economic and social fabric as suburbs with more concentrated populations could these originally rural parishes maintain parochial schools. The presence of Catholic schools was directly related to the degree of urbanization.

Even within the more congested City, patterns of dispersal often determined the presence or absence of a parish school. The Church's policy of allowing each ethnic group its own parishes affected those less numerous nationals like the Belgians, Dutch, Hungarians, and even to an extent, the French, all of whom had difficulty maintaining congregations in sufficient geographic concentration to support an ethnic school. Cultural attitudes brought from the old world also produced variations of commitment to the parochial school. Thus, all the major Catholic national groupings struggled to construct their own educational systems except the immigrant Italians, who cared little about the parochial school, or for that matter, the Catholic parish itself.

Catholic school fortunes in Chicago, then, as measured by enrollment and the percentage of parishes with schools, depended to a great extent on immigration rates, economic conditions, degree of urbanization, and the size and attitude of ethnic groups.

But of far greater importance than these relatively specific factors, the more pervasive social climate that defined the Catholic Church's position in the City as a whole profoundly affected the development of parochial schooling. Broadly speaking, the history of Chicago Catholic education, viewed in its social context, falls into three distinct, though chronologically overlapping phases. In the first phase, from the beginnings into the 1920's, the Church and its enterprises endured a prolonged period of tribulation. Its essentially immigrant status, the poverty of its constituents, and above all, the general atmosphere of suspicion and hostility toward Catholicism as a religion put the Church in a decidedly disadvantageous position, which made the achievement of its educational goals difficult in the extreme. Yet, the alien status itself generated enthusiasm for a separate system of schooling. Ironically, tribulation contributed significantly to the success of the Catholic educational effort.

The second phase, with roots sunk well back into the nineteenth century and its time of tribulation, came to fruition during the 1920's as a period of transition. As an astute commentator observed in 1927, "for Catholics the period of tribulation is over, and the future is bright with promise." [12] From one point of view, Catholic education in Chicago endured tribulations from its beginning to the present; from another, its future always seemed bright with promise. But looked at in careful historical perspective, these simultaneous themes of tribulation and promise converged, in the 1920's, marking an important watershed. The growth of Catholic power in the City, the progressive assimilation of the Church's ethnic groups, and their attendant social and residential mobility had melded by this decade into the dominant theme.

In many respects, the third phase, the post-1920's, seemed to fulfill the promise of a bright future, particularly in the vast expansion of the Catholic system into the City's outer ring and the suburbs. Yet, success itself ultimately produced a burden that, cyclically, threw the enterprise back into a period of anguished tribulation, this time caused by a quite different set of social circumstances associated with rising costs of education, the racial crisis, and profound changes in the Church itself.

2

The Religious Factor

In 1835, Lyman Beecher, president of Cincinnati's Lane Theological Seminary and renowned Presbyterian minister, published a little book entitled *A Plea for the West*. Beecher's plea exposed what he considered a papal plot to control the United States through massive Catholic immigration into the nation's mid-section. In one sense, it merely added two hundred odd pages to the volume of nativist literature that, by the mid-1830's, had "become a part of the regular industry of the country, as much as the making of nutmeg or the construction of clocks." [1] But Beecher's focus on the Midwest as the ultimate battleground added a new geographic dimension. He argued that the impending struggle would be won or lost in the Midwestern classroom. With intended reference to the contrast perceived between Protestantism and Catholicism, Beecher contended: "It is equally clear that the conflict which is to decide the destiny of the west will be a conflict of institutions for the education of her sons, for purposes of superstition or evangelical light, of despotism or liberty." [2] If Catholic children could be exposed to the common or public school, reasoned Beecher, they would learn to think for themselves and inevitably cast off the shackles of Roman despotism. Thus, *A Plea for the West* was in essense a plea for the common school.

As if in response to Beecher's plea, Yankee ministers moved westward to states like Illinois, filled with zeal for such common schools as were already taking shape in the East. During the 1830's, a group of Presbyterian and Congregational ministers founded the Illinois Teachers Association. They began publication of the *Common School Advocate* and systematically lobbied for funds in the State Legislature.[3] This marriage of Protestantism and the common school movement did not, of course, necessarily spell Beecher-style nativism. Protestant clergymen, as social and cultural leaders concerned about the nation's welfare, were prominent in the common school movement from its beginnings in the East. As denominational spokesmen they participated in the sometimes acerbic squabbles over what form of religion to teach in the schools and, by the 1830's, had fairly unanimously agreed that the common school should endorse a religion common to the majority—nondenominational Protestantism. Following their congregations into the Midwest, these Eastern clergymen brought with them concern for the common school. No doubt this historical fusion between Protestant church and public school, enhanced by a strong nativist undercurrent, provided significant impetus for Catholics to create an alternate system of parochial schools.

In Chicago this certainly held true. Indeed, the little settlement on the southwest shore of Lake Michigan could not have begun its meteoric rise to major urban status at a time better suited to direct the ancient religious rivalries into an instant civic tradition, in large part founded on the schools. The very composition of the infant city's population in the early decades ensured an outbreak of the nativism already endemic in the Midwest. Early civic leaders, after the first few years of French–Canadian influence, derived almost exclusively from Eastern Protestant stock. The City's lower classes, the Irish and the German who had immigrated directly from Europe, mostly belonged to the Catholic Church. "Animosities held by some

Protestants toward the power of Rome" appeared almost instantly, and in 1834 one Protestant divine prayed by night in front of the lone Catholic Church that "no evil should come to Chicago from its presence." [4]

On the school front, developments proved nothing less than predictable. The better established Protestants controlled the town's social and political institutions, as if by birthright. While Chicago's immigrant Catholics struggled to secure their shanties from the elements, the city fathers in 1834 allocated the first public monies from the education fund to two already existing institutions, one taught by Miss Eliza Chappell in the Presbyterian church and the other by Mr. Granville Spratt in a Baptist church on South Water Street. The following year, at a meeting in the First Presbyterian Church, the town was divided into school districts, which effectively instituted a system of public education.[5] Nothing seemed unusual in this loose yet obvious liaison between Protestant church and public support of education. It was taken for granted that, in the promising new educational program, Protestant teachers would read to the children from the King James Bible, the established practice in common schools of the East.

During the 1830's, the Catholics of Chicago registered no recorded public protest. Struggling to maintain a single log cabin church constructed in 1833 near the river at Lake Street, they did announce that "we are going to open a school." [6] But the school failed to materialize, probably due to the extremely unsettled character of early Catholic life in the City. When William J. Quarter, Chicago's first Catholic bishop, arrived ten years later, he found just one small church that had gone through five pastors in a turbulent decade. He also found several thousand immigrant Irish and German Catholics, whose children went to the public schools if they attended school at all.

Though no record remains that Quarter openly opposed the public schools, he immediately went about establishing his own. So successful was he that, at the time of his sudden death in 1848, Chicago Catholics had a college for boys, a private academy for girls, and elementary schools in three of the City's four parishes. The bishop never seriously considered the possibility of anything but separate schooling for his Catholic flock. Quarter's earlier experiences as a priest in New York City, where the Church's objections to Protestant domination of the public schools had ended in bitter defeat, may have determined his policy. Probably, also, warnings from the national hierarchy about "efforts made to poison the fountains of public education, by giving it a sectarian hue" [7] influenced the bishop's action. Since the First Provincial Council of Baltimore in 1829, the Catholic bishops had publicly complained that "the schoolboy can scarcely find a book in which some one or more of our institutions or practices is not exhibited for otherwise than it really is." [8] But almost certainly the public school Quarter found in Chicago helped settle the issue. Though Catholics constituted roughly one-third of the City's population in the 1840's, they never held more than one position at a time on the seven-member Board of School Inspectors, and sometimes none at all. Protestant teachers commanded the classrooms and enforced reading of the King James Bible, and a foreign visitor reported that "Irish children who attend the City's schools often become Protestants." [9] Thus, despite the absence of public controversy during the 1840's, de facto Protestant control of the public schools certainly constituted a major factor in Chicago Catholicism's commitment to parochial education.

By the early 1850's, Chicago Catholics had launched a newspaper of their own, and for the first time in the burgeoning young city, the religious antagonisms that had smoldered for two decades exploded into the public forum, with the schools the burning issue. In the City's public schools, complained the nascent *Western Tablet*, Catholic children "are taught to feel ashamed of the creed of their forefathers, which is often assailed, travestied, and ridiculed by anti-Catholic and prejudiced teachers." [10] To combat this pernicious evil, argued the *Tablet*, Catholics had resorted to schools of their own, which already accounted for the education of a thousand of the City's children. Yet they were denied a share of the school fund and "forced by compulsive taxation to pay for the schooling of others." [11]

Catholic leaders labeled the public schools as "Atheistical, godless, and pernicious—prolific hotbeds of prostitution, indecency, blasphemy, naivery and crime." [12] Catholic parents inclined to entrust a child to such a school were urged: "Let him rather never know how to write his name, or spell his way through the plainest paragraph of a newspaper, or perform the simplest calculation, than become the bound and chained slave of Satan, than rise up at the last dread day of account to curse you in all the unavailing repentance and bitterness of final despair." [13]

The adversary counterattacked with equal disregard for the demands of temperance. In defense of reading the Bible in public school, the *Chicago Tribune* argued: "So long as we do so, we are saved from all attacks of Romanism, and can bid defiance to the snares of Papacy and the delusions of Priestcraft." The Bible, said the *Tribune*, "dispels the darkness" Catholic priests "so sedulously endeavor to create—it ruins their plans, and discomfits their schemes, and they hate it." As for education in Catholic schools, "every traveler in Europe and every intelligent American knows how ignorant are the masses in Spain, Portugal and Italy" where the Church controls education. The Catholic demand for a share of tax money met immediate opposition from the City's secular and religious press.[14] The *Tribune* argued that dividing the school fund would bring the religious sects too much into politics and undermine the institutions of democracy. In 1854, when mayoral candidate Isaac Millikin declared in favor of giving Catholics a share of the school fund, the *Tribune* warned that "the enemies of free schools and political and religious liberty will vote, without exception, for Millikin." Even the normally secluded professors of St. Mary's College were accused of "coming into the wards of the City to influence votes. . . . Nothing less than the subversion of our School System, and the appropriation of its funds to sectarian purposes, could induce them to take such a course." When Millikin actually won, the *Tribune*, blaming election fraud, warned that matters would change when the "Know Nothings come to town." [15] They came in 1855 and swept the City election after a campaign in which "the

Catholic question almost precipitated a religious war." [16] The defenders of public education rejoiced in this foiling of the first Catholic advance on the public treasury and smugly justified their victory, pointing out that the City's indigent Papists were "in the main non-taxpayers anyway." [17]

The religio-educational battle of the 1850's settled nothing. Protestants still controlled the schools, enforced the King James Bible, and defended the public till. Catholics still chafed under the alleged injustice and struggled to construct an educational system of their own. But the public expression of rancor did produce one effect. It greatly deepened already entrenched hatreds and set the stage for decades of many-sided, bitter, and sometimes almost comic controversy over the schools. The evidence strongly suggests that, at least by the 1850's, a profound suspicion, if not hatred, of public education had become firmly fixed in the Chicago Catholic consciousness. In the ensuing years, this attitude fed on sufficient evidence of religious discrimination in the City's public schools to perpetuate itself even after the major sources of discontent had been eliminated. At the same time, events of the 1850's only served to confirm the worst fears of the Church's opponents. As many had believed all along, Catholics seemed bent on both unjustly securing a share of tax money for their own institutions and gaining control of the public schools. The many specific controversies that emerged over the decades invariably found Catholics the underdog and contributed to their period of tribulation in Chicago. Yet, the conflict itself served as a catalyst to the development of Catholic education. Without the enemy, such a vast and all inclusive parochial system would never have come to be.

The battles raged in the main on two fronts—one centering on the public schools, the other on the parochial. Catholics, at least, always viewed these as two aspects of the same war against the religious adversary.

The Church found its stance on the public schools of necessity fraught with ambiguities. On the one hand, at least in its origins, the public school appeared as the hated citadel of Protestantism, a direct

threat to the faith of Catholic children. On the other, not only did
the Catholic populace have a stake in these schools through their
taxes, but during the first hundred years an estimated half of the
Catholic children, either by economic necessity or parental choice,
attended public school. Thus, even as they struggled to establish and
expand a parochial school alternative, Catholics took a keen and
often belligerent interest in the conduct of public education.

The City's Protestants, of course, fought to defend the public
schools from Roman conquest. As Protestants saw the issue, the
Church grieved that the public schools were "not under the control
of Catholic Priests" and did not teach "the peculiar traits upon
which Catholicism is based." The Catholic hierarchy, "shameless and
ungrateful zealots," with "the dust of some old despotism yet on
their shoes," were accused of "reaching out for the control of that
which they will use for the religious and political enslavement of all
who come within their control." [18]

Catholics defined the issue quite another way. They had to secure
the interests of Catholic children attending public schools. Their first
objective was to de-Protestantize the public school curriculum. This
included not only doing away with the "heretical" King James Bible
but banning scripture reading altogether from the schools. Though
the *Tribune* exaggerated in contending that the Church believed the
Bible "was intended to be read only by the few, the Priests," [19]
standard Catholic teaching did hold that the Church alone could
interpret the Bible's meaning. To Catholics, the accepted practice in
public schools of reading scripture without note or comment
smacked squarely of Protestantism.

In their struggle against this form of discrimination, Catholics
found allies in Chicago by the 1860's. The City's Jews objected to
reading the New Testament in the schools. Unitarians and Universal-
ists, more liberal Protestants, and a handful of articulate atheists and
agnostics also argued the case against religion in the public schools.
By the late 1860's, even the *Chicago Tribune*, reversing its earlier
stand, agreed that despite its value, Bible reading in the schools
could only cause dissension.[20] Finally, in 1875, the Chicago school

board banned the Bible by a decisive vote of 11 to 2.[21] Though some
contended that Catholics engineered the movement, in fact only one
Catholic served on the school board that banned the Bible. And
some opponents of the Church even viewed the move as a blow to
Catholic interests in depriving them "of the slightest foundation for
charging that Catholic pupils are forced to listen to Protestant
teaching; it takes from them the only good excuse they have ever had
for an attempt to break down the system." [22]

But Catholics found still other excuses ready at hand. For one
thing, the question of public school religion did not die with the
Board's decision in 1875. More militant Protestant groups continually
sought its reinstatement, always against the opposition of Catholics,
Jews, liberal Protestants, and non-believers.[23] Finally, in 1910, the
Illinois Supreme Court, in a case brought by Catholics of Scott
County, declared reading the Bible in public schools unconstitutional. Despite attempts by the Illinois State Teachers Association to
revive the issue in 1911 and 1912, Chicago Catholics rejoiced that
here at least was a battle definitively won.[24]

Their rejoicing proved premature. The Bible readers next moved
to outflank the Supreme Court by changing the constitution. In 1920,
the framers of a new constitution included a provision for Bible
reading, but Illinois voters rejected the entire constitution. Again in
1925, a bill went before the State Legislature to amend the
constitution in favor of Bible reading, but it too failed. Throughout
the 1920's, Catholics accused Protestants of trying to make the "little
red schoolhouse" a "vestibule of the Sunday School." [25] Chicago
Protestant groups, in 1926, endeavored to "bring the public schools
into a scheme of week day religious instruction," but due to the
alleged "silent opposition of the Catholic Church" the plan did not
gain acceptance.[26]

Thus, over a period of fifty years following the initial victory,
Catholics and their unlikely allies succeeded, against repeated
opposition, in keeping the Bible out of the City's public schools. Yet,
success required constant vigilance, and even as they fought to
de-Protestantize the schools, Catholic leaders often used the very

necessity of battle as proof that the public schools were alien turf
unfit for Catholic children. Then too, for Catholics the King James
Bible stood merely as the most odious symbol of Protestant influence.
Textbooks and certain aspects of the curriculum also offended their
religious and moral sensibilities from time to time. For example, in
1895, they complained that Barnes' *History of the United States* used
in public schools contained factual errors about the Catholic Church.
In 1903, the diocesan newspaper objected again that "the general
history officially approved for the schools and in compulsory use
reeks with insidious or open assault upon the most precious
knowledge and traditions of the Roman Catholic element of
Chicago's citizenship." In 1906, the editor, objecting to the lack of
Catholics on the school board's textbook committee, warned against
adoption of a book which referred to Joan of Arc's visions as
"delusions" resulting from "disease" and in which "every devoted
Catholic is systematically misrepresented." [27]

The question of sex education in the public schools after 1912
generated still more heat. When the ex-president of Harvard,
Charles Eliot, advocated including sex hygiene in the curriculum, the
editor answered that "some men live too long and talk too often."
But when the Chicago school board took up the issue, the *New
World* got down to business, first calling the program "another
incursion of the spirit of organized public paternalism into the
regions and the sacred privacy of the family and the home." (See
Appendix C for a discussion of the general policies of the *New
World.*) A week later the editor, though admitting the gravity of the
problem, opposed the program on grounds that the public schools, in
having to divorce the physical aspects of sex from the moral and
religious, could not possibly handle it adequately. When the school
board approved what was then called "personal purity," the editor
predicted disaster for a program that could only encourage the pupils
to "be chaste or you will be diseased" and that would have to use
untrained personnel. Vindication came a few months later when
someone submitted expressions used in sex hygiene lectures to the
Assistant Attorney General in Washington, who labeled them

"unmailable under the provisions of section 211 of the Criminal Code of 1909"; and the editor demanded that the school board ban sex lectures the United States Government could not even allow in the mails.[28]

The atmosphere in the schools, of course, was determined not merely by textbook and curriculum committees, but more immediately by the teachers themselves. The alleged bigotry of public school teachers constituted the earliest Catholic complaints in Chicago. Redress of this wrong could only be accomplished through changes in the teacher force, and it began to be achieved as the daughters of Catholic immigrants aspired to this moderately respectable but not very lucrative profession. The Church welcomed and encouraged the development, and Catholic girls' high schools and academies sought to prepare their students for teaching positions in the public schools. By the 1890's, Irish girls were seeking such appointments in large numbers.

The movement posed another threat to Protestant hegemony and precipitated a new set of controversies. In 1903, a school board ruling seemed to discriminate against Catholics entering the teaching profession. The school board ruled that though graduates of the Normal School could obtain immediate employment in the public schools, graduates of other colleges had to have, in addition, from two to four years' teaching experience elsewhere. Though this move probably reflected, at least in part, the contemporary struggle to further legitimize formal teacher education programs, Archbishop James E. Quigley, in an address to the Chicago Catholic Women's League, took it as an indirect attack on Catholic colleges, which, in principle, threatened their very existence. "If a School Board can make attendance at a Normal School a condition to employment in the public schools," argued Quigley, "why may not some city charter of the future or amendment to the constitution of the state, make attendance at the public common schools a condition to employment in any branch of public service." After heated debate, which included allegations of another plot to keep Catholic teachers out of the public schools, by June of 1904 the school board dropped the ruling due to a critical need of more teachers in the City's schools. In 1906, Superintendent of Schools Edwin G. Cooley decided to require entrance exams only of those coming from high schools not approved by the principal of the Normal School and the superintendent of schools, which meant in effect that mainly Catholic school graduates would be examined. The *New World* called this open discrimination. The Cooley plan did not prevail, but the question was raised again in 1915, this time when superintendent Ella Flagg Young, testifying before a state committee investigating the Chicago school board, proposed a quota system by which the board would assign to each high school, both public and private, a fixed number of places in the Normal School. Because for years several Catholic schools had been supplying a disproportionate number of future teachers, the *New World* saw this as one more bigoted effort to limit the number of Catholic teachers in the public schools.[29] Again in 1920, the school board efficiency committee on admissions to the Normal School recommended that the top one-quarter of each high school's graduates, public and non-public, should automatically gain admission to the Normal School without examination. Catholics interpreted this, too, as a quota system to limit the number of Catholic teachers: "The real harm concealed in the recommendation is in the fact that if 25% be taken from the public high schools there would be no vacancy for ours. This is concealed, but must be known to those who drew up the report." [30]

Far more blatant was the alleged discrimination against Catholic teachers in the Chicago suburbs. In 1917, the *New World* complained that "right here in Cook County it is impossible in some school districts for a Catholic to secure a position as a teacher." The situation was still the same in 1924: "There is no secret about it. The education agencies know it. Within a radius of ten miles of Chicago, almost within a stone's throw of its city limits, it is openly advertised that Catholics will not be permitted to teach in certain places. Right here in Cook County there are a dozen places where school trustees will not hire a Catholic girl for the grades or for high schools." Such discrimination in the suburbs also had a telling effect on prospective high school teachers in the City. Chicago at the time hired only experienced high school teachers. But many Chicago Catholics could not get their experience in the suburban schools and therefore could not be hired in the City either.[31]

Curricular matters, personnel policies, and the like were decided by the Chicago Board of Education. Naturally, Catholics sought adequate representation in that body. Through most of its history, Chicago's school board was appointed, first directly by the Common Council, and after 1872, by the mayor with advice and consent of the Council. The best evidence available indicates that throughout most of the City's first century, Catholics did not achieve representation proportionate to their numbers. Thus, of all the people who served on the school board between 1840 and 1875 Catholics made up about 10 percent, between 1876 and 1900 about 16 percent, and between 1901 and 1925 about 26 percent. Only once, in the early 20's, did they constitute a majority.[32] Further, Church authorities often complained that Catholics appointed to the board were but "nominal sons of the Church." They saw the matter in purely political terms. For example, in 1901 when the reformers wished to "take the schools out of politics," the New World answered: "If keeping the schools in touch with the common people and under the control of the common people is to be called keeping them in politics, then the longer they are kept in politics the better." In 1906, with board vacancies about to be filled, Catholics argued for proportionate representation, insisting that it be Catholic with a capital "C." When Catholics held only three places on the 21-member board during Mayor Fred Busse's tenure, in 1907, the New World complained that though the Mayor himself was not consciously bigoted, many of his advisors "are as bloated with ignorant prejudices as the average Methodist Parson." And later, with board appointments due again, the editor reminded his readers of "their duty to see that Catholics who are appointed as members of the Board of Education are verily representative and intelligent Catholics with courage enough to oppose anything that may be detrimental to the Catholics as a body or a jeopardy to Catholic truth and teaching." And in 1915, with a movement afoot to restrict board membership to those whose children attend or did attend the public schools, the paper threatened: "If school board membership is restricted as is proposed, that cry 'no taxation without representation,' will be raised once more to good effect." [33]

The question of taxation, of course, constituted one more ground for Catholic insistence on a measure of influence in public school affairs and another target for angry invective. Keenly aware that Chicago Catholics could ill afford high taxes, that half the Catholic children did not benefit from public education, and that every improvement in the public schools threatened the competitive chances of the parochial, Church spokesmen generally favored keeping educational expenditures to a minimum and tended to support only those programs from which Catholics might directly benefit. In 1901, Catholics brought suit in the circuit court of Cook County against the Board of Education for exceeding its state mandate in appropriating funds for textbooks for other than the needy. One of the plaintiffs was Thomas Brenan, a Catholic member of the school board. The case was won, but the advocates of free textbooks pressed the cause. When, in 1903, the State Legislature debated one of the many free textbook bills introduced over a period of years, the *New World* warned that "as advocated the scope of the new bill is distinctly socialistic." And when, in 1908, Chicago's school board again moved in the same direction, the Catholic weekly alleged: "the gentlemen in charge of the public schools have all turned socialists." While consistently endorsing free textbooks for the needy, the *New World* saw no reason to supply them for those able to pay: "The man who is not willing to buy textbooks for his children is not worthy of his children." When, in 1921, a bill was presented for referendum to the voters "whereby all school children are to be given free textbooks," the *New World* went on the warpath again: "This is needless and mischievous. It is needless because at the present time all children unable to purchase textbooks are given them without cost. . . . It is mischievous because of the misleading word 'free.' . . . The dodge is another scheme to increase taxation."

Finally, after a quarter century of agitation over the free textbook issue, Chicago started giving textbooks to all children in 1922. The *New World* blamed the "apathy of the voters" and warned that "the politicians, the book agent, the publisher, the second hand book dealer" would now engage in "a scrimmage" in the lucrative textbook market.[34]

Catholic leaders also adopted a generally cautious attitude toward the many pedagogical innovations advocated in the vast educational upheavals around the turn of the century. They opposed most as "fads," especially if costly. In this they fell back on the Illinois State Constitution to justify the limits set to legitimate public action: "The Constitution of the State defines the function of the public schools to be the furnishing of a good common school education." Anything that went beyond their definition of a common school education earned the "fad" label. The teaching of foreign language fell for a time under this stricture. In 1893, the *New World* gleefully reported that " 'modeling in clay'—that is, making mud pies—will not be taught at public expense." In 1901, it endorsed the resolutions of a group of "teachers and taxpayers" of Chicago against the Civic Federation-sponsored bill for "Nature Study, Domestic Economy, Manual Training, Child Study, Medical Inspection, Algebra, Latin and other subjects in the elementary schools requiring special teachers with high salaries." In the following years, though forced to accept the permanence of many "fads," the *New World* continued to complain about "extravagant appropriations" for such programs. In 1910, as "social progressivism" began to hit the schools with full force, Superintendent Ella Flagg Young proposed establishing social centers in the public schools to be used by mothers after school hours and by fourteen- to eighteen-year-olds in the evening, to keep them out of the dance halls and saloons. The *New World* objected that "experience elsewhere has proved that the public school's social center is a costly and useless fad." The attack against fads continued well into the 1920's. "In the field of pedagogy every year sees a new prophet," complained the Catholic editor. "There is nothing too fantastic to be tried. . . . The children are the laboratory. . . . The teacher must follow along in whatever fantastic wake that a rudderless ship creates." [35]

Catholic opposition to public school expenditures no doubt stemmed in part from a general aversion to higher taxes. It also derived from a genuine suspicion, shared by many in Chicago, of the innovations that seemed to be transforming the function of public education after the 1890's. But the *Chicago Tribune* was guilty of only a slight exaggeration in 1890 when it accused Catholics of opposing appropriations for public schools "in the hope that they may cripple their efficiency and take the first step toward breaking them down." [36] A Catholic tax dollar spent on the public school was a dollar taken away from the parochial school. Equally important, from economic necessity parochial schools stuck to the basics of education, the three R's. Each new expensive service provided in the public school increased its attraction over the parochial school. Catholic leaders saw the issue clearly. For example, in marshaling opposition against the first specter of Federal aid in 1919, the Chicago Archbishop argued privately, in Catholic circles, that federal funds would create a "colossus which would practically prevent competition . . . so that our poor little parish schools would be like pygmies alongside this overfed monster of a state school." Federal aid would provide public schools, he said, with "dental laboratories, physicians, trained nurses, physical instructors in attendance, practically free restaurants, gymnasiums, baths, etc." "How long," he asked, "will our schools—not withstanding their splendid reputation—continue to compete with the state schools?" It would be "only a question of time when our people would be weaned away from the support and use of the Catholic parochial school." [37]

More than anything else, Catholics saw the proliferation of public school programs as a threat to their own schools. For this reason they did not wish the public schools to prosper. The religious hostility branded so early into the City's consciousness had fixed the Catholic attitude in its opposition to the public school. Thus, despite repeated efforts to de-Protestantize the schools and win a measure of control for themselves, the real Catholic effort went into the building of a competitive system. In this endeavor, too, Catholics met with opposition that contributed much to the Church's time of tribulation but served also as a spur to greater effort.

Protestants had moved quickly to safeguard the treasury from Catholic incursions. Early state laws regulating the expenditure of tax money for education were nebulous about the allocation of funds. In many localities, as in early Chicago itself, much of the money went to denominational schools. But the threat of popery in the Midwest prompted a new law in 1855 that effectively excluded nonpublic schools from public funds.[38] Catholics could muster no opposition to passage of this law, so devoid of political power were they at the time. The state constitution of 1870 still further secured the public coffers. At the Constitutional Convention, the Methodist Episcopal church submitted a resolution "prohibiting the legislature from making any grants of money or land, either directly or indirectly, to sectarian or denominational schools, and we request all Protestant denominations to unite with us in this prayer." [39] The resolution's wording and the brief debate that followed clearly identified the Catholic Church as the object of exclusion. Not a single Catholic served as delegate to the convention,[40] and the Illinois voters ratified the provision. Yet Catholics never really gave up the fight to gain a share of tax funds for their schools. In 1875, they proposed an amendment to the state constitution, without success, and raised the issue again in the 1890's, "adding to an atmosphere of strife already heavily charged." [41] The yearly payment of taxes for the support of public schools to the exclusion of their own served as a perennial reminder of what seemed to them the prejudice of the Church's enemies.

Even the freedom to conduct their own schools for a time seemed threatened. In July of 1889, a Republican legislature passed the Edwards Law. Under the guise of strengthening the state's regulation of school attendance, a provision obviously inimical to nonpublic schools was slipped through. The Edwards Law stipulated that only those schools approved by local boards of education could satisfy the compulsory attendance requirements. This, of course, meant subjection of all parochial schools to local school boards. Outraged Catholics organized for repeal. With the gubernatorial elections forthcoming in 1892, the Catholic bishops of Illinois declared in a letter to all their constituents: "We denounce this law as a violation of our constitutional rights, and hold that those who favor it are unworthy of the support of enlightened and fair minded voters. Let us use all right and honorable means to have it repealed." [42] The German-Catholic organizations of Illinois established a vigilance committee in Springfield. And German Lutherans and Catholics were urged to unite, at least for this issue. [43] The November defeat of the long-entrenched Republicans brought the law's speedy repeal. Whether or not it was true, the *New World* believed that Governor Altgeld had ridden to victory on the votes of Illinois Germans, both Catholic and Lutheran, who switched to the Democratic camp over the Edwards Law. Suspicion of the Republican party and its alleged ties to the anti-immigrant American Protective Association (APA) remained high. More than a decade after the Edwards issue, the *New World* reminded its readers that the Republican candidate for Governor had earlier opposed repeal of the law. [44]

The near disaster of the Edwards Law seems to have awakened Catholics to the permanent need for watchfulness. The German Catholics kept a vigilance committee in the state capitol, and the diocesan newspaper agitated over every potentially dangerous issue. Catholics developed an almost paranoic reaction to legislation that seemed to pose even an indirect threat to their own schools. For example, in 1895 a seemingly innocuous law slipped through the legislature requiring every school, public and nonpublic, to fly an American flag under penalty of a daily three- to ten-dollar fine for noncompliance. Seeing in the law another attempt to harass the already financially strapped Catholic schools, the *New World*, again crying APAism, blamed the Republicans for its passage, and asked: "Has the state the right to impose an expense like this on the parochial schools?" In 1899, the Rogers Bill to prevent the granting of bogus college degrees went before the state legislature. Rogers wanted a six-member commission appointed by the governor to set standards for colleges and universities and a minimum $100,000 endowment as a prerequisite for degree granting. The *New World* admitted the need for regulation; but, probably seeing a threat to most Catholic colleges, opposed the $100,000 endowment, suggesting a minimum property and capital investment requirement instead. Not all such legislation, of course, was actually directed against Catholic schools. Yet, the highly charged religious atmosphere of the time invited suspicion of every new educational proposal. And, in 1924, the *New World* was probably not entirely unjustified in its accusation that "captious laws, catch penny regulations, and devious tests were all compiled to trip us up." [45]

Then, too, what they failed to do by legislation and constitutional provision, the Church's adversaries tried to effect by polemic and persuasion. The *Chicago Tribune*, for example, consistently attempted to drive a wedge between Catholic clergy and layman on the parochial school question. "It is only in rare cases that Catholics keep their children from the public schools of their own motion," argued the *Tribune* in 1875. Since "the days of unquestioning obedience are passed" and "the power of the Roman Catholic church over its members . . . is not so great as it was," the *Tribune* foresaw by 1890 the decline of parochial schooling, claiming that only the clergy believed in the Catholic school. When the Third Council of Baltimore decreed a school in every parish, the *Tribune* boasted that the decree could not be enforced in Chicago, completely ignoring the fact that 90 percent of the City's parishes already had schools. In 1890, when from Catholic pulpits the people were told that "no child could be admitted to the sacraments of confirmation and communion unless it had attended a parochial school," the *Tribune* scoffed that "probabilities are that the request of the clergy will have no apparent effect on parochial school attendance." It also went to absurd lengths to prove that Chicago's Catholics did not attend parochial schools, in 1890 claiming that only 20 percent of Catholic children did.[46] Either the *Tribune* needed a better statistician or it deliberately distorted the Catholic school's

drawing power. In 1890, 19 percent of the City's school children
attended Catholic schools. If these were only 20 percent of all the
Catholic children, then Catholics made up almost the total public
school population, an obvious impossibility. But, as one observer of
the Chicago situation remarked more than three decades later, in the
realm of religious rivalry, "nothing seems too preposterous for
belief." [47]

The *Tribune* also endeavored to discredit the Catholic school as an
educational institution. In 1890 it asked its readers to look to the
nineteenth ward to see the "perfect fruits" of Catholic education.
"In that Ward is the great Twelfth Street Jesuit Church. . . . There
are six parochial schools with nearly 5,000 pupils belonging to that
Church." Yet the products of these schools consistently returned the
"scaley" Johnny Powers to the City Council. The record, thought the
Tribune, "proves pretty clearly that the blending of religion and
education in parochial schools from which such great things are
promised does not lessen the number of tough voters in the
nineteenth ward." A few weeks later the *Tribune* asked again of the
Catholic schools, "For what great men is America indebted to them?
They have taught hundreds of thousands of children. Who among
them all has climbed the ladder of honorable fame?" "The public
schools," said the *Tribune*, "are admittedly superior to the church
schools." Even "the vast majority of Roman Catholics" were said to
regard the parochial schools "as inferior and inefficient as compared
to the common schools." And when, in the mid-90's, the public
schools could not accommodate all the children, the alleged reason
was that Catholics were abandoning the parochial schools. "Even the
Catholics themselves admit they are not as good as the public
schools." [48]

The *Tribune* was correct, of course, in its assertion that Catholic
authorities strenuously promoted parochial schools. Each September
before school opened, and at other times as well, Catholic pulpit and
press rang with denunciations of godless public education and
extolled the glories of parochial schooling. But the evidence does not
support the contention that they had to badger an unwilling laity. In

truth, for the immigrant Catholic and his children, the Church school offered sanctuary from intolerance and bigotry. As one historian observed about the 1890's, "whatever the signs of growing tolerance among the various sects" in Chicago, "few, if any, included the Roman Catholics." [49] To many Catholics, the parochial school was a symbol of defiance against the established order that so despised their religion. Each experience of real or imagined hostility drew Catholics into a tighter unity centered in the parish and parochial school. They met charges of Catholic school inferiority with resolve to build still more and better schools. The very existence of an enemy produced greater dedication to the cause of parochial education. Catholic spokesmen mockingly advised that the *Tribune* attacks should be read "rather for amusement than for instruction." [50] But the real refutation came in the continued expansion of the parochial school system itself. Every year new schools opened and enrollments grew. This was the Catholic answer to the public school and to the critics of Catholic education.

Predictions that Catholic education would die on the ecclesiastical vine were not fulfilled. On the contrary, by 1930, the several parochial elementary schools and the one thousand pupils of 1852 had grown to 323 schools and 168,000 pupils in the entire tricounty area. Fewer than 10 percent of the Catholic parishes had no school, and most of these parishes were simply too small to support one. The movement spread into areas other than the parochial elementary school, too. Catholic high schools countered public high schools; the Church's own universities countered state and private ones. Catholics developed their own social centers to counter Protestant oriented settlement houses, launched the Catholic Youth Organization in response to the YMCA, and so on. The approximately 2,500 youths in Catholic secondary schools in 1900 grew to over 18,000 in 1930, and another 5,000 students attended Chicago's six Catholic colleges and universities, all founded since the turn of the century. Five more institutions cared for and schooled 3,400 Catholic dependent children, and eighteen settlement-type institutions offered educational programs of various kinds in poverty areas. In addition, summer camps, homes for young Catholic workers, night schools for adults, and other institutions contributed to the well-founded impression that the Church competed vigorously at almost every educational level.

Always the Church institution or program was presented as an antidote to the pernicious public or secular one. Thus, the Catholic high school would prevent youth from being "plunged into the icy broth of a secular, godless high school." The launching of a Catholic women's college in Chicago would save the young woman from attending Northwestern or the University of Chicago "at great danger to her faith." Such institutions were dismissed as teaching "strange doctrines"; they were "diabolical," "materialistic," full of "rowdyism," lacking in "moral atmosphere," "under the influence of socialism," "full of debauchery and drunkenness," and "subversive of all religious belief." Catholic settlement houses, pictured as battling for immigrant youth and their parents against the inhospitable city and the Protestant social worker, found themselves and their rivals in conspicuous proximity. In 1892, for example, two years after Jane Addams established Hull House on the near west side, Catholic laymen organized a similar program for the Italians of the same district. Even Catholic resident institutions for dependent and delinquent children originated at least in part from reaction to the peril of receiving instruction from teachers of another or no religious belief.[51]

In only one area did Catholics not seriously compete, and this merely underscored the nature of the conflict. The Church did very little to provide religious instruction for its children in public schools. In the 1870's, the Diocese did launch an effort to create a widespread Sunday school program; yet "this was never meant to be a permanent experiment but rather an insufficient alternative pending the erection of its own system of education." Many parishes organized Sunday schools, but the work remained haphazard and unenthusiastic. In the 1890's, a Catholic clergyman observed that "our Sunday schools lack interest and are poorly attended." In 1912, with approbation of the bishop, Catholic laymen organized the

Catholic Instruction League to set up "catechism centers" for Catholic children in the public schools, but their efforts focused on pockets in the inner city where Protestant missions proselytized immigrant children of unchurched parents.[52] Before 1930, the Diocese itself organized no catechetical effort to reach the Catholic public school child. The lack of enthusiasm for Sunday school religion programs in the face of comprehensive efforts at every other level simply confirmed Catholic antagonism to public schooling. Such programs would have implied cooperation with the enemy. "While we must not neglect" the Catholic children in public school, argued Archbishop Mundelein in the 1920's, "we should not attract them to these institutions in preference to our own." [53]

Without the common enemy against which to rally, Catholics would probably have founded schools in Chicago anyway, but not on such a grand, systematic, comprehensive scale. It was the backdrop of rabid anti-Catholicism in Chicago generally and the alleged Protestant bias of the public schools in particular that prompted a total effort to build within the City a Catholic educational island. First in the nativist and the Know-Nothing movements, later in the machinations of the American Protective Association, and always in the City's suspicious and often hostile Protestant establishment, the advocates of Catholic education found a compelling incentive for the parochial school.

3

The Ethnic Factor I

The conflict between Catholic and public institutions in Chicago stemmed not merely from the fact that Catholics professed an alien religion. Most Catholics also came from ethnic stock foreign to the nation's mainstream. And nowhere did the inevitable cultural conflict center more than in the schools. Catholic ethnics, most of them of Celtic, Germanic, Slavic, or Latin origin, found the public schools of Chicago generously endowed with a distasteful Anglo-Saxon flavor that represented American public education's typical response to its mandate for Americanizing the immigrant child. The curriculum, the textbooks, and, most importantly, the teachers tended to impress a single mold rooted in the English language as the only legitimate medium of expression, English literature and history as essential to the American experience, and Anglo-Saxon virtue as the foundation of national character. One nonethnic observer claimed in 1897, with only slight exaggeration, that "you can search the records in vain to find" in the Chicago schools "any recognition of the need for special adaptation of the system to the foreign clientage. There is only one course of study for all." [1] The prevalent opinion and the practice in the schools agreed with the important Harper Commission report of 1898, that "a large proportion of our children comes from families where English is barely known, and where under the best conditions, the ideas and traditions of the home are utterly opposed to the requirements of American citizenship." [2] Even the more understanding and sympathetic voices from the settlement house movement could not quite escape the assumption that "the children and their parents may speak Polish, Hungarian, Russian or Yiddish; but these same children are to be trained for a civic life that has grown of American experience and Anglo-Saxon tradition." [3] Some educators did profess to meet the newcomers on their own ground. For example, Ella Flagg Young, whose career as teacher, principal of the Chicago Normal School, and superintendent of the Chicago schools spanned the period of heavy immigration before and after the turn of the nineteenth century, claimed the public school as a successful ethnic melting pot. Yet, her book, *Isolation in the School*, published in 1901, established rather clearly who, in her view, was to be melted: "It is the free public school," argued Young, "that has made the child of foreign parentage strive to take on the habits of thought that would identify him with the people whose ancestors were merged into this social and political society at an earlier date than were his." Indeed, Young observed with approval, despite her recorded objections to uniformity in the schools, that "the differences growing out of the social customs of the many nations into which long ago the races had divided have been brought into the public school to be minimized, obliterated, homogenized in the process of unification." [4]

Though most immigrants agreed that their children must be trained in the "American experience" and even, as the Harper Commission put it, that the "essential purpose of the American school system is to form American citizens," [5] they did not see what that had to do with the "Anglo-Saxon tradition." The immigrant found nothing in the "ideas and traditions" of his home "utterly opposed to the requirements of American citizenship." He resented the implication that in the public school his social customs would be "minimized" and "obliterated." Why could he not be an American and remain Irish or Polish or German too?

Immigrant groups fought back against this view of Americanism. They struggled to expunge insulting passages from the textbooks, to have their own heritage recognized, to force introduction of their languages into the schools. Sometimes they succeeded. By 1865 the Chicago Germans won the teaching of German in the public schools. The Irish vigorously and bitterly opposed the Anglo-Saxon bias. Thus, on a January evening in 1900, Irish board member Thomas Brenan rose in the chambers of the Chicago school board and blurted: "I am in favor of having the children of the public schools read about the noble exploits of all countries and peoples, but I cannot see any lesson to be learned from the bloody history of England." Despite the contention of an Anglo-Saxon member that "the history of England is indissolubly linked with that of the United States, and should be taught in the schools," the predominantly Irish *New World* argued that children would do better left unexposed to "the ramping Anglo-Saxon glowering on his native heath." [6] In 1904, the school board actually dropped the teaching of English history from the City's elementary schools.

Yet victories were few, gains slight, and they left ugly scars. The Germans had to fight off repeated attempts to remove their language from the schools. Other groups battled unsuccessfuly for years to introduce theirs, and even then gained but minor and grudging concessions. The Harper Commission report expressed hope that "demand for instruction in their language on the part of foreign-born citizens will gradually diminish." [7] The next edition of a textbook might remove a slur against the Irish, include mention of Pulaski's Polish origins or Columbus' Italian. But always the situation demanded vigilance. In 1896, for example, an article in the *Primary School*, intended for use as an object lesson in public schools, depicted the life of Irish peasants as "worse than it is" and implied their belief in fairies. The students of Hyde Park High School advertised their 1906 play with store window placards portraying a bulldog-like "Mrs. Mulchahy, or the typical Irish woman." The *New World* reprinted the picture and devoted a full page to calling it "an insult to the Irish race." [8] This periodic occurrence of ethnic insult and the persistent resistance to accommodation of "alien" cultural aspiration kept national groups in mind of the public school's essential bias.

In contrast, the Chicago Catholic school offered an enticing alternative. The Catholic Church had agonized before over the problem of cultural accommodation. With mass movement into the new nation it had to struggle again. The resulting effort, though fraught with tribulation, produced a resolution decidedly amiable to ethnic interests.

Since the Council of Trent in the sixteenth century, the Catholic Church had centralized its government, with stress laid on oneness in belief and practice, against the divisive threat of the Reformation. In France, Germany, Poland, through most of Europe, priests offered Mass in the "universal" Latin language, using an identical rite. But not everything could be the same. The children might learn their religion from one catechism, but necessarily translated into their own tongue. The faithful made their confessions and heard sermons in the only language most of them knew, and sang their hymns in the tongue of their fathers. They built churches in the styles that best expressed their cultural heritage. Each nation celebrated the feast days of its favorite saints with special and often extravagant ceremony. Thus, while for the most part one in faith and essential practice, European Catholics could not slough off linguistic and cultural differences. Nor need they do so as long as they remained within national boundaries. Within a country it mattered little to which parish one belonged. Church authorities simply divided each diocese into congregations with defined territorial limits. Unlike in most Protestant denominations, the Catholics' place of residence determined their parish membership.

But in the United States, and particularly in urban centers, the Catholic Church ran squarely into a situation that could not be handled in the old European way. What would happen when, within the geographic limits of one territorial parish, there lived immigrants from Ireland, Germany, Bohemia, Poland, and Italy? In what language would sermons be preached and confessions heard? In which style of architecture would the church be built? Which saints would merit special honor? Nothing in Church law covered the situation. While national groups clamored for recognition, bishops struggled for ad hoc solutions to the problem. Some argued in favor of rapid "Americanization," without concession to national custom. Others, as in St. Louis, compromised by creating separate ethnic "chapels" legally subordinate to the local territorial parish. Still others gave free and equal rein to each group. The problem precipitated a national crisis within the Church, one not officially resolved until the late 1880's in favor of separate national parishes of equal status with the territorial.[9]

The bishops of Chicago took no part in this controversy. Instead, they responded with a pragmatism that quickly became the hallmark of Chicago Catholicism. Without fanfare or appeal to law or principle, the very first bishop set the precedent that his successors followed, without exception, for almost a century.

When William J. Quarter arrived in Chicago in 1843, he found a single congregation made up of Irish and Germans and the few remaining French. The parish's ethnic flavor, after its founding in 1833, had shifted over the first difficult decade with a succession of French, Irish, and German pastors. Each group enjoyed separate services in its own tongue when a sufficient variety of priests could be had.[10] But by the time Quarter arrived, the Irish and Germans had increased enough to require the addition of new parishes. The bishop first shrewdly secured hierarchic authority by creating a corporation sole, recognized by the State of Illinois, which made the Bishop of Chicago forever proprietor of all parish property in the diocese.[11] He then established three new parishes. One, he decided, would be a territorial parish to complement the original congregation, which was now also designated as exclusively for the English speaking. The other two were for the Germans. "It is a matter of great concern to me," he wrote "to erect a church for the Germans residing here in Chicago and to build a school for the daily instruction of their children." [12] Quarter's action in providing separately for the Germans marked the parting of the ways. By the time Rome had ratified the existence of ethnic parishes in the United States in 1887, in addition to the thirty-five Irish-dominated territorial ones, there were eighteen German, six Polish, five Bohemian, and two French Catholic parishes in Chicago. Each enjoyed equal status. By 1900, 55.4 percent of all Catholic school children attended officially ethnic schools, and the other 44.6 percent the officially territorial but de facto Irish schools. For the next three decades, these percentages remained substantially the same.

CATHOLIC ELEMENTARY SCHOOLS
City of Chicago
1870–1930
Ethnic Enrollments

Ethnic Affiliation°	1870	1880	1890	1900	1910	1920	1930
Territorial °°	7,712	11,138	18,167	22,153	42,150	50,772	68,203
German	2,700	3,976	6,884	11,352	14,311	13,347	11,307
Polish	100	875	3,799	12,276	21,318	35,862	49,517
Bohemian	100	650	1,752	2,174	3,198	2,553	1,888
French		74	451	1,115	1,271	1,343	1,567
Lithuanian				133	794	3,237	3,738
Italian				435	702	3,053	3,746
Slovak					375	1,980	2,686
Belgian					310		
Negro						208	981
Croatian						380	1,158
Slovene							325
Total	10,612	16,713	31,053	49,638	84,429	112,735	145,116

° Figures for ethnic groups are based on the known affiliation of the school at the time. They do not include children of one group who might have attended the school of another.
°° Territorial parishes were open to anyone, but were chiefly attended by the Irish.

No doubt the Chicago Church's accommodation on the ethnic question stemmed in part from purely practical considerations. With nationalism running so high, why risk internal strife in a diocese already overburdened with the problems of rapid expansion? To buck the ethnic current seemed humanly impossible, anyway. Priests and teaching sisters themselves often arrived speaking little or no English, and unfamiliar with any but the mother culture. They could only teach what they knew. Then too, nationalism stimulated effort and achievement as Catholic competed against Catholic for educational glory. Each faction extolled its heroes—the Irish Sisters of Mercy who struggled through the mire of the early City's streets to their several schools; the Polish Father Vincent Barzynski whose single-handed efforts resulted in six new parishes and schools, a college, an orphanage, a newspaper, and the Polish Roman Catholic Union; the Sisters of St. Casimir who with zealous devotion transmitted their national heritage to Lithuanian children; and so on.[13] Perhaps also, the Church's liberal concessions to nationalism reflected its defiance of the nativist prejudice against foreigners. It may also have resulted simply from genuine recognition of the value inherent in the many national cultures that made up the City's Catholic population.

But beyond these considerations, Catholic leaders clearly recognized that the freedom granted Chicago's ethnics worked to the Church's advantage, keeping them within the fold. In the ethnic parish, the immigrant need fear no insult, real or imagined. In the parochial school, his children learned the mother language and culture from priests and teachers reared in the same tradition themselves. Home and school functioned in harmony. Catholic leaders made capital of the parochial school's ethnic attraction. Over against the "infamous" public school "dominated by an unfair and comparatively small faction," who persistently tried to use it to teach the rising generation of immigrant children "that they were the descendents of a class of commercial marauders in England styling themselves the great Anglo-Saxon race," [14] Catholic protagonists posed the parochial school where children would learn the ethnic truth.

So clear to Church spokesmen was the Catholic school's ethnic edge over the public school that some strove to perpetuate it by opposing any concession to national interests in the public schools. While condemning the public school for failure to "take into consideration . . . the mother tongue of our children," [15] they sometimes opposed the introduction of foreign languages in public schools. In 1879, for example, after frequent squabbles over the German question, the public school board voted to drop the teaching of German. The Chicago *Arbeiter Zeitung* complained that "nativism dominates our school board supported by several Catholics who in their own interest welcome any measure which would weaken the public school system, so much hated by them." [16] After reversal of the decision the following year, Catholics still objected, convinced that the practice drew German children away from the parochial schools. In opposing foreign language programs in the schools, Catholics joined with nativist Americans, but for different reasons. After 1890, the Polish National Alliance and the Polish Roman Catholic Union in Chicago clashed over the teaching of Polish in the public schools. The predominantly Catholic but more secular and nationalistic Alliance pressured the school board for two decades, and in 1911, finally succeeded in having Polish introduced into a Chicago public high school. The National Alliance cared less whether the children attended Catholic or public schools as long as they could study Polish. The Roman Catholic Union, on the other hand, saw the introduction of Polish into public schools as a threat to the drawing power of the parochial schools. They grew "violently angry" over the 1911 outcome, and the feud between these two groups continued for years.[17] The Bohemian Free Thinkers and Bohemian Catholics engaged in a similar struggle.

Catholic leaders understood full well that many children were sent to parochial schools not only for religious reasons. Their schools offered what the public schools did not. Both to attack the public

school's Anglo-Saxonism and to oppose its de-Anglo-Saxonization
made perfect sense. Either way, the parochial school would gain.

Yet, despite its obvious advantages, the ethnic parochial school did
not return pure profit. Above all, in dollars and cents, it produced
extravagant inefficiency and waste. Even without the diversity of
national schools, the Catholic practice of allowing each parish its
own school, however large or small, did not make for economy. But
the presence of several distinct national school systems, each overlaid
on the other, resulted in absurd lack of coordination and prodigious
economic waste in a diocese where "lack of funds" was the common
plaint.

The diseconomy could be observed in the physical geography of
the City itself. By 1906 for example, in an area of less than one
square mile, the Back of the Yards district housed nine Catholic
churches, each with its school. The nine parishes represented seven
different nationalities. Children on their way to school passed not
only the local public school but several parochial as well. Each
school-day morning the young scholars sorted themselves into their
respective national habitats. Fluctuating fortunes in these various
schools reflected not a coordinated educational policy but merely the
flux of the district's in and out migration. Thus in 1910, the German
school had 1,172 pupils, the Lithuanian only 175. Each school
prospered or declined independently of the others. The Irish parish
of St. Rose, in 1900 "the center of the religious life of the district,"
declined into the "smallest and most unpretentious of them all" by
1930.[18] Though the Irish school lost three-fifths of its pupils between
1900 and 1910, the nearby Eastern European institutions struggled
to provide for 4,500 more. Yet, for a Pole or Lithuanian or Slovak to
attend St. Rose before the last Irish child had departed was
unthinkable. As one school stood almost empty, another stood
a-building just across the street or down the block.

The same pattern emerged in every area of heavy Catholic
immigration. On the near northwest side, for example, Irish and
Germans built the first parishes and schools. Then in the decades
following the 1870's, the Poles came and "in a short space of time,

built several parishes of their own," even as the Irish and Germans departed. Between 1890 and 1900, the Polish school enrollments increased by over 100 percent while the Irish decreased by over 33 percent. Annunciation parish alone once numbered over 1,000 families. By 1916, though "diminished to almost a shadow of its former self," the parish, with the 150 families that remained, struggled to maintain itself as an Irish institution, while the Poles tightened their grip on the rolling mill district.[19] The Germans fared the same. Between 1873 and 1905 the Poles set up three parishes that formed a triangle around the original northwest side German parish of St. Boniface. By 1915, the Poles had crowded over 7,000 pupils into the three schools of these parishes, while at St. Boniface, "with ever increasing impetus, the old German families were leaving the neighborhood for the more attractive outskirts of the city." Attendance at the school declined from 1,200 in 1900 to 200 in 1916. The crisis between St. Boniface and the encircling Polish strongholds produced a comedy of ethnic errors. First, the strongly nationalistic German pastor tried "every promising means" to "keep his own people clustered around the church." The efforts included successful lobbying for newly paved streets, sewer installation, and even the 10-acre Eckert Park. Meanwhile, he spoke publicly against the Poles, snubbed them in the streets, and made them generally unwelcome in parish and school. But to no avail. The Germans departed anyway, and the parish income no longer met expenses, nor could it even pay interest on the debt. Finally, in 1916, the Archbishop appointed a new, more realistic German pastor who welcomed the Poles and laboriously learned their language. For his efforts he earned the bitter accusations of neighboring Polish pastors for enticing their parishioners into the German church.[20]

One found the same phenomenon in every other workingman's district—Bridgeport, Pullman, South Chicago, the lower west side, and even to an extent, in the zone of emergence adjoining the workingman's districts—an intense concentration of Catholic churches and schools, each functioning in almost total isolation, each with its own growth and decline. The Church's ethnic policy did not make for efficient management.

Nor did it contribute much to the Lord's injunction: "Love one another." Indeed, the disharmony, friction, and sometimes open antagonism between the Catholic ethnics contributed more than its share to the Chicago Church's time of tribulation. Rivalry between Catholic co-religionists often ran high. Each group failed to appreciate the customs of the other. The frugal German and his meticulous *Hausfrau* often despised what seemed slovenly in the carefree "shanty" Irish. Even in religion, the Irish settled for "simplicity," while the German reveled in "the most solemn celebration" of sacred feasts.[21] The mutual suspicion and dislike that drove the two into segregated churches and schools sometimes spilled into open hostility, to a point in fact that prompted the *New World* in 1897 to ask in near despair, "Will anyone tell us why it is that the Irish and German Catholics cannot get along together?" [22] The Polish, on the other hand, mistrusted both. As relative latecomers, they felt the disdain reserved for foreigners not only from the native mainstream but from their better established religious compatriots whose egos could only feed on the discomfort of those more foreign than themselves. The Poles resented the Irish and German Catholic "establishment" and strove to establish themselves. Thus, in 1911, the Polish National Alliance's *Dziennik Zwiazkowy* urged the building of more Polish schools, with the warning that "if we neglect this worthy and noble matter, our enemies, the Irish and Germans will gain. . . . They can more easily keep us under their yoke." [23]

But the Poles, in turn, attempted to yoke other still more recent and less numerous neighbors from overseas. When the Lithuanians founded their first parish in 1886, they had to engage Polish sisters for the schools, since no Lithuanian teachers had as yet arrived in Chicago. This apparent act of cooperation resulted in a bitter complaint to diocesan authorities thirteen years later, signed by 1,500 Lithuanian parishioners, about the "Polish Sisters, incompetent to speak the Lithuanian language and who through ignorance convert our children into Poles." The situation further deteriorated when Lithuanian girls began joining the religious order of their Polish teachers. Lithuanian priests agitated among these renegade Lithuanian sisters, urging them either to form a separate Lithuanian province of the order or to break off entirely to join the Sisters of St. Casimir, a Lithuanian religious group formed to conduct parochial schools for Lithuanian immigrants in America. Eventually this group took over all the Lithuanian schools in Chicago and eliminated the threat to Lithuanian children.[24] While the Lithuanians had their differences with the Poles, the Slovaks had theirs with the Bohemians. In the early days, the Slovaks worshipped at Bohemian churches, and then the Bohemian Benedictines staffed the first Slovak church of St. Michael's. Slovak boys of the parish joined the Bohemian Benedictine monastery at Lisle, Illinois, and the girls entered the convent there. But the professed harmony of religious life failed to eradicate national differences. .By 1927, the Slovak monks broke away from the Bohemian Benedictines and began years of querulous negotiations to gain control of St. Michael's parish in Chicago. The Slovak Sisters, too, formed their own community and agitated, with the help of Slovak parishes, to "take over all other Slovak schools" from the Bohemian Benedictines.[25]

Many Catholic ethnics first attended the churches and schools of a better established group, related in language and customs. Thus, Bohemians worshipped with Germans; Poles and Slovaks with Bohemians. Croatians and Slovenes first attended Bohemian churches, too; they then shared facilities and finally broke off to form completely separate parishes.[26] What began in cooperation often ended in anger and recrimination. Such was the seamless cloak of Catholic unity in Chicago. And always, striving to weave the separate threads together stood the Bishop of Chicago at the episcopal loom, himself the periodic object of vitriolic broadside and vicious ethnic rumor.

The first line of attack focused on the bishop's throne itself. This the Irish secured and maintained, save for the brief incumbency of a Flemish Jesuit from 1849 to 1853, until 1916. After that it passed to a third generation American of German descent who acknowledged no ethnic affiliation whatever. As early as the 1840's, disgruntled Germans pressed for at least a coadjutor bishop who "could talk their language fluently and understand their customs." [27] Later, in the 1880's, Chicago Germans joined a national movement demanding totally separate bishoprics in the United States. By 1908, Polish pressure had secured at least a Polish auxiliary bishop for Chicago, the first in the United States. As late as the 1920's, Poles, Lithuanians, and Slovaks each demanded separate bishoprics.[28] On this point the Bishop of Chicago, like Rome itself, held firm. Thus in 1927, Archbishop Mundelein stood "as much opposed to the making of a Slovak Bishop to look after the interests of the Slovaks resident here as I was to the making of a Polish Bishop or a German Bishop for the same reason." [29]

The second line of attack on episcopal authority had to do with parish autonomy. Unlike certain other dioceses, Chicago always provided equal status to the national and territorial parishes. Yet equal status also meant equal subjection to episcopal rule. In particular, it meant that the bishops held title to each parish's property and reserved the right to appoint every parish priest. In some cases, this practice led directly to defection from the Church and even schism. Thus, the parishioners of the original Czech parish refused to turn over their deed. A lengthy lawsuit during the 1870's, eventually decided in favor of the bishop, caused many Czech parishioners to leave the Church.[30] In the 1890's, dispute over the appointment of a pastor in the Polish St. Hedwig's parish led to the formation of the schismatic Polish National Church in Chicago.[31] Sometimes the principle of episcopal control conflicted with customs established in the mother country. In Lithuania, for example, lay trustees held the parish property and even nominated pastors. Attempts to do the same in Chicago led to bitter disagreement in 1906 and formation of the Lithuanian National Church. On occasion, too, unique circumstances in their country of origin put national groups into direct conflict with Church authorities. Thus, the Church's traditional alliance with Bohemia's Austrian occupiers drove many Czechs from the Catholic fold in Europe itself and produced a deep antipathy to hierarchic authority in those who remained. In Chicago, though few became Protestants, many called themselves "Free Thinkers," and not more than half actually practiced the Catholic faith. Those that did resented the Church's institutional authority, which from the Austrian experience they saw as antagonistic to Czech nationalism. As late as 1917, after another acrimonious dispute with Bohemians in Cicero, the Archbishop complained bitterly that the "exaggerated spirit of nationalism that is rampant today among the various Slav races," amounted "almost to a mania in some cases." [32]

Bishops agonized over the excruciating ethnic dilemma; and sometimes one ecclesiastic's expedient decision came back to plague his hapless successor. For example, to counter the Lithuanian schism, Archbishop Quigley appointed extreme nationalists to Lithuanian pastorates after 1906. But, within a decade, their contentiousness forced Archbishop Mundelein to replace some of these pastors with other, more moderate nationalists. Despite an optimistic report from the diocesan chancellor, in 1919, that "the Lithuanian parishes, always a source of trouble in the Archdiocese, are now in a most peaceful condition," [33] trouble brewed again by the 1920's. Some of the newer priests, though of Lithuanian descent, favored the introduction of English. In January of 1925, Lithuanian nationalists passed out handbills at Sunday Masses urging parishioners to "uprise for the Lithuanian nationalism in our church, which we by our own labor and hard-earned pennies have built up and are upkeeping to this day." "Our Lithuanian church is the only stronghold for our Lithuanian nationality in America," they argued. "Let us defend it from Americanization. . . . Away with the English sermons from Lithuanian churches and, you traitors, and Americanizing priests, get out from our Lithuanian parishes." [34] An angry delegation met with the Archbishop, who, though again insisting on his right to appoint pastors, assured the nationals of having not "the least intention for infringing the rights of the Lithuanian language." [35]

Yet, surprisingly, the lid to this ethnic boiling pot never blew. In the Polish schism, only three new Chicago parishes were formed and even these declined after 1900. The Lithuanian separatists gained an even smaller following. Though parishioners defected here and there in protest against an alleged violation of their national rights, the vast majority held true to the church of their fathers. Indeed, despite smoldering tensions, the Church still offered more freedom of ethnic expression than could be found in the City's public institutions. Before 1916, no record remains that any Catholic bishop ever refused permission for the establishment of a national parish or even failed to appoint priests of the same nationality; and each national parish chose its own community of sisters to teach in the schools. After its formation in 1887, the diocesan board of school supervisors always reflected a careful ethnic balance.

Some prelates even distinguished their tenure by sedulous cultivation of ethnic goodwill. Thus, the *Chicago Tribune* listed as Patrick A. Feehan's major accomplishment "in the first place, the diplomatic handling of the Irish, German, Polish, Bohemian, French and Italian elements in the diocese." [36] During a reign of over 20 years which spanned the first two decades of the great second immigrant wave from Southern and Eastern Europe, he was always, it was said, "anxious to give a parish to any number of people who could give evidence that they were able to support a priest." When the State Legislature in 1889 passed a law requiring all schools to use English as the sole medium of instruction, Feehan supported the Catholic ethnics in their successful struggle for its repeal. His successor, James E. Quigley, who presided during the years of maximum immigration from 1902 to 1915, always provided parishes "with priests of their own nationality" [37] and promoted the founding of 20 parishes for the recalcitrant Italians. Even George Mundelein, in 1916, though not personally in favor of perpetuating the ethnic system, "endeavored to show a spirit of fairness" [38] to each nationality, always supplied them with priests of their own, and allowed the formation of new national parishes when necessary. Prior to 1916, no restrictions whatever controlled the language of the school curriculum; and after that the national language and culture could still be taught and catechism offered in the mother tongue. Despite the tribulation, ethnic interests actually thrived under the Church's permissive management in Chicago.

Whether the ethnic school actually enhanced the children's experience, depended, of course, on how one viewed the purpose of American education. To those for whom Americanization meant the obliteration of cultural differences brought from Europe, the ethnic school could only be seen as divisive. But those who saw Americanization as a fusion of diverse cultural strands into a new social whole had to admit that the Catholic school in Chicago eased the immigrant's transition from the old world to the new and, in the process, enriched the City's life. Whatever the judgment, from the Church's more narrowly parochial point of view, its ethnic policy clearly helped cement the immigrant's loyalty while cutting deep into the pull of the public school. On balance, the ethnic factor, and in particular, the Church's permissive handling of it in Chicago, despite the tribulation, produced a substantial net gain for the Catholic educational enterprise.

4

The Ethnic Factor II

A Catholic newspaper report on the Chicago Church's schools in 1852 completely omitted mention of the City's two German Catholic schools. The omission, though acknowledged later with apologies, symbolized the extent to which Catholics themselves from the very early decades in Chicago thought of their schools as quite distinct ethnic systems. Fifty years later, when the diocesan newspaper published a special 154-page edition to commemorate the beginning of the new century, it organized the section on Catholic schools along ethnic lines, with each group treated as a separate system.[1] The article merely mirrored reality. Almost overwhelmingly, the history of Catholic education in Chicago for the first 100 years was the history of its separate ethnic systems. Each system developed or failed to develop in large part independently of the others.

To the French probably belongs the honor of having first imparted instruction under Catholic auspices at this early portage between Lake Michigan and the Illinois waterways. From 1674 to 1675, the Jesuit Père Jacques Marquette wintered on the banks of the Chicago River and, in keeping with missionary practice, almost certainly offered religious instruction to the local Indians. Within twenty years, another French Jesuit founded the Angel Guardian Mission at this outpost for French traders. In 1699, a visitor reported that "several girls of a certain age and many boys were taught" there.[2] But the mission closed about 1700, and after that, except for an occasional missionary visit, Indians and Frenchmen lived without priest or church or Catholic school. Frenchmen constituted the charter membership of Chicago's first Catholic parish in 1833. But that was their one moment of glory in the City's modern Catholic history. Within two years they were swamped by the more numerous Irish and German immigrants. Not until 1852 did French Catholics open a parish and school of their own, only to lose it again within another two years due to an invasion of Irishmen.[3] In 1864, the bishop gave them a lot on the near west side where the new parish and school of Notre Dame de Chicago acted as a magnet for the French Catholics "dispersed in all parts of the city." [4] During the late '80's and the '90's, French Catholics founded parishes in industrial West Pullman, near the stockyards, and in Brighton Park "for the French speaking people of the southwest side." [5] The school enrollment of these several French parishes never exceeded a total of 1,500 pupils at its zenith. Yet, whenever possible, the French Catholics preferred to have their children educated among their own.

Most of nineteenth-century Catholic Chicago belonged to the Irish and Germans. Until the late 1860's, their schools accounted for 100 percent of the parochial school enrollment. They still made up over 80 percent in 1890. The Germans were predominant on the north side and to an extent on the northwest, the Irish on the west and south sides. Yet each had representation everywhere else. Where one went to found a parish the other was sure to follow. For example, after the Germans established their first parish on the north side, in 1846, Irishmen "who could not understand the German sermons" soon founded their own just a block away.[6] A little further north, two more German and Irish churches were put up in the late 1850's, this time separated by three blocks.[7] By the end of the century, the north side Germans had 4,081 pupils in four parish schools south of Irving Park Road; the Irish had 2,040 in four smaller schools of their own.

On the northwest side everyone took for granted that Irish and German Catholics went to separate churches and schools. Here, by the 1860's, each had founded parishes, separated in distance by a short walk but in language and culture by the gulf that divided Teuton from Celt. Later, when the two groups pushed further north and west into the Humbolt Park distirict in the 1880's, "all Catholic settlers, without distinction of race and language, joined hands and the result was that two new parishes were established: St. Sylvester for all the English speaking settlers, and St. Aloysius for the Germans." [8] Even "joining of hands" resulted in separate facilities.

To the Irish belonged the west side. From their original parish of St. Patrick's just west of the river they fanned out after the 1840's into fourteen parishes east of Cicero Avenue by 1900. In 1910, their west side schools enrolled almost 12,000 pupils. Yet, in the shadows of Irish churches could also be found the smaller German ones. In the early 1840's, the City's largest German colony resided just west of Chicago's downtown, where parish and school thrived until commercial expansion spelled its doom. In the 1850's, Germans moved across the river into St. Francis of Assisi parish, just down 12th Street from the huge Irish church of the Holy Family. Though actually surrounded by Holy Family's five branch schools, which educated 5,000 children by 1890, the German parish schooled 900 *kinder* of its own. By 1900, the Germans had a total of four parish schools on the west side, but always sandwiched between the larger Irish parishes.

On the south side, the story repeated itself. In heavily Irish Bridgeport, the three Irish schools were matched by two German before 1883. The Germans moved first into Back of the Yards with a parish and school in 1879. The Irish followed with one of their own by 1881. The pattern was the same in every workingman's community. It could also be found in the zones of emergence. For example, in Englewood and West Englewood, the three German parishes built between 1886 and 1901 were countered by four Irish between 1886 and 1904. Further east, the Irish opened Holy Cross parish in

Woodlawn in 1891; the Germans followed three years later with St. Clara's.

In the City, except for the north side, the Irish Catholics outnumbered the German. Yet, in every section, first in working-man's areas, later in zones of emergence, both groups had their separate constituencies.

Outside the City proper, patterns of settlement and occupational choice served to siphon off the two groups into even more distinct communities. The prairie farming land of Cook, Lake, and DuPage counties held particular attraction for the Germans. For example, by 1870, there lay to the west a "long chain of parishes founded by the early German settlers on that wide expanse of prairie land stretching from Chicago to Aurora." [9] To the north and south, too, German farmers founded parishes in rural settlements like New Trier, Niles Center, Buffalo Grove, Fremont Center, Volo, Blue Island, and New Strassburg. In all, by 1870, there were 16 German parishes in a wide arc around the City, all but three in distinctly rural communities. Most of the Irish had had enough of farm life on their native sod, with only a few finding their way into agricultural villages like Wauconda, Meehan's settlement, and Wadsworth in Lake County. But most "suburban" Irish in the nineteenth century lived in canal worker settlements like Sag Bridge and Lemont. Yet even outside Chicago, when Irish and German Catholics found themselves thrown together, they founded separate parishes. In Waukegan, each had a parish before 1870. In Lemont, the Irish canal worker parish founded in the 1840's did not suit the Germans who arrived in the 1860's to work the nearby quarries, and after a brief experiment in ecumenism, they founded their own.[10]

Each parish throughout the Diocese was staffed by priests of its respective nationality. The German school children were taught first by laymen and then by the German School Sisters of Notre Dame and German branches of the Franciscan, Bendedictine, and Holy Cross Orders. The Irish had their Sisters of Mercy and Sisters of Charity and others from the Emerald Isle. Societies like the Ancient

Order of Hibernians promoted a program of Irish history in "those schools in which the great majority of the children are of Irish parentage," [11] and even granted special "diplomas" to those who completed the program. At the secondary level, Irish Christian Brothers, Sisters of Mercy, and Sisters of Charity opened schools in Irish parishes or Irish neighborhoods. The Germans had for a brief time their own branch of the University of St. Mary's of the Lake. They also founded several private academies for girls and a high school for boys and girls in St. Michael's parish. Even orphans were segregated. The Diocese itself had run an orphanage since 1849, and the Christian Brothers had cared for and schooled delinquent boys in connection with St. Bridget's Irish parish in delinquency-prone Bridgeport after 1859. But in 1865, the German Catholics decided to form their own orphanage, supported by contributions from all German parishes.[12] In a word, aside from allegiance to a single bishop, Irish and German Catholics rendered the Diocese into two quite separate systems.

The massive new immigration from Southern and Eastern Europe after 1880 rendered it into even more. By 1850, a few Polish immigrants began settling on the near northwest side close to the industries that lined the Chicago River, but not until 1867 could they muster enough resources to found a parish.[13] Despite this relatively late start in the young city, the following decades saw the Poles rise to a position that challenged Irish and German hegemony. By 1900, the enrollment in Polish schools outnumbered the German. From the original parish of St. Stanislaus Kostka, the Polish population spread out over the northwest side into 17 new parishes by 1920, when their schools here numbered 17,000 children, 75 percent of the Catholic school enrollment in the area.

The Poles also formed large, tightly knit colonies outside their major settlement on the northwest side. Large Polish parishes and schools could be found wherever industry located in Chicago, after the 1890's. By 1920, 3,557 pupils in three Polish schools of South Chicago accounted for 96 percent of the Catholic school enrollment there, and in the area around the stockyards 42 percent of the

Catholic school pupils attended Polish schools. Even on the lower west side, usually considered a Bohemian stronghold, 50 percent of the Catholic enrollment belonged to Polish schools in 1920. In all, by 1930, the Poles had 42 schools in Chicago itself and 12 more outside the City, mostly in such industrial suburbs as Calumet City, Chicago Heights, Cicero, Blue Island, Harvey, Lemont, Argo, and North Chicago. The Polish Felician Sisters, the Sisters of the Resurrection, and the Sisters of the Holy Family of Nazareth all set up their mother houses in Chicago and staffed most of the Polish schools. The others were staffed by Polish branches of the Franciscans and School Sisters of Notre Dame. In the early years, most of these sisters came from Poland, and as late as the mid-1920's an official report indicated that many could speak but broken English.[14]

The Catholic schools served as major vehicles for preservation of the Polish language in every Polish colony. A reporter for a Chicago newspaper in 1903 found that, although Polish parents were anxious to have their children learn English, "these children never sacrifice their native language. In the parochial schools . . . they are taught in English for four hours a day and the balance of the time in Polish, Polish history, literature and kindred subjects being studied in the native tongue." [15] The groundwork in Polish language and culture laid at school was bolstered by participation in Polish debating societies, clubs, and leagues of all sorts, fostered by the parishes. In 1917, a University of Chicago student debater charged that in the Back of the Yards Catholic schools "English is taught as a mere ornamental language as is French in high school. It is a fact that children born in these colonies speak English with the greatest difficulty." An irate Polish pastor answered, asserting that in the Polish schools of the district "all the branches are taught in the English language with the exception of catechism and one or two subjects immediately related to the mother country." He did not observe, however, that catechism in addition to two other subjects constituted a sizable portion of the curriculum.[16]

Of all the ethnic groups, the Poles were also the most persistent in maintaining a system of distinctively ethnic secondary schools in

Chicago. By 1890, two private secondary institutions had already been founded for Polish Catholics in their original settlement on the near northwest side. These were described in 1912 as having "a spirit sincerely filled with love for all that is Polish." By 1910, Holy Trinity parochial high school had been added in the same area to give the Polish boy "mastery of the language of his forefathers together with a deep appreciation of the ideals and traditions of the Polish people." The 1920's saw two more private girls' high schools on the far northwest side where Poles had then begun to move. Resurrection High School was described as "exclusively for Polish girls whose aim is to be developed into prominent citizens, and managers of families with a soul Polish and religious throughout." The other school, Good Counsel, was founded "to serve the general needs of higher education for Polish families located in that section of the city." During this period, the Polish Educational Aid Society was busy "promoting the cause of the higher education of Polish boys and girls by paying whole or part tuitions in Polish Catholic high schools for children who graduate from parochial school and whose parents cannot afford such tuitions." [17]

The Poles seemed determined to organize an all-inclusive system of their own. In 1908, they even completed plans for a Polish National University in Chicago, to be affiliated with the Catholic University of America in Washington, D.C. When this university failed to materialize, the Chicago Poles eventually settled for sponsoring a chair of Polish literature at Loyola University. Long after the turn of the century, the large majority of Catholic Poles still lived in a world apart, with their own parishes, schools, social organizations, orphanages, and newspapers. The official diocesan paper carried little Polish news, and the editors complained that, being unable to read Polish, they could not include news from the Polish Catholic papers. As one Chicago Polish commentator put it, "what the oppressive hand of Prussian, Russian, and Austrian could not accomplish, was not to be permitted to happen in a benevolent land of freedom of worship and speech." [18]

What the foreigner's oppressive hand could not accomplish against the Pole, it did not accomplish either against his neighbors from Eastern Europe. Bohemian Catholics, for example, settled in self-contained neighborhoods, built their churches and schools, and jealously maintained their national customs against the Americanizers and their Catholicity against free-thinking fellow countrymen. The first few Bohemians in Chicago lived on the near north side about 1855, but, by the 1860's, they had settled mainly on the near west side. "Here developed between 1860 and 1870, the first large and characteristically Czech settlement, in which all occupations were represented, and where the Bohemian language could be used exclusively." In 1863 they built the combination church–school of St. Wenceslaus in the heart of this district. But by the 1870's, the main Bohemian body began inching away. Bohemian Catholics first moved across the river, into Bridgeport, and founded a parish and school there. But in Bridgeport, due to a fire ordinance, they could not build the small frame cottages they favored, and the parish never thrived. The main body simply moved further west and slightly south of the original settlement, into the lower west side. In this area known as "Pilsen," they founded St. Procopius parish in 1875. It became the center of Czech Catholic activity in Chicago, with a school that numbered 1,300 pupils by 1895, the largest Bohemian school in the country. Moved by the "longing in the vast majority of Bohemians to have their own home," the colony pushed ever westward along the lower west side, eventually expanding into Cicero and Berwyn and establishing a string of Catholic parishes and schools as it went. By 1914, the 10th, 11th, 12th, and 34th wards, stretching along the lower west side to the city limits, numbered over 80,000 first- and second-generation Bohemians, 30 percent of the area's total population and 77 percent of all Czechs in Chicago at the time. In this area were six of the nine Bohemian Catholic churches and schools. The others could be found in Bridgeport and the Back of the Yards, and one was on the northwest side. By 1909, the Czechs had a parish and school in Berwyn and by 1919 another in Cicero.[19]

They kept alive the flames of nationalism in various ways. The National Alliance of Czech Catholics maintained a committee on education, which was especially concerned with promoting the Czech language. It sponsored literary contests in the schools, offered forums, lectures, and discussions on Czech history and culture, and printed pamphlets on current topics. In 1930, the District Alliance of this organization still sponsored lectures on Czech history and culture in all Bohemian parishes. But the schools themselves did the major job of transmitting Czech culture to the young. Every Bohemian parish had its school, and as late as the 1920's each still gave two hours daily to instruction in Czech. In addition, the children often participated in school plays and programs, given in Czech, for the benefit of the parish. As early as 1876, a Czech literary society had been formed to "prepare and publish Czech readers for the schools." The first teachers were laymen, but with the rise in enrollment, Bohemian members of the Benedictines, Franciscans, and School Sisters of Notre Dame gradually took over the schools and recruited and trained Bohemian girls to carry on the work. In 1912, the Bohemian Benedictine Sisters opened a girls' boarding school in Lisle, Illinois. In 1887, the Bohemian Benedictine Monks founded St. Procopius College "to preserve . . . ethnic consciousness or nationality" among the Czechs of the lower west side. Fifteen years later, they moved to rural Lisle where the college became the chief center for the study of Czech Catholic culture in the United States. By 1898, the Bohemians had their own orphanage for boys and girls, also at Lisle. The Czechs, too, maintained a completely self-sufficient Catholicism, independent of the main Catholic body.[20]

A few Lithuanians had come to Chicago around 1870. By 1886, they founded St. George parish in Bridgeport. But the real growth of Lithuanian Catholicism did not begin until 1900. Between 1900 and 1914 the Lithuanians founded nine parishes in Chicago, one on the northwest side, two on the lower west side, two near the stockyards and another just west in Brighton Park, one in the South Chicago steel mill district, one in Roseland, and another in West Pullman—all located near industry. Outside Chicago, too, one found Lithuanian parishes where the workers were—in Waukegan, Chicago Heights, and Cicero. The Lithuanians quickly founded parochial schools in all these parishes. By 1913, the Sisters of St. Casimir, founded to conduct schools for Lithuanian immigrants to the United States, made Chicago their base of operations. By 1925, they had taken over all the Lithuanian schools. And in 1911, they founded St. Casimir Academy, a private secondary school in the Marquette Park section of the southwest side. Here, as in their parochial elementary schools, "believing that the best of European culture should be preserved in American children of foreign ancestry," the sisters strove to inculcate "Lithuanian literature, customs, culture and history." The Lithuanians looked above all to their schools as a means to preserve "the rights of the Lithuanian language." [21]

A small group of Slovaks had settled on the near west side in the early 1880's, but were too few in number to found their own parish; their first parish was not founded until 1898, when they built St. Michael's church near the stockyards. This area became the best known Slovakian settlement in Chicago, and by 1920, the parish was the largest one of that nationality in the United States. The school enrolled over 1,000 pupils. As late as the 1920's, during the first six months of first grade, the children of this school had to be taught entirely in Slovakian so unfamiliar were they with English.[22] The Slovaks also founded other parishes, always in the industrial areas where their immigrants settled near the factories. In 1907 they founded one near the Pullman works. With the opening of the school here "many of the families living in the north, south, and even the west outskirts of Pullman moved into the Roseland district so that their children could have easy access to the new school." [23] They founded another in 1909 near the South Chicago steel mills and two more between 1911 and 1914 on the northwest side for Slovak workers in the Northwestern Railroad yards. Two pockets of Slovak workers also formed on the lower west side, where they founded two other parishes by 1914. Though somewhat scattered throughout the City, the Slovaks gathered about their churches where they could hear sermons and confess in Slovakian through the 1920's. Every parish save the one in South Chicago had its school.

A small number of Slovenian and Croatian Catholics began

settling in Chicago in the 1890's. For a time they worshipped in a Bohemian church on the lower west side, then formed a joint parish of their own, and finally, by 1913, split into separate units. Between 1900 and 1913 the Croatians founded four parishes and the Slovenians two. Their small congregations made the maintenance of schools difficult, but by the 1920's all had schools except one Slovenian congregation. The schools proved a magnet in attracting parishioners. For example, the pastor of Slovenian St. Stephen's reported in 1923 that "Many are moving nearer St. Stephen's to give their children the benefit of a Catholic education." [24]

A few Flemish Belgians drifted into Chicago during the late nineteenth century, but settled in scattered locations. From time to time, Flemish Jesuits from St. Ignatius College ministered to their needs, but not until 1903 had enough Flemish Catholics settled on the northwest side near the Deering works to form a separate parish. The congregation remained small, and again parishioners resorted to the founding of a school "to draw the Belgians around St. John Berchmans." [25]

Dutch Catholics, too, attempted to preserve cultural ties by founding their own church. In 1900, enough Dutch had settled in the Pullman area to ask for a "Hollandish speaking parish." They founded St. Willibrord's, but the congregation remained small and could support no school until the late 1920's.[26]

A very small group of Hungarian Catholics also settled in Chicago, especially in the little community of Burnside on the south side. Here, in 1904, they established Our Lady of Hungary church; but this group, too, because of its small size, did not open a school for over thirty years.[27]

There was also an assortment of Middle-Eastern Catholics who followed a different liturgy than the Europeans and therefore had to found their own churches. The Syrians established St. John the Baptist parish in 1910 on the lower west side,[28] and in 1911, a group of Assyro-Chaldeans founded St. Ephrem's parish on the northwest side.[29] But these parishes had no schools until the 1930's. Shortly after 1900, Ukranian Catholics, who followed an Eastern rite and had been granted their own bishops in the United States, founded parishes in Chicago too; these included St. Mary's in Back of the Yards and St. Nicholas on the northwest side. Neither of these parishes had schools before 1930, though, starting in 1909, St. Nicholas conducted after-school classes in religion and in Ukranian language and culture.[30]

The small groups of ethnic Catholics, probably because they were smaller and often scattered, had considerable difficulty in founding and maintaining their own parishes and schools. Yet, all seemed to share one characteristic with the large groups: the effort. Indeed every group, whatever its size, struggled to build separate parishes and schools—with one notable exception.

The Italians distinguished themselves for their disinterest not only in the parochial school but in the Catholic parish itself. With every other Catholic group, ecclesiastical authorities struggled to keep enthusiasm for the national parish within reasonable bounds. But with the Italians, the struggle went into providing churches and schools they would not build for themselves.

In 1870, a few Italian priests of the Servite order entered the City, intending to cooperate in the building of a parish for their countrymen who were just beginning to settle there. "The time had not arrived, however, when the Italian population could be formed into anything resembling good working material for a parish." [31] Finally, in 1881, the Italians did establish Assumption parish on the near north side at Illinois and Orleans Streets, but they opened no school until 1899.

By that time the number of foreign-born Italians had risen to over 16,000, and Protestant ministers and settlement workers had begun working in the Italian colonies. To counteract this influence, groups of non-Italian Catholics, encouraged by the bishop, organized Sunday schools for Italian children. The first two of these were opened in 1898 on the near south side and in Englewood by a group of laywomen. At the same time, attempts were made by "prominent Catholic ladies from all parts of the city" to raise funds "to erect a church in the center of the Italian district" on the near west side.

The result was a mission Sunday school on Forquer Street. In 1899, the *New World* exhorted Catholics to help the Italian missions in Chicago because these immigrants were poor and without a tradition of building and supporting churches "by voluntary contributions, as the Irish and Germans and Poles have done." The Irish administrator of the west side mission asked his fellow Catholics: "Can we remain indifferent while in the most congested neighborhood of Chicago, children are growing up in the gutter like social weeds, to become afterward perhaps a menace to our garden city?" Probably referring to Jane Addams at nearby Hull House, he also warned that Italian children were being drawn away from the Church by "well meaning non-Catholic philanthropists." By June of 1899, enough help had come to lay the cornerstone of a church for the west side Guardian Angel mission. But even with the construction of a church the enterprise remained "chiefly supported by the generosity of outsiders." By 1903, Guardian Angel had 1,000 Italian families and 1,433 children in the Sunday school taught by 125 teachers from all parts of the City and suburbs. The Sunday school became a favorite among Catholic public school teachers, and for years William J. Bogan, later superintendent of the Chicago public schools, served as its director. But still the parish remained a mission without a full-time day school.[32]

The "Italian problem" became a cause of major concern. The *New World* complained that "experience has simply proved that the Italians will not send their children to the parochial schools if they have to pay for them there, and experience has also fully proved that when Italian children go to the public schools in nine cases out of ten they lose all religious faith." [33] Chicago Catholicism had not experienced disinterest like this before and had always relied heavily on the initiative of the people themselves. Not until the more energetic Archbishop Quigley arrived in 1903 did the Diocese itself take remedial action for the Italians. At the time there was just one full-fledged parish, on the near north side.[34] In addition, missions operated on the near west side, the near south side, and in

Englewood. But in the decade from 1900 until 1910, the number of Italian immigrants in Chicago increased from 16,000 to 45,000.

Quigley responded to the problem by building churches for the Italians on his own initiative. By 1906, there were nine Italian parishes in the City, all but one founded by Archbishop Quigley with help from the Diocese. In 1910, with 45,000 native-born Italians and another 28,000 of Italian parentage in Chicago, there were ten Italian parishes, but only one had a school.[35] This was extraordinary in a diocese where most of the parishes had schools. Indeed, despite his efforts, in 1913 Quigley had to report to Rome that "the Italians who come from Southern Italy and Sicily are unexcelled in their ignorance of religion. . . . There are sufficient parochial schools for all the children of immigrants, except the Italians." [36]

Only through outside help were the Italian parishes able to open schools. German sisters conducted a school for the Italian children of Santa Maria Incoronata parish after 1915. And in 1917, Archbishop Mundelein asked "different communities [of sisters] to contribute toward the educational training of the Italians." [37] When Pastor Louis Giambastiani of St. Philip Benizi parish on the near north side appealed to the Archdiocese for help to open a school in 1918, he reported that Methodists, Presbyterians, Episcopalians, Seventh Day Adventists, and "anarchists" were working among the Italians of his parish. "How can I fight all these religious enemies without a school or encouragement of any kind," he pleaded. "I am thoroughly convinced that you people do not build a school because you do not realize the *absolute necessity* of it. If you would you would gladly meet any sacrifice that may be required." He complained that after seven years of labor "all the fruit of the past is a large crowd of young people growing around the church that don't care neither for church or God. They are practical atheists. Why? They did not have a Catholic school." Giambastiani admitted failure to get support for his enterprise from the people themselves in this "chaotic parish." The Archdiocese responded by allocating $65,000 for a school, which was opened in 1919.[38]

As late as 1919, the Italian districts of Chicago were still very much considered mission territory. In a letter to the Apostolic Delegate in Washington, the Chancellor of the Archdiocese reported that the Archbishop "has provided schools for them and has provided accommodations for over 3,000 Italian children, who are being taught by the religious of various communities, who have given their service gratis. This work alone has cost the Archdiocese $21,000 a year." [39] Meanwhile, Archbishop Mundelein decided to force the Italian parishes to "stand on their own feet," complaining of them that "quite a few of those already existing in Chicago are only able to continue in existence because they receive help from me, something which cannot be said of any of the other various groups of churches in the city." He began to cut off aid. For example, St. Anthony's parish had been created "with the understanding that the school would be supported by the Archdiocese's fund." For years the Archdiocese had paid all interest, sisters' salaries, janitors' wages, and the gas, electricity, telephone, coal, and repair bills. But in March, 1921, Mundelein reduced the aid to a monthly allotment of $300 and then, in December, cut off support altogether, to the pastor's chagrin. [40] The problem of making the Italian parishes, and especially their schools, self-supporting was to cause considerable difficulty for years to come.

And despite past aid, the result was not impressive. By 1920 diocesan authorities had helped found ten Italian parishes, but there were still only 3,053 children in their schools. As late as 1930, one observer reported that on the west side around Loomis Street "There are four public schools, with 12,000 children, ninety-eight percent of them Italian Catholic, in attendance." [41] By 1930, when Italians made up the second largest group of predominantly Catholic foreign-born peoples in the City, only 3,700 children attended their parochial schools. Indeed, though Polish immigrants outnumbered Italians by only two to one, there were thirteen times as many Polish children in the Polish Catholic schools. [42] Italians simply did not send their children to the parochial schools.

There were, of course, Italian children in some of the non-Italian parochial schools. Yet, oddly enough, despite the difficulty in building and maintaining Italian churches and schools, the Italians did not move readily into the parishes of other nationalities. For example, not until 1917, when the neighboring population had become almost exclusively Italian, did their children begin attending the previously Irish Holy Family parish on the near west side.[43] Similarly, the nearby German St. Francis of Assisi parish had to recruit Italian membership after its original German parishoners had all moved away.[44] In fact, between 1890 and 1930, while the already existing Irish and German schools on the near west side were being reduced by almost 5,000 pupils, three brand new churches and schools were built for the Italians in the same locality. When the Italian frequented the Catholic church and school at all, he seemed to prefer one exclusively his own. At least he shared this latter characteristic with the other Catholic ethnics.

5

The Poverty Factor

Differences of wealth separated Chicago's Catholics from the City's mainstream almost as much as did religion and national origin. For over a hundred years after Chicago's founding in 1833, Catholics populated the City's poverty zones in far greater proportions than the citizenry in general. The burden of poverty, though it did not bring Catholics into direct conflict with the rest of Chicago society as the differences in religion and national origin did, nevertheless played a crucial role in the Church's period of tribulation. Surprisingly, it also contributed to the growth of Catholic education, at least at the elementary level.

The Chicago Church struggled for lack of funds from the very first year of its existence. In 1833, the City's original Catholic community took an option on a piece of land at Lake Street, and built a small frame church with their own hands. But they could not raise sufficient money to pay for the property and had to cart the building off to what was then a cheaper and less desirable site at Michigan and Madison Avenues. When Bishop Quarter arrived in 1843 to assume control of the new diocese, his responsibilities included debts of $3,000 on this church, $1,000 on an adjoining lot, and $400 on a piece of land for a cemetery, all bearing interest at 12 percent annually. The debt seemed "especially onerous in view of the poverty of the Catholic immigrants who constituted most of the congregation." The parishioners could not make payments, and the Bishop and his brother "paid it with their own private means." [1]

"We are poor indeed," he wrote, and petitioned old friends in New York and the missionary Society for the Propagation of the Faith in France for aid.[2] In 1845, he spent four months in New York City begging for help to build a Catholic college to educate boys for the priesthood and professions. At the same time he laid plans for a girls' school, but poverty again intervened. "If I had the means," he wrote, "I would set on foot an establishment of religious ladies, for the education of poor female children of the diocese." [3] Quarter finally succeeded in funding these schools through gifts from the Propagation of the Faith and contributions from the East. In 1847, he optimistically established a preparatory school for the university, which was also to give boys "an opportunity to prepare themselves for the various business departments of life." [4] But few Chicago Catholic families of that era had the means to offer their boys a secondary school education or even to prepare them for business, and this school's pretentions to secondary school status soon faded. In 1851, it became St. Joseph's free school for boys, an elementary institution for the poor. To assist the destitute Germans, Quarter wrote to the missionary Leopoldine Society in Germany that "as yet the Germans have no church of their own." [5] The letter brought funds from the Fatherland to help erect two modest German churches and schools in 1846.

Such were the inauspicious beginnings of Catholic institutional life in Chicago. Each of the first parishes and schools had to be financed in part by benefactors in Europe or the East, and even at that, the results proved less than grandiose. According to an 1852 description, which contrasted the "splendid brick structures" of the public schools with Catholic institutions, the latter were physically not much to brag about. "The fact is," wrote the diocesan newspaper, "that all our school houses are wretched wooden buildings, in which our children are crowded together for want of space." One was "a hired tenement"; another "occupies ground that does not belong to us"; and all the rest stood "on ground that has been acquired and should be used for other purposes, and where scarcely any room is left for the diversion of the children." One such was "the decayed frame cabin, which cumbers the Bishop's lot, near the corner of Michigan Avenue and Madison Street, just behind the cabin which he himself occupies as a dwelling house." [6] Writing in 1852, James Van de Velde, the second Catholic bishop of Chicago, complained that "poverty is so great that there is not a single parish even among those longest established, which is sufficiently provided with the necessary equipment for the celebration of the sacred rites." [7] He hardly exaggerated. St. Patrick's church was "a rambling shack at the corner of Randolph and Des Plaines." North of the river, after five years, the construction of Holy Name church "was at a standstill due to lack of funds." St. Louis church at Poke and Sherman on the "untamed south side" remained "as poor in this world's goods as it was rich in dissensions." "The whole region was unkempt and a bedlam." [8]

One Catholic institution that did not share in the physical wretchedness was the "university" that Bishop Quarter founded as the first Catholic educational enterprise in Chicago. After two makeshift years in the old frame church of St. Mary's, by dint of persistent begging in New York, the bishop was able to purchase a full city block north of the River at Chicago Avenue and what later became State Street. Here he erected by 1846 a "beautiful, architectural three-story wooden edifice, with brick basement and colonnade front, surrounded on all sides with native forest trees." [9] This building and the complete seminary and collegiate program it offered quickly became the pride of Chicago Catholicism. But just as quickly it turned into an albatross about the episcopal neck. The "university's" dismal failure to remain solvent, coupled with incessant wrangling over its management, very soon overshadowed the institution's modest physical grandeur. Before the university's final demise in 1866, its troubles led to the resignation of two bishops and contributed to the mental breakdown of another.[10] The institution was first run by diocesan clergy, then leased to the Holy Cross order, and then taken back again by the Diocese; and its struggles proved rather conclusively that Chicago could not yet support a Catholic university. Indeed, by the mid-1850's, in a futile attempt to attract enough students, St. Mary's had to open a secondary department. By 1861, the collegiate program accounted for only 37 of the 156 students. Efforts to enlarge its capacity in 1864 only put the school more heavily in debt. Despite appeals for aid in the already destitute parishes, the financial problems could not be solved. In 1866, the lay students were dismissed, as were the seminarians two years later. The buildings served as an orphanage until their final destruction in the Great Fire of 1871.

The unhappy history of St. Mary's University typified the degree to which poverty deterred the effort to provide schooling above the elementary level. Both the cost to the Church of such institutions and the expense for a Catholic family in tuition and foregone income held enrollments in secondary schools below the expected level throughout the first century of Catholic life in Chicago. Of the forty private Catholic secondary institutions founded before 1900, one-half never saw the light of the new century, many because of financial difficulties. Several exclusive girls' convent academies, like the one conducted by the elite Madames of the Sacred Heart, did thrive, though enrollments remained small, and they survived by attracting the daughters of Chicago's non-Catholic "first families." [11] The several Catholic "colleges" for boys, though originally modeled on the European gymnasium with highly academic curricula, all reverted heavily to commercial programs. Even the well-regarded Jesuit college of St. Ignatius, founded in 1870, offered a commercial track, since throughout the nineteenth century few boys could see their way through the complete collegiate program. For example, when future mayor Carter Harrison II, a non-Catholic, graduated from St. Ignatius in 1881, he constituted exactly 50 percent of his class.[12]

Despite an increase of over 600 percent in Catholic secondary school enrollments between 1900 and 1930, growth did not keep

pace with the general increase in high school attendance. The public
high schools grew by over 1000 percent during the same period. The
end of the 1920's found Catholic high schools with only 13.8 percent
of the combined public–Catholic enrollment in Chicago and 7.6
percent in the suburbs. Further, 58 percent of Catholic elementary
school graduates attended public high schools. Poverty clearly
accounted for most of the unsatisfactory showing. Catholic authorities claimed that "more of our graduates would attend the Catholic
high schools . . . if means could be devised to keep the tuition
lower." And the diocesan newspaper warned "that the poor may be
excluded by the high cost of education that no one can control." [13]

The failure to compete more successfully at advanced educational
levels through all these years, of course, merely reflected the main
Catholic body's general destitution. Catholics who came to the City
in the early decades, aside from a few French traders, were chiefly
poor Irish and German immigrants. The Irish, who made up the bulk
of early Catholic immigration, arrived without means and without
education. Forced into the hardest and most menial of occupations,
"many found employment in the construction of public works and
utilities and in the building of railways and canals, and as factory
workers." "They made up in a very real sense the very first
proletariat of the budding metropolis," living in what newspapers of
the day described as "shanties" and "rookeries." By the 1850's and
1860's, the north side Irish were still described as "crowded in
unsanitary shanties which provided little shelter from the cruelties of
the weather," while others settled along the Bridgeport canal "where
offensive odors befouled the air." The German Catholics did not fare
much better. Some came to Chicago as craftsmen and small
shopkeepers, but most were common laborers. In the early decades,
the Protestant Ladies Benevolent Association had "mostly Catholics
from Ireland and Germany" as objects of their charity among the
impoverished.[14]

These Catholic immigrants supplied the muscle to build and
maintain the canals and railroads that made Chicago the commercial
capital of the Midwest. They built the McCormick reapers, slaugh-

tered and dressed the cattle and hogs of the Armours and Swifts, planed, cut, and stacked the lumber in the many mills along the river, made the bricks, and sweated in the foundaries and steel mills of the robust young city. The mills, the factories, the slaughterhouses, the real estate offices, the professions, the newspapers, on the other hand, belong chiefly to native-born entrepreneurs attracted to the city of potential wealth from the East. Almost exclusively they were Protestants. Such was the economic gulf that separated the Catholic laborer from his Protestant employer.

In the early decades, one could not so easily delineate poverty geographically in Chicago. The town, lacking the amenities of modern rapid transit, remained highly compact. "Stone and brick houses, standing shoulder to shoulder with dingy and squalid shanties" characterized the 1850's and 1860's. The businessman, however affluent, had to live near his business, the factory owner near his factory. Thus, Chicago produced "an extraordinary melange of the Broadway of New York and little shanties, of Parisian buildings mixed in some way with backwoods life." Poverty and wealth lived side by side, separated perhaps by a block here or a railroad crossing there.[15]

Yet descriptions of the day left little doubt where most Catholics belonged. For example, though St. John's parish, founded in 1859, bordered the fashionable south side Gold Coast of Michigan and Prairie Avenues, its "worshipers were the toilers in the industrial district that held, as well as the stockyards, the Rock Island and Illinois Central shops, the county hospital, Toby's Packing House, and Libby's at 14th Street. The lumber district along the river also employed many of the parishioners." [16] Similarly, both Catholic and secular Chicago hailed the coming of the Jesuits in 1857 as a momentous event. But their choice of a location for a parish and school hardly merited a reputation gained in Europe for educating kings and scholars. Their first church on the empty prairie at 12th Street and Blue Island Avenue attracted mainly Irish squatters from the north side "point" district, who simply "loaded their cabins on lumber wagons and moved them into the wide prairies of the parish," where they also squatted. Though within 20 years the parish had developed the largest and most inclusive parochial educational establishment in the United States, it still "drew to its arms the working men who lived in the small wooden houses scattered over the windswept prairie near the railroad buildings and the lumber yards." Two future mayors of Chicago grew up just north of this parish in the wealthy Washington Avenue district during the 1870's and 1880's. Carter Harrison II admitted to excursions into Holy Family turf only when "a gang could be gathered together on Saturday to afford protection from gangs of Micks . . . mostly boys of the parish of the Holy Family on 12th Street." And William Hale (Big Bill) Thompson later recounted with respect boyhood forays into Holy Family land where "the tough Irish boys hated rich men's sons." The sons of west side rich men fared even worse when they ventured slightly north into St. Columkille's territory where "the Irish were even tougher. They waylaid rich boys venturing into the woods beyond Whiskey Point Road or fought them when they swam in the district's limestone quarries." [17]

Though rich and poor were separated by but a few city blocks, the social and economic gulf that divided them was wide indeed. There could be no question into which group the overwhelming majority of Catholic Chicagoans belonged. Bishop James Duggan summarized the situation tersely enough in 1869: "The truth is that our Catholics are poor. They are numerous but not wealthy." [18]

Their lack of wealth was put to a severe test just two years later when the Great Fire leveled much of the City. "A great part of the material equipment of the Catholic Church in Chicago in churches, schools and institutions, representing years of self-sacrificing toil and generosity on the part of clergy and laity, was involved in the common disaster." [19] The fire swept away eight of the twenty-four Catholic churches in Chicago, together with their schools and convents, plus four private academies and an orphan asylum. It was said that "no cause suffered more deplorably from the great conflagration . . . than that of the Roman Catholic Church." [20]

The rebuilding necessitated by the fire had hardly been completed when the great new wave of immigration after 1880 unloaded hundreds of thousands of Catholic Poles, Slovaks, Lithuanians, Bohemians, Ukranians, Croatians, Slovenes, and Italians on the Chicago Church, all as destitute as the Irish and Germans who continued to find their way across the sea and to Chicago. Poverty, indeed, made the bishops' work "sad and taxing." Parishioners who could "aid but little in providing means for the celebration of the Mass" could aid even less in providing schools for the Catholic children.[21]

By the last third of the nineteenth century, improved transportation served to separate rich and poor geographically. The more affluent gravitated to the beautiful north and south lakefront, to the west side Washington Boulevard axis away from the commerce and industry of the Chicago River, and to the more spacious city fringes. The workers settled near industrial and commercial sites. Here, in the shadow of belching smoke stacks and near the squeal of dying pigs the laborer could slog without cost through the mud of unpaved streets to his long day's work. In these areas—the older, residentially blighted commercial sections surrounding the city center, along the branches of the river, near the noisy railroads, around the stockyards, and in the southeast Chicago industrial areas adjoining the Calumet River—one found most of the Catholic population.

It was on this infertile soil, where people lived in "conditions as bad as any in the world" according to contemporary accounts, that the Catholic parochial school system had its roots.[22] By 1890, 77 percent of the Catholic school pupils resided in these poor working-man's areas, compared to only 45 percent of the public school children. Catholic schools that year accounted for 19 percent of the total public–Catholic elementary school enrollment in Chicago, but in the poverty areas the proportion was much higher. For example, in wards 5 to 9 where workingman's houses, usually two to a lot, clustered around the industries located along both sides of the south branch of the Chicago River, 17 Catholic schools served 14,000 children, 40 percent of the public–Catholic school total in the area, more than twice the city-wide average, and almost one-half of all the

Catholic school children in the entire city. In contrast, wards 2, 3, and 4 on the lakefront directly to the east had only two Catholic schools, both bordering on the River wards, from which most of their 1,300 pupils came. A near-contemporary comparision of River wards 5 and 6 with the lake district revealed over-all death rates two and one-quarter times higher and infant mortality six times higher in the former, which had no hospitals, while the lake district had seven. "In the lake region is intelligence, wealth, comfort and all that makes life enjoyable; on the other hand is ignorance, want, misery and degradation." [23] The geographic cleavage between wealth and poverty strongly coincided with that between Protestant and Catholic. The lake district had twenty-two Protestant churches, the River wards only six "struggling" Protestant congregations.

In every poverty zone, the proportion in Catholic schools exceeded that for Chicago as a whole in 1890. In every sector the industrial and commercial wards had the highest proportion in Catholic schools. Thus, the inner city west side wards 18 and 19, both manufacturing centers where houses were "packed as full of human beings as they will hold" and "nearly all the vacant ground" was occupied by buildings, had 38.1 percent of its children in Catholic schools. The more affluent wards 12 and 13 further west, "home wards" with "large and modern" houses occupied by their owners, had only 12.5 percent. On the near northwest side the "great manufacturing" ward 16 and the "very crowded" ward 17 had 27.7 percent in Catholic schools. The intermediate ward 14, which was then "rapidly filling up with homes," and the "distinctively suburban" ward 15 had only 11.8 percent. On the far northwest side, in ward 27, still "a series of small towns separated by farms of 400 acres," Catholic schools accounted for only 2 percent of all pupils. In short, judging by school enrollment, Catholics of 1890 found themselves severely overrepresented in workingman's areas and underrepresented in the middle class.[24]

Twenty-five years later the situation had changed very little. Only in one section of Chicago's poverty zone did Catholic school enrollments fail to increase substantially by 1915. This was on the

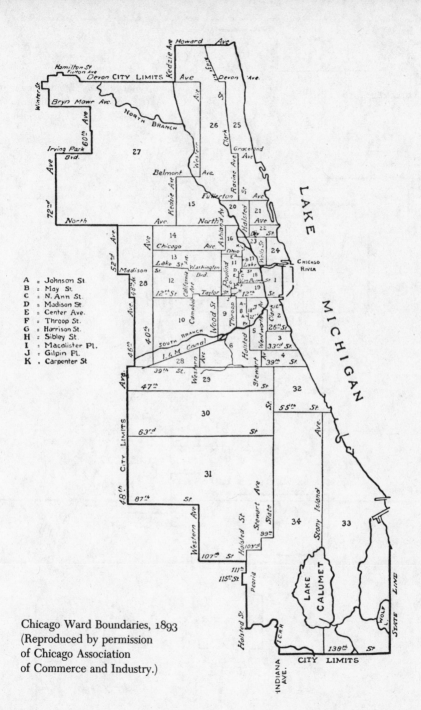

A = Johnson St.
B = May St.
C = N. Ann St.
D = Madison St.
E = Center Ave.
F = Throop St.
G = Harrison St.
H = Sibley St.
I = Macalister Pl.
J = Gilpin Pl.
K = Carpenter St

Chicago Ward Boundaries, 1893
(Reproduced by permission
of Chicago Association
of Commerce and Industry.)

WARD BOUNDARIES IN CHICAGO, 1893

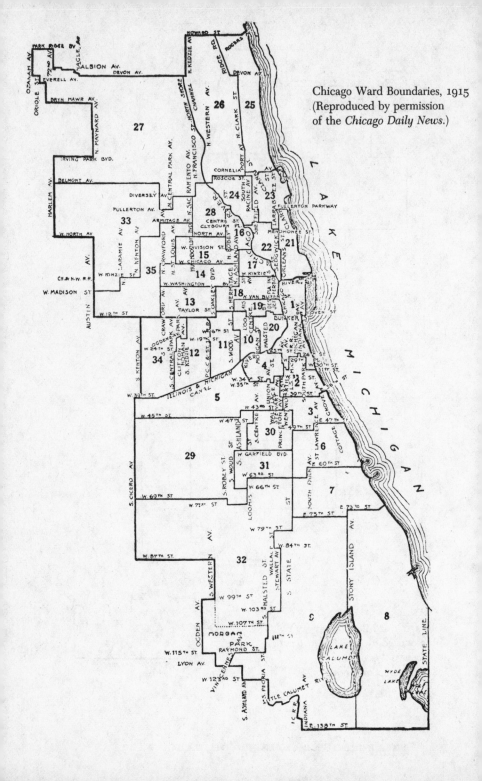

Chicago Ward Boundaries, 1915
(Reproduced by permission
of the *Chicago Daily News*.)

near west and lower west sides where the Irish, German, and Bohemian Catholics were displaced after 1890 by Eastern European Jews, Greek Orthodox, and Italian Catholics who were not interested in parochial schools. Everywhere else Catholic poverty boomed. Though in the entire City, only 22.8 percent attended Catholic schools in 1915, the northwest side inner city wards 16 and 17 had a whopping 47 percent, largely due to the great Polish migration to the northwest side. Since 1890, Catholic school enrollments had increased over 400 percent in this district, parts of which were so congested that an equal density in the entire city would have resulted in a Chicago population of over 32 million.[25] On the southwest side, wards 4, 5, and 30, which included both the industrial river district and the stockyards, had 43 percent in Catholic schools. Parish schools around the stockyards alone grew from seven with 4,000 children in 1900 to twelve with over 12000.

In South Chicago, 37.7 percent attended Catholic schools by 1915. Here, development of the steel mills after 1880 had brought a steady influx of Catholic workers into this low, marshy area, where by 1900 the raising of streets without installation of proper drainage created a stagnant "Venice" through "almost the entire year." Many homes had to be built on stilts. Open ditches were "clogged with silt, garbage, and refuse; privy vaults and cesspools overflowed the surrounding ground after each rainfall." Even the one natural asset—a view of the lake—was "cut off from most of the territory by the steel mills." [26] The condition of Catholic parishes in this area reflected the general malaise. In 1882, Immaculate Conception church began in an empty store; then for years it existed in a basement that served as church and school. The first pastor lived in a remodeled woodshed. At Saints Peter and Paul, "the main source of revenues of the church for many years depended on fairs and entertainments." At St. Francis de Sales, "in the mornings the children would go to the coal sheds of the railroad yards and gather up pieces of coal for the stoves in the inadequate classrooms." [27] Yet, somehow, such schools stayed in business, and enrollments here doubled between 1900 and 1920. They increased even more further south in the industrial Pullman area, where the two schools and 360 pupils of 1900 were eight schools and 2,645 pupils by 1920.

In all, the City's poverty area Catholic schools increased their enrollments by fully 70 percent between 1900 and 1920. Wherever commerce and industry expanded in Chicago during these years, there Catholic parishes and schools expanded too.

This was true even in the suburbs. The two decades after 1900 saw the opening of 46 new suburban parishes and 35 schools. Enrollments increased to 12,169 in twenty years, a growth of over 400 percent. But most of the increase came from the development of industrial and workingman's suburbs around Chicago; these included Chicago Heights and West Hammond, steel industry towns to the south, and Cicero to the west, where the installation of a huge General Electric plant caused a heavy influx of workingmen. By 1920, the lower class towns of Blue Island, Chicago Heights, West Hammond, Harvey, Posen, Lemont, Summit, Cicero, Melrose Park, and Waukegan accounted for 64 percent of the Catholic suburban enrollment. Much of the rest came from such outlying country towns as Buffalo Grove, Fremont Center, Naperville, Volo, and Lombard. As late as 1930, the industrial suburbs still registered 60 percent of the Catholic pupils outside Chicago. Though Catholic schools accounted for only 17.8 percent of all eligible school children in suburban Cook, Lake, and DuPage counties, there were 30.5 percent in Cicero, 27.5 percent in Chicago Heights, 47.2 percent in Calumet City, and 37.3 percent in Harvey.[28] Whether urban or suburban, the Catholic Church remained the church of the workingman, its schools the schools of the workingman's children.

Yet, surprisingly, the lower class status of its communicants through all these decades did not appreciably deter the Church's educational program at the elementary school level. Despite the constant complaint that parishes "were short of funds," the schools endured. In 1883, the Bishop of Chicago had proudly reported to Rome that "in almost all the parishes of the diocese there are Catholic schools. . . . It is a heavy burden to maintain these schools because, since all the churches are supported by the voluntary

district of the west side" or the congregation for the "employees of the steel mills and manufacturing plants." In such churches he felt a "warmth of understanding and tolerance" and "met his fellow worshippers on a plane of equality." [33]

The Church, of necessity, prided itself in catering to the working-man. In 1897, the *New World* reported that "a Protestant minister declared last Sunday in this city, that not one-tenth of those who attend Protestant churches are laboring people. He should have known that the Catholic Church is the church of the working man." Catholic leaders boasted that "In each of the Catholic churches there are some five or six Masses each Sunday forenoon, and each of these Masses is crowded with a congregation consisting largely of working people." [34] The claims were not exaggerated. One historian of the period declared that "when a worker belonged to any church, it was fairly always the Catholic one. The Church knew that its adherents were chiefly immigrant workingmen, while nearly all the businessmen were Protestant." [35] Even in the 1920's, University of Chicago political scientist and erstwhile politician Charles Merriam reported that "the business leadership in Chicago was largely Protestant and the labor movement predominantly Catholic." [36]

In the parochial school, the immigrant workingman's children found the same "understanding and tolerance" and met with other children on the same "plane of equality." The children derived from similar humble origins; and, perhaps more important, the teachers knew and shared their lot. Most religious teaching orders had come as immigrants from Europe themselves and drew their recruits from the workingman's ranks. They lived next to the school, worked for a pittance, and of necessity suffered under the common poverty.

Literature of the period points to a strong solidarity based on economic struggle. Years spent worshipping or attending school in empty storefronts or unfinished church basements somehow created pride, not discouragement. The very "fairs and entertainments" necessary to maintain church and school brought the people together in a closer unity of purpose. Children picking coal in the nearby railroad yards to feed the schoolroom stoves developed a sense of participation, together with the meager contributions of their parents, in building a common enterprise. Even the economic necessity of the combination churches and schools, with worship conducted in the auditorium, helped fuse religion and schooling in the Catholic consciousness. Parish histories written years later on the occasion of a jubilee or anniversary revealed a distinct nostalgia for the hard times that drew parishioners together in common toil, and looked back with reverence on the origins of a parish in a stable next to infamous "bubbly creek" or in a cabin on the windy prairie.

Thus, poverty, like nationality and religion, while contributing to making the first century of Catholic life in Chicago a time of tribulation, also provided a basis for group solidarity and pride. As one speaker put the matter, at Archbishop Feehan's silver jubilee celebration in 1890, "If non-Catholic Chicago can with just pride call attention to its colleges, universities and libraries, rich and noble in wealth and endowments from millionaire friends and patrons, so can Catholic Chicago ask consideration for what the devotion and generosity of its comparatively poor people have accomplished in building and maintaining institutions for practical education and advanced learning, but particularly in the establishment and support of the numerous and efficient parochial school." [37]

II

A FUTURE BRIGHT
WITH PROMISE—
THE 1920's

6

Out of the Smoke Zone into the Ozone

Though 1930 found Catholic school children still overrepresented in the workingman's areas of the City and its suburbs, the Catholic population had not remained socioeconomically stagnant. The preponderance of churches and schools in the commercial–industrial zones and the continued growth of enrollments there through the 1920's masked the fact that residential and social mobility was increasing on an ever expanding scale. In fact, though little noticed at the time, the 1920's marked a definite turning point in Chicago Catholicism's socioeconomic fortunes. For the first time, growth in the middle class sections outstripped that in the poverty zones.

The Chicago Catholic population had been staging toward this shift for decades. The first and most dramatic exit from the workingman's areas took place during the 1890's on the near west and lower west sides, when the Irish, German, and Bohemian Catholics were displaced by Russian Jews, Greek Orthodox, and the Italian Catholics who did not support parochial schools. In the west side wards east of Ashland Avenue, Catholic schools enrolled 39 percent of the children in 1890. By 1915 they enrolled only 13 percent. The single great Irish workingman's parish of the Holy Family, where almost 5,000 pupils in five schools accounted for one-sixth of all Chicago Catholic school children in 1890, lost one-half its pupils in less than a decade, and by 1920, fewer than 1,000 remained. Enrollment at the neighboring German school at St. Francis of Assisi declined from 900 in 1890 to under 400 in 1910. Most of the displaced Catholic population simply moved further west to somewhat better neighborhoods where their children made up over one-quarter of the school enrollment by 1920. This turnover of peoples on the west side merely underscored a less perceptible trend in all of the workingman's areas. On the west side, older Catholic groups gave way to newer, largely non-Catholic ones, making the transition highly visible in depopulated parishes and schools. Elsewhere, as established Catholic workingmen moved out, newcomers took their places, filling up and expanding older parishes and schools, thus creating an illusion of stability.

For example, as early as the late 1880's, parishes and schools began spreading southward from the stockyard area with the flow of the earlier and by now more prosperous Irish and German families out of the district. Visitation parish well illustrates the development. Founded in 1886 on the southern fringe of the stockyards at 51st Street, by 1892 Visitation was moved to 55th Street, just then developing into spacious Garfield Boulevard, the new residential center of the parish. By 1900, over 600 pupils attended Visitation school, children of people who were said to "own their own homes, have no fear of immediate starvation, work every day, and find their motive interest in the church and its activities." Similarly, further to the east on Garfield Boulevard, St. Anne's, established in 1868 as a country parish, in the 1890's filled up with refugees from the stockyards, and developed into a parish without "evidence of great wealth or of pinching poverty." Its school, too, enrolled over 600 children by 1900. Englewood and West Englewood also welcomed masses of the neither rich nor poor "who to this time had attended the established parishes to the north." By the turn of the century, there were eight Catholic parishes with four schools and 1,500 pupils in the area. After the Englewood "El" brought better transportation into downtown Chicago in 1907, these communities developed still

further, and by 1920, eleven churches and nine schools educated
almost 5,000 children of Catholics who, though hardly affluent, at
least lived in communities of "comfortable homes" and well
constructed apartment buildings. Many of these people probably
resembled the not too fictitious and not very middle class father of
Studs Lonigan who had moved from a boyhood in poverty-ridden
"Canaryville" to St. Anselm's parish at Michigan Avenue and 61st
Street just south of Washington Park.[1]

Similar developments took place all over the City as somewhat
better circumstanced Catholics moved out of the inner circle into an
intermediate zone of emergence characterized by neither wealth nor
poverty. It was here that shop foremen, skilled laborers, and the like
bought their modest but not uncomfortable homes. Between 1900
and 1920 Catholic schools in these areas added over 18,000 pupils, a
growth of over 240 percent. They increased by another 12,000
during the 1920's.

Long before the 1920's, too, Catholics had not entirely escaped the
solid middle class, or even the upper middle class. The Chicago
Church had always boasted a visible, though admittedly small body
of the more well-to-do. One sign of its presence could be found in the
cultural and social activities it sponsored. In 1854, for example,
Chicago's more prominent Catholics founded the Chicago Catholic
Institute "to establish a Catholic library and reading rooms" and "to
provide for the delivery of lectures." By 1868, the Union Catholic
Library, "composed of the cream of the Catholics of Chicago,"
blessed the City with its presence. "A valuable library was collected
and the most noted American lecturers were brought here." This was
succeeded by the Columbus Club, which reached a zenith in the
1890's, when it "contained amongst its membership the most worthy
of the Catholic population of Chicago." And then 1893 saw the
organization of the Catholic Women's League, with a middle class
membership, which, in addition to settlement work in the poorer
neighborhoods, sponsored lecture series and discussion clubs.[2] The
quality of the new diocesan newspaper begun in 1892 also reflected
the presence of an audience with at least enough leisure for concern

about public and cultural affairs on a rather high intellectual level.[3]

This cream of Catholic society attended parishes usually just on the fringe of more opulent neighborhoods. Thus, in the 1860's and 1870's, on the near south side, St. John's parish, while including within its boundaries the industrial district for the most part, also encompassed "a slice of the elite over on the Gold Coast of Michigan and Prairie Avenues." [4] A little further south, St. James parish by the 1880's, though committed mainly to the poor, also numbered among its parishoners a few "men of social and civic prominence." [5] In 1880, despite opposition from a majority of Protestants "bitterly opposed to having a Catholic church located in their midst," the parish of Holy Angels was started on Oakwood Boulevard near the Lake, in an area just recently "laid out for a choice and exclusive suburb." Holy Angels became one of the City's "most influential parishes" and was the first predominantly middle class parish on the south side.[6]

On the west side, two Catholic churches were located in the late 1860's and early 1870's along Jackson Boulevard, on the border of the posh Washington Avenue area. This section became "the highway of the 'high toned' Irish." These parishes were later spoken of by a former resident, probably with some exaggeration, as "the heart of a great residential section made up, not of people of wealth, but of those of the upper middle class. . . . It was a district, too, that in its heyday was almost solidly Catholic." Not all the parishioners, of course, came from the upper middle class. More typically, the founding of St. Malachy's in 1882 just off Washington Boulevard at Western Avenue brought "great numbers of Catholics; some of them came to work at the carbarns that were over on Western Avenue, others came to be in the fine new residential section." [7] Thus, well before the 1890's one could find a few parishes, usually bordering the wealthier neighborhoods, that housed a combination of workers and the more well-to-do. By the 1890's, earlier immigrant families had already reached their third generation, and the exceptional new-comer made good faster than that. The history of these relative few was all but lost in the overwhelming fact of the immigrant poor. But they were there.

During the next three decades they could be seen with increasing frequency. On the south side, commercial expansion and aging housing pushed the Gold Coast ever further outward. During the 1890's, for example, Kenwood became a haven for "wealthy stockyard executives and members of fashionable families moving southward from the older Gold Coast." [8] Some Catholics found their way into the Kenwood area, so few at first that in 1903 Archbishop Quigley "felt misgivings about founding a parish here at all. It was so largely Protestant that it was doubtful if a Catholic church could be supported." But he made the gamble and opened St. Ambrose church. It developed slowly, indeed; but by 1920, had achieved a reputation as perhaps the highest status Catholic congregation in Chicago. Its school enrolled over 350 children. Further to the west along fashionable South Parkway, Corpus Christi parish, founded in 1901, was also said to be "attended by the influential and cultured people." [9] By 1920, 450 children attended this parish's school. In middle class Hyde Park, Woodlawn, and South Shore, too, Catholic parishes prospered. In all, by 1920, the seven Catholic schools of these three communities enrolled over 3,000 pupils. Though not Chicago's most affluent areas at the time, they were not communities to be ashamed of.

The same could be said about middle class Catholicism's growth on the west side after 1890. St. Mel's parish had existed since 1878 on the far side of Garfield Park. Until the 1890's, when extension of the elevated made the community more desirable, the church and its school served mainly workers in the Chicago and Northwestern carshops to the north. But after the 1890's, St. Mel's thrived in a neighborhood of "spacious thoroughfares" and "substantial homes." [10] By the end of the century, there were two more parishes in this area of West Garfield Park, and by 1920 the three schools enrolled almost 3,000 pupils. Still further west in the middle class sections of Austin on the City's border the Church founded three more new parishes between 1908 and 1911, in addition to St. Catherine of Siena, there since 1889. By 1920, these four parishes schooled 1,832 pupils.

On the north side, too, through the late nineteenth and early twentieth centuries, Catholics strung a series of parishes near the narrow strip of preferred residential areas that spread progressively northward along the lakefront. Like the south side Gold Coast parishes, most of these included slices of the lakefront elite. Thus, the old cathedral parish of the Holy Name on the near north side, after 50 years of serving first Irish immigrants and then a cosmopolitan hodgepodge of slum dwellers and transients, by the 1890's bridged both the slum to the west and the Gold Coast then developing as the City's most prestigious area to the east. Most parishioners came from very modest or worse circumstances, though "the principal pews were regularly filled by many of the wealthier people of the City, who preferred a residence in the parish." [11]

Later parishes to the north also reflected the mixed nature of Chicago's north side. Thus, Our Lady of Mt. Carmel on Belmont Avenue just a few blocks from the Lake saw "the blending of the rich and the poor into a working unit." Influential people like Edward N. Hurley, Mrs. Lester Armour, and Mrs. Roger Sullivan attended this parish, but there were also "the middle class people who live in the neighborhood of the church, and, from the west boundary, some who know real poverty." St. Mary's of the Lake at 4200 Sheridan Road had become by 1920 a "strange combination of the wealthy, middle class, poor, and that great army of transients." Its membership in the 1920's included people like superintendent of public schools William J. Bogan and ex-Mayor and Governor Edward Dunne. St. Ita's at 5500 Broadway became a parish "attended by many of the wealthy and influential Catholics of the city. A great number of them live at the Edgewater Beach Hotel." [12] This "great number," an obvious exaggeration, did include during the 1920's mayor William Dever and coffee manufacturer Thomas J. Webb.

At the City's northern fringe, Rogers Park was annexed in 1893; because of its superior transport to the Loop and nearness to the

Lake, it developed into a solidly middle class residential community after 1900. When the Jesuits decided to found Loyola University there in 1906, they were followed by a migration of second- and third-generation Irish who came from their older west side establishment in Holy Family parish. By 1920, there were 1,500 children in the three Catholic schools of this area. If the development of parochial schools in Rogers Park was sparked by an infusion from the west side, other Catholics, and especially the Germans, had been moving along the normal residential mobility routes into substantial north side communities from the near north side since at least 1900. By 1920, Lake View, Uptown, and Lincoln Square had 13 Catholic schools and over 6,000 pupils.

Yet, by 1920, most middle class communities along the north, south, and west sides had reached residential maturity. Only in those areas at the outer extremities did Catholic school enrollment grow substantially during the '20's, and even there expansion proved modest. Thus, in Austin on the west, South Shore on the south, and West Ridge on the north, Catholic enrollments climbed by a total of 3,000 pupils during the 1920's. But it was the far northwest and southwest sides, opened up by improved public transportation and especially by the advent of the automobile, that bore the brunt of Catholic migration in the 1920's.

Some of the parishes and schools in these communities were already in existence, at railroad junctions or even near truck farms, before the great building boom of the '20's brought them into the life of the City. For example, in south side Auburn Gresham, St. Leo's at its founding in 1885 served mainly workers in the railroad yards not far away, but during the 1920's it became a parish of "peaceful and substantial homes." Similarly, St. Kilian, in 1905, serviced about 75 families in an Auburn Gresham area still made up mostly of truck farms. But after 1920, "many people from more crowded parishes moved southward into the neighborhood and within the boundaries of St. Kilian's parish, where they purchased or built homes." In fact, so many people moved that between 1916 and 1926 three more parishes and schools had to be opened in this area of brick bungalows and small apartment houses. By 1930, there were five schools and 3,900 children. Similar developments took place all over the south side—two new parishes and schools in the brick bungalow community of Grand Crossing; another in middle class Chatham; one in the "suburban island" of Avalon Park; and, finally in 1924, the first Catholic parish in upper middle class Beverly, "one of the prettiest residential districts inside Chicago." "Attracted by the favorable home conditions," Catholic families poured into these south side communities during the 1920's.[13] Their children added 4,700 pupils to the Catholic schools there.

Events on the far northwest side closely paralleled those on the southwest. In 1910, not a single Catholic school existed in the mostly undeveloped areas of Edison Park, Norwood Park, Jefferson Park, Forest Glen, North Park, and Portage Park. But during the 1920's, each of these communities felt the "impact of sub-dividing and building booms" as "the advent of the automobile helped to overcome the lack of adequate transportation." Catholics seeking better housing settled in these "commuter suburbs" within the city limits, where they could enjoy a "residential community zoned primarily for single family homes."[14] By 1930, there were ten parishes and schools there, with 4,800 pupils, 71 percent of them added during the 1920's.

The trend in the City could not be mistaken. Though still greatly outnumbered by 1930, Catholics spilling out of their previous areas of densest settlement in the workingman's northwest and southwest inner city had fixed upon the spacious far northwest and southwest sides to fulfill their dreams of escaping the congested life of the City.

Without doubt, the 1920's marked a watershed in the socioeconomic makeup of the City's Catholic schools. True, 1930 still found the workingman's areas with 49 percent of the total Catholic enrollment compared to only 36 percent of the total public school enrollment. True, by 1930, Catholic schools accounted for 34 percent of the total public-Catholic school population in the poverty areas, just 25.8 percent in the intermediate zone of emergence, and only 19 percent in the middle class communities. True, in other words, the burden of poverty in Chicago still weighed most heavily on Catholic shoulders. But the burden had lightened. Forty years earlier, 77 percent of the Catholic pupils had attended schools in laboring class areas. Forty years earlier, Catholic schools had accounted for less than 5 percent of the total enrollment in the City's middle class sections. But the situation changed for the better with each decade. And it was the booming '20's that tipped the balance, with just over two-fifths of Catholic school growth taking place in the middle class areas, just under two-fifths in the zone of emergence, and only one-fifth in the poverty areas. For the first time, growth in the middle class and intermediate sections outstripped that of the inner city. In 1930, for the first time in history, Catholic Chicago had less than one-half its pupils in poverty area schools.

In the suburbs, too, the 1920's brought a boom in Catholic activity. Only 1,571 children attended the 17 Catholic schools in the tricounty area outside Chicago in 1890, an average of only 90 pupils per school. Most of these parishes were either rural or in small industrial towns like Lemont where three schools educated 470 children of that town's quarry workers. The two decades after 1900 saw a rapid growth of suburban Catholic parishes and schools. By 1920, there were 55 schools and 12,169 pupils. Though most of the growth had taken place in the new industrial suburbs, there was some evidence of a middle class suburban trend as early as 1900.

In 1890, probably only St. Mary's in north shore Evanston with its 121 children and possibly St. Joseph's in nearby Wilmette with its 176 could be called suburban in the true sense, and even these parishes were the bequest of earlier farming communities. But by 1900, Evanston had added another Catholic parish, and school enrollments went up over 500 percent. Spurred by the development of rapid transit into Chicago, the north shore middle class suburbs of Evanston, Wilmette, and Hubbard Woods had five parochial schools and 1,385 pupils by 1910. In the next decade, the movement quickened still more. On the north shore, three schools in Evanston, two in Wilmette, and one each in Hubbard Woods, Highland Park, Lake Forest, and Niles Center enrolled over 2,000 children by 1920.

Meanwhile Chicago's west side Catholics had launched their suburban trek. In 1907, at the founding of Ascension and St. Edmund's
parishes in Oak Park, "Catholics were few in number and scattered."
They experienced "an undercurrent of opposition" from the predominantly Protestant citizenry of this highly desirable locale.[15] But by
1920, their two schools numbered over 500 pupils. In addition, there
were now schools further west in Forest Park and Maywood.

But it was the 1920's that saw the beginnings of real middle class
Catholic suburban migration in proportions approaching a mass
movement. Real estate developers quickly recognized the new trend,
and for the first time advertised prominently in the diocesan
newspaper. Some appealed to secular advantages like living among
the "residences of well-to-do people" in Libertyville with its
accessibility to Chicago via the new Skokie Valley route of the North
Shore Line or the nearness of the "Crystal Vista" development on
Crystal Lake to golf courses for both men and women. Others
focused on the Catholic mentality. Sites in Mundelein, Illinois,
offered a "wonderful view of the seminary grounds." In Hillside,
"the modern Catholic village of Cook County," where "church,
school and social facilities offer an ideal haven for the Catholic
family," one could live "in the shadows of Mater Dolorosa seminary." Westchester promised no seminary shadows, but it did have
"big values in lots near the new church and school." For those who
preferred to move "out of the smoke zone into the ozone," Glen
Ellyn, "the most ideal suburb west of Chicago," beckoned with its
homesites "in the new parish of St. Petronilla" and a personal
invitation from the pastor to "become residents." [16]

The developers, of course, knew they had a market. Many
Catholic families were eager to move. During the 1920's, 22 new
parishes and 33 schools sprung up in the suburbs. Older parishes
grew larger and could open schools for the first time. By 1930, 89
percent of the 99 suburban parishes had schools, with almost 24,000
pupils. The 24,000 suburban pupils, of course, still did not approach
the 145,000 in the City's Catholic schools. Nor did they match the

suburban public school enrollment. In 1930, Catholic schools accounted for only 17.8 percent of the total suburban school enrollment, compared to 27.9 percent in Chicago itself. Further, 60 percent of the Catholic suburban school children still came from the workingman's suburbs. Catholic schools enrolled one-third of the pupils in industrial suburbs like Cicero, Chicago Heights, Calumet City, and Harvey, but only 12.2 percent in middle class Evanston and 14.2 percent in Oak Park. There were even fewer Catholics in the better suburbs than in the City's middle class communities.

Still, they were present and increasing rapidly. During the 1920's alone, Catholic school enrollment tripled in these middle class suburbs. On the north shore, Evanston had added another school and one was opened in Glenview. In all, the northern middle class suburbs enrolled almost 3,000 children by 1930. The western suburbs had developed to an even greater extent. Oak Park alone added two more schools and more than doubled its 1920 enrollment. St. Luke's, in wealthy River Forest since 1887, now opened a school as "many people moved out of the city and erected new homes." [17] Maywood added a new parish and school, as did Hillside. Further west there were schools in Elmhurst, Lombard, Glen Ellyn, and Wheaton. Parishes in the northwestern and southwestern suburbs also began growing and established schools for the first time: River Grove, Forest Park, Park Ridge, DesPlaines, Arlington Heights to the northwest; Lyons, Brookfield, LaGrange, and Downers Grove to the southwest.

Thus, by 1930, Catholics in the suburbs had made considerable progress, adding 60 parishes in the 40 years since 1890. Of the 71 new schools established in these 40 years, almost one-half were opened in the 1920's. Of the 22,000 pupils added in four decades, over one-half came in the 1920's. Further, during this decade, the Church opened its first large suburban high schools, one in Evanston and another in Oak Park. Though schools in the workingman's towns still predominated, those in the middle class communities grew the fastest during the 1920's. The same could be said of the suburbs as of the City: the 1920's marked a watershed in the socioeconomic fortunes of metropolitan Chicago Catholics. The Protestant "Jones's" remained far in front; but the gap had been narrowed.

The "Church of the workingman" was elated. Indeed, though taking pride in maintaining the allegiance of the common laborer, Catholic leaders had never really rested easy with the prospect of remaining a church of the urban proletariat. The unease stemmed not from dislike for the workingman, but from concern over the evils of congested urban living. For this reason, the *New World*, by the 1890's, actually promoted the establishment of rural settlements for Catholic immigrants to save them from the degenerate city. In the editor's view, it was "the country life, from which have sprung the greatest and best and strongest and most virtuous public men this country has produced." Yet the country, he argued, had been "practically abandoned to the Protestant sects" while the Catholic population was "congested in the cities." In 1899, the nationally influential Bishop of Peoria, John Lancaster Spalding, addressed the same theme before a Chicago audience in Holy Name Cathedral. It was "the weakness of the Church in America," Spalding argued, that "our Catholics are massed in these centers where they live for the most part in hired rooms where, having no proper home, they are driven into the street or saloon, where the daily record of crime is spread before their eyes to harden and corrupt, where parents have little control over the associations of their children." Spalding complained that workers were "obliged to toil seven days in the week without opportunity to cultivate or keep alive either their mental or religious or moral nature." The Bishop of Peoria attributed the surprising religious vitality of Catholic urban immigrants to the "spiritual treasure which they brought from the Old World, where they were tillers of the soil." The *New World* fully agreed: "If the cities were not constantly renewing their youth from the country, their population would become wholly degenerate, and they would go to ruin. . . . It is the country life that holds the destiny of the future. It is the country life that survives." [18]

But the country life did not survive. The rural frontier had already closed. Jobs and the future lay in the city. The Catholic immigrant could not be shunted away. He massed in the congested city. Yet, by the 1920's, with the development of better rapid transit and the advent of the automobile, a new possibility emerged for the growing numbers of Catholics who could afford it. One could work in the city and live in the country, or at least on the city's more spacious and amenable outskirts. The descendant of Europe's peasantry could become once again, if not a full-fledged tiller of the soil, at least a Saturday trimmer of crabgrass and shrubbery. The Church's spokesmen enthusiastically encouraged the movement "out of the smoke zone into the ozone." As the *New World* put the new alternative, "in America where homes are largely migratory, they fix themselves in proximity to the place of employment. Factories, shops, and offices are confined within narrow limits. About these spring up miserably congested residence areas, the consequence of the worker's anxiety to be close to his work. He must be careful, though, that in buying this convenience he does not sacrifice vital interests of his family. There is no question that the outlying districts and suburban towns are far to be preferred as home sites, particularly when there are children. . . . There may be an objection against the time that must be spent in reaching the place of employment. That is where parental selfishness injects itself, often unconsciously. The alternative to the worker's sacrifice of an hour spent in commuting, is withholding from the children the environment that is little less than vital for them, and forcing them to live under conditions that are a constant menace to their physical and moral well-being." [19]

No doubt the laws of economics and of human self-interest proved more compelling than the editor's pen. Though, as he had suggested, it was "not possible for every family to seek the benefit of a home on the outskirts of the city," for many Catholics the lure of newer and better housing in less congested surroundings happily coincided with bigger bank rolls. Catholic school enrollment during the 1920's told the story. Catholic immigrants to Chicago had, of necessity, begun on the bottom of the socioeconomic heap. By 1930 they still claimed the largest piece of the bottom. But the change had clearly begun.

Though their school system remained heavily lower class, by 1930, the future was apparent. With the closing of large-scale immigration from heavily Catholic countries during the 1920's, the Catholic ghettos of the inner city would inevitably dry up. The Church in Chicago had boasted of its hold on the workingman while fearing the ultimate consequences of serving only him. But in the 1920's, it joyfully prepared for a more pleasant future in tree-lined suburbs.

7

Slaying the Ethnic Dragon

To even the fairly close observer, the Chicago Catholic Church of the 1920's must have seemed still a babel of ethnic separatism. As late as 1930, 56 percent of Chicago's Catholics belonged to national parishes, and 53 percent of Catholic school pupils attended ethnic schools. Yet by the end of the 1920's, the ethnic parish's fate had already been sealed. The end would not come quickly or easily; in fact, the last gasp would never be heard at all. But the long period of decline had clearly begun. It was determined in part by the nation's anti-immigration laws of the 1920's, which cut off the source of ethnic renewal. It was also determined in part by the strong personality of the new Archbishop after 1916, whose firm but politically realistic policies undermined the structural foundations of Catholic nationalism in Chicago.

But more than national or church policies, the exigencies of urban life had for decades taken their toll of ethnic cohesiveness. The shifting urban job market, the lure of better housing, the opening of new areas for development, the spread of trolley and bus lines, the quest for economic betterment, all these conflicted with the immigrant's inclination to live among his own. Nor could he control the mobility of his children. The movement had gone largely unperceived behind the more momentous and obvious fact of massive immigration, mutual suspicion, and ethnic rivalry. Yet with each new generation, the process of dispersal found the members of each group rubbing shoulders more closely with the others. Long before the 1920's, a few who had their finger on the Catholic pulse could feel the eventual outcome. In 1904, the unusually observant editor of the *New World* predicted of the ethnic enclaves that the "friction resulting from association with other races will gradually disintegrate these colonies. Temporary segregation," he argued, "has its advantages; it protects, to some extent, religion and race. It is impossible, however, that such a status should continue. . . . The importance of having all these nationalities touch at certain points with the great Catholic body, therefore, is apparent." [1] The editor did not speak in a vacuum. By 1904, some nationalities had already touched with the great Catholic body, or at least with one another.

With good reason, the process of dispersion affected certain groups earlier and more easily than others. The smaller groups, the French, Belgians, and Dutch, for example, simply lacked the numbers to establish new institutions when their members departed the original colony. The larger but longer established groups, in particular the Irish and Germans who constituted the backbone of Chicago Catholicism throughout the nineteenth century, with each new generation found less reason to remain apart.

Perhaps the French experience foreshadowed better than any other what would eventually happen to all. Before 1840 the original French were squeezed out of Chicago's first Catholic church by the more numerous Irish and Germans. In the 1850's, they established another parish of their own, but lost it to Irish invaders before 1860. For a time after 1864, Notre Dame de Chicago on the near west side attracted French Catholics previously dispersed all over the City. Around this church they "began to settle more permanently, bought houses, and started in business." [2] But after 1900, due to an "invasion of manufacturing interests . . . and the consequent shift in population," the French people gradually drifted west or scattered elsewhere, and by 1918, "but a handful of families" remained.[3]

Though the church itself continued offering French sermons for old parishioners who wished to return on Sundays, the school was open to any child in the neighborhood. In other parts of the City, the French attempted to establish colonies centered in a parish, too; but these inevitably met the same fate. St. John the Baptist near the stockyards in the 1890's served 500 French families huddled near the church. But by 1900, many Frenchmen were already moving away, and the Irish and the Germans made up one-half the congregation. Similarly, the French parish in West Pullman, though still recruiting Canadian priests in 1930, had long since gone cosmopolitan as the earlier French workers departed. The only French parish that maintained a solid ethnic identity through the 1920's was St. Joseph and St. Anne in Brighton Park. Of the approximately 18,000 French Catholics in Chicago by the late 1920's, only about 2,700 were reported in the three officially French and two French-English parishes. The urban dynamic had apparently absorbed the rest into "the great Catholic body." [4]

The forces that disintegrated the French acted even more rapidly on such later but less numerous arrivals as the Flemish Belgians and the Dutch. The Belgian attempt, in 1907, to draw their people around a single northwest side church by founding a school ended in but temporary success. By 1916, so many had already moved away from St. John Berchmans that it had to become "an American or cosmopolitan parish." Though many Belgians still considered it their church and celebrated important feast days there, after 1916 people of other origins, especially the ever-present, northwest side Poles, took it over.[5] Similarly, the Dutch Catholics had founded their lone church at the turn of the century in south Chicago's Pullman area when most found employment in the industries there. But gradually they departed and by the 1920's, people of all nationalities attended.[6] Neither the Belgians nor the Dutch were sufficient in number to build more schools as their people dispersed.

What happened to these national groups because of size, happened to others simply as a function of time. The earlier the arrival, the sooner economic betterment led to residential mobility and its related assimilation. Most significantly, those two great protagonists of early Catholic Chicago—the Irish and the Germans—found the argument for self-segregation less compelling with each new decade.

As early as the 1870's, Irish and Germans formed a shaky alliance over the issue of Sunday closing laws, and in 1889 formed another to oppose the Edwards Law that threatened extinction for their parochial schools. By 1904, a German–Irish musical and literary society met together on St. Patrick's day, and a German quartet sang *"Das Tragen von dem Grün."* In the decade before World War I, Teuton and Celt found themselves drawn together in dislike of the purported Anglo-Saxon attempt to make the United States "a tail to the British kite." They formed an Irish–German alliance in opposition to American flirtation with England. By 1910, the Irish editor of the *New World* welcomed a "pact and union" of the Ancient Order of Hibernians and the German Catholic Societies. He urged both to live together in harmony, and ended with a *"Hoch das Deutschland!"* By 1913, the Irish-dominated diocesan paper ran, in addition to its traditional "Around the Emerald Isle," a column conspicuously balanced on the other side of the same page, "News of the Fatherland." [7] But it was in the parishes—where the people were—that the real accommodation between the two groups took place on an ever-increasing scale.

Shortly after the turn of the century, one found growing indications in the German churches themselves that German Catholic nationalism was dying in Chicago, even on the heavily German north side. Thus, just two years after an exclusively German group founded St. Gregory's parish in 1904, by common consent two of the three Sunday sermons were preached in English. The English sermons attracted a "great influx of Celtic parishioners" who lived conveniently nearby, and St. Gregory's "was fast losing its reputation as a German parish." At the inception of St. Clement's parish in 1905 just north of Fullerton Avenue, the German parishioners demanded that one-half of the Sunday sermons be in English. But "after seven years trial as a bi-lingual parish, it was found that there was little call for and still less need of continuing the use of the German language." In

1912, St. Clement's became a territorial parish serving all the local residents. After that, though German names continued to predominate, many Irishmen, too, showed up in the lists of active parishioners.[8]

After 1905, the Germans founded just one more parish, St. Williams on the northwest side, and even this was listed as "German–English" from the beginning. By 1916, twenty-six of the old German parishes reported English and German services, and only nine had German exclusively.[9] In 1917, Archbishop Mundelein stated that "I have before me at the present time the application of several large German parishes which of late years have used the English language to the greatest extent in sermons and in instructions and who now ask that parochial limits be set them and that now or shortly in the future they be declared entirely English-speaking parishes." Even in the old Chicago *Deutschland* of the near north side, where the latest arrivals from the fatherland continued to settle, one found signs of Americanization. Thus, in 1916, a German father at St. Michael's, who had obviously not himself benefited much from exposure to English, asked the Archbishop "If the teachings in St. Michael's school or the preference can't be inglish [sic] more than German. I am sending three children to this school and they tell me they insist that have to learn German." Thus, even before World War I, German Catholicism in Chicago had already progressed far along the Americanizing path. The war, with its strong anti-German sentiment, and the end of immigration and the high mobility of the booming '20's pushed it beyond recall. The movement needed no prodding from Church authorities.[10]

The 1920's simply confirmed the already established pattern. Many second- and third-generation Irish and German Catholics migrating from the central city found their way into the long-established German farming community parishes, especially on the far north side and in north shore suburbs. These people worked a transformation. Thus, by 1927, old St. Henry's in Rogers Park became the parish church for all Catholics in the locality, regardless of nationality.[11] The same year gave "English-speaking boundary lines" to the formerly German St. Nicholas parish in Evanston. In many parts of the inner city, too, German pastors complained that "not many German Catholics in easy circumstances come here and those of that kind belonging move away as soon as they can." Such parishes could not survive as national units, and one by one they were given "boundary lines" and opened "also for English-speaking." The trend could not be mistaken. The better-established Germans abandoned the workingman's parishes, and there were no Germans to take their place. Those moving out felt little desire to preserve the language and culture of the fatherland. By the late 1920's, it was said of the German parishes that "they are German-American with the emphasis on the latter. . . . Theoretically they remain German churches, and the names of their pew holders still indicate a strong German following, but in many cases the parish is most cosmopolitan." A few years later, when Cardinal Mundelein addressed a letter to the "predominantly German" churches of the City, he included only eight on the list.[12]

The German transformation of their national parishes into English-speaking territorial ones, of course, was complemented by the movement of many Germans into the territorial parishes previously dominated by the Irish. As early as 1883, a report to Rome stated that "many German children use English and choose to join the English-speaking churches." [13] Parishes like Holy Name, the original Irish parish on the north side, numbered many Germans by the end of the nineteenth century. By the 1890's, one found an increasing number of regular territorial parishes organized jointly by Irish and Germans. Thus, in 1892, a group of Catholic women headed by Mrs. John Doyle and Mrs. Lewis Kreuder collaborated in forming Our Lady of Lourdes in "a center of the German population" of Ravenswood, an indication of some cooperation between Irish and German even then.[14] Several of the first parishioners in the predominantly Irish St. Ita's parish in 1900 were of German origin. And the parishioners of St. Sebastian's church in 1912 were described as "exclusively American, those of German and Irish descent predominating." [15] All these parishes existed on the north side where German churches abounded, within rather easy reach of those who preferred. When north shore suburban Wilmette needed a new parish in 1904, Edward Kirchberg and Edward Dolan, two names not easily associated in earlier years, circulated the petition. More and more the new territorial parishes were described as "made up of people of Irish and German extraction." In the secondary schools, too, the originally Irish or German institutions, though their respective nationalities still predominated, generally had a generous mixture of both nationalities as well in the first decades of the twentieth century. And in 1924, when Catholics in the north shore suburbs decided they wanted a boy's high school, the pastors of Irish St. Mary's parish in Evanston and German Sacred Heart parish in Hubbard Woods jointly petitioned the Archbishop for permission to build.[16]

Not all welcomed these changes, of course. For example, at St. Gregory's on the north side where the Germans had accepted Irishmen since before 1910, some of the old guard tried to force the Irish into nearby St. Ita's in the 1920's. The pastor had to fight this move with a sermon that charged: "Nationalism is a heresy like anything else against the dogma of Christianity." [17] For their part, the more loyal sons and daughters of St. Patrick still endeavored "to teach Irish history in the parochial schools in which the children of Irish-Americans are in the majority." [18] In the 1920's, the Ancient Order of Hibernians sponsored essay contests on Irish history for parochial school children. Indeed, for many, old loyalties died very slowly, and not uncommonly parishioners by-passed the nearby parish for the more distant Irish or German church and school to be at home among their own.

Yet, the evidence leaves little doubt that for Irish and German both, the ethnic boiling pot had begun to fuse into the melting pot.

The process may have been hastened, too, by the loss of many older parishes to more recent immigrants. In the inner city, both the Irish and Germans had learned that survival depended upon acceptance of other nationalities. This was not given easily, and then only out of necessity. Yet, the experience must have driven home the lesson that in a big and changing city like Chicago only a cosmopolitan Catholicism could thrive.

For example, by the 1880's, the "mixing of nationalities" around the original German church of St. Peter's at Polk and Clark Streets had all but destroyed its original character. This parish now had "little more to do with Germans, except for the German priest, a good German club, and a number of old-time German members who have not yet succumbed to the pressure of the railroads and the entrance of many questionable elements into the neighborhood around the church." In the 1890's, Germans made a feeble attempt to maintain the identity of St. Peter's school by offering a "class for teaching of the German language to those who wish to learn it." But the neighborhood had become "one of the most vile in the world," and the parish membership was reduced to 35 families, among them a handful of old-time Germans, plus Irish, Italians, Greeks, Arabians, and Blacks.[19] Thus, the German Catholics learned their first lesson in the hard facts of urban ecology quite early; but hardly the last.

The first daughter church of St. Peter's suffered a like fate. St. Francis of Assisi thrived on the near west side into the 1890's when the area filled up with Russian Jews and Italians, and the Germans moved further west. The pastor tried desperately to stave off disaster, and even built a new church in 1904 after the old had been destroyed by fire. But by 1910, "the fate of the parish was sealed. No human power could alter it." The school enrollment had fallen from over 900 in 1890 to less than 400, and most of the pupils were not German. Faced with extinction, the pastor then turned to the only potential parishioners in the neighborhood—the unchurched Italians. The Italian had to be coaxed, especially to join a non-Italian parish. In 1917, the district "was thoroughly canvassed; every Italian family visited; in every home the cause of Catholic education explained. In a short time St. Francis school was popularized in the district. In the meantime the large school of sixteen rooms, long in disuse, and the auditorium were renovated and equipped again as of old, for educational purposes." After a twenty-year struggle against decline, necessity forced St. Francis parish to take the only path possible short of complete collapse—to abandon its original German affiliation.[20]

The fate that undid St. Francis and St. Peter's parishes dealt equally harshly with almost every German church in the poverty zone, save on the near north side. Thus, the Germans had not only begun to mix with their former hated rivals, the Irish, but had sacrificed some of their most cherished church property to newcomers. This experience must surely have paved the way for a more reasonable or at least a more pragmatic approach to the question of erecting more parishes of their own.

The Irish endured the same experience, only more so. Because their parishes remained legally open to anyone, the Irish were more vulnerable. Most of their original parishes near the city center saw complete changeovers in nationality prior to the 1920's. On the near north side, for example, well before the end of the nineteenth century, the Irish abandoned Holy Name parish to transients and Italians and a handful of the cosmopolitan wealthy along the Gold Coast. Then in 1904, St. Dominic's parish was carved out of Holy Name's western section. "The one thousand families that formed the new unit were almost entirely Irish." But within sixteen years the parish underwent a radical transformation. The locality was "invaded by factories and by an Italian population, thus causing the original members of the parish to seek places of residence in parishes further north." The school filled up with children "of Italian parentage, and not a few, also, of parents of other nationalities." [21]

On the near northwest side, the original Irish parish of St. Columkille reached its zenith about 1905 with a school enrollment of 1,234 pupils, but shortly afterwards expanding business and commerce encroached on the neighborhood. "An influx of strangers made its way into the district, and the people of the parish, always desirous of pleasant home surroundings, resented this, so many of the parishioners 'packed up and left for parts unknown.' The first realization of their departure was made evident in the decrease in the school attendance." Matters got so bad that the school had to close for a time. But rather than abandon the plant altogether, the

parish finally appealed for pupils from any nationality, and "the
school reopened to accomodate children of all nationalities attending
the public school. About 300 flocked to old St. Columkille's and
mingled in the respective grades." [22] After the 1880's, commercial
expansion and ethnic change also began to hit St. Stephen's parish on
the northwest side. In 1910, the Irish sisters who taught in the school
withdrew because "the surroundings make the place in every way
undesirable." With few children left in the school, the sisters felt that
"our going will work no hardship on the people of St. Stephen's."
The Irish parishioners had all but disappeared, and the church was
"attended almost entirely by the Polish people of the district."
Finally, in 1916, the Poles took it over completely as a national
parish.[23]

On the west side, the pride of Irish Catholicism in Chicago, Holy
Family parish, succumbed to the influx of Jews and Italians before
the nineteenth century had run its course. On the lower west side, its
daughter parish of the Sacred Heart was increasingly "made up of
many nationalities including Bohemian, Slovak, Irish, Polish, German, Lithuanian, Italian, Austrian, Croatian, Spanish and Belgian."
Even in such heavily industrial areas on the south side as Bridgeport
and Back of the Yards, some Irish parishes began to decline after
1910. For example, All Saints at 25th and Wallace, the home of Peter
Finley Dunne's famous Mister Dooley, became by 1930 "one of the
most cosmopolitan parishes of the city. It numbers many nationalities
in its fold, principal among them the Irish, Mexican, German, Italian,
and Polish." On the south side along the lakefront the old Irish parish
of St. John's had long ago fallen to industry and the vice district. By
1924, St. Elizabeth church was given over to Black Catholics. Others
like St. James, Holy Angels, Corpus Christi, and St. Anselm, though
still holding on, were all but depopulated by the spreading Black
Belt. Thus, the Irish, like the Germans, lost much dearly bought
property to more recent immigrants. As early as 1915, the often
socially sensitive editor of the *New World* had commented that
"parishes that were once composed of Irish or German communicants are soon filled up with other nationalities." [24]

No doubt the transformation of Irish and German parishes, the growing entente between the influential Teuton and Celt, and the accelerating mobility created a social climate that favored or at least made possible firmer action from the episcopal throne itself. No bishop of Chicago had ever moved against the national churches. But the man who occupied that position after 1916 was inclined to swift decision. Within a month of his arrival in Chicago, Archbishop Mundelein decreed that henceforth all the schools would teach their major subjects in English.[25] He also adopted a policy, though never officially promulgated, of discouraging the founding of new national parishes or the expansion of old ones. Yet, the new Archbishop did not deceive himself. His throne still rested on an ethnic powder keg. Most Irish and Germans would not protest. The more recently arrived Italians, though large in numbers and still confined mostly to their little Italys, seemed not to concern themselves with church affairs. Smaller groups, like the French, Dutch, and Belgians, had already all but dissipated their meager forces. But the masses from Eastern Europe—Bohemians, Lithuanians, Slovaks, Slovenes, Croatians, and most of all the Poles—remained largely unassimilated. These people made up almost 40 percent of the City's Catholic population in 1916. Their fierce nationalism demanded extreme caution and forced the princely prelate into uncharacteristic compromise. Though insisting on English in the schools, he allowed teaching of the native language and culture and even catechism in the mother tongue. Though opposed in principle to the formation of new national parishes, where expediency dictated he permitted them. Yet, on balance, despite concessions accompanied by complaints about the "exaggerated spirit of nationalism that is rampant today among the various Slav races," [26] for the most part Mundelein held the line against the Eastern European ethnics.

By the end of the 1920's, for example, Bohemian nationalism had been contained by a combination of the Archbishop's maneuvering and the natural process of dispersion. When, in 1925, a group of Bohemian laymen in Berwyn asked for a second parish where "the gospel shall be preached to us in our mother tongue and the pastor, being of our own blood, will comfort us in the confessional in the language that we best understand," the plea fell on deaf ears.[27] More important, the growth of existing Bohemian parishes ceased. In fact, between 1910 and 1930 enrollment in the City's Bohemian schools declined by 40 percent. Despite some expansion in heavily Bohemian Cicero and Berwyn, total enrollment in the entire Diocese did not increase. Though all the Czech parish schools except the original St. Wenceslaus vigorously maintained their ethnic identities through the 1920's, they were actually dying on the vine.[28] Bohemian immigration to Chicago peaked by 1920, and many children of earlier immigrants were finding their way out of little Bohemia into other parts of the City and other parishes. The enduring solidity of the lower west side Bohemian colony only obscured their departure. Mundelein could afford to step backward occasionally without jeopardizing the final verdict. Besides, the Bohemian schools never accounted for more than 5 percent of the diocesan total. Though perhaps causing trouble for Church authorities disproportionate to their numbers, the Bohemians did not constitute a major power bloc in Catholic Chicago.

The same was true of most other Eastern European groups. By 1930, despite considerable growth during the 1920's, the Slovenes had just three small schools in their parishes and the Croatians four schools, which averaged fewer than 300 pupils each. The lone Hungarian parish had no school at all. The somewhat larger Slovak group managed to add 700 to their school enrollments during the 1920's, and one new parish. But this was listed as English and Slovak from its inception and embraced "the members of all other nationalities." [29] Further, in some of the older Slovak schools, the intense ethnicity of former years began to decline. This was especially true in areas of mixed nationality. For example, on the northwest side, Slovak workers in the Northwestern Railroad yards lived among Poles, Italians, Czechs, Ukranians, Germans, and Irish. Of their two parish schools in this locality, by 1924 one offered just fifteen minutes a day of Slovak instruction to the three upper grades, and the other taught only religion in the mother tongue. On the lower west side, St. Joseph parish school offered just two half hours a week of Slovak instruction and that outside regular school hours. These schools were still Slovak to be sure, but not to the extent of former years.[30]

The Lithuanian question posed a somewhat different problem. Throughout the 1920's, the Archbishop attempted to appease the Lithuanian nationals striving to protect "the rights of the Lithuanian language" in church and school. The list of approved Lithuanian textbooks published by the newly created diocesan school board in 1916 "greatly dissatisfied the Lithuanian priests." They demanded a Lithuanian as supervisor of their own schools and complained that "the present supervisor did not handle the matter successfully for us, probably because he does not know our language and therefore cannot judge what is good and what not for our schools with reference to Lithuanian books." Mundelein tried to placate Lithuanian desires without granting them their own superintendent. He instructed the existing supervisor to cooperate more fully with the angered Lithuanian priests, but was told later that the attempt had been "unsuccessful, notwithstanding repeated efforts on my part." The Lithuanians, in fact, continued to teach their language and literature, as well as religion, from textbooks of their own choosing. Their schools continued this practice into the 1930's. Yet, Mundelein's policy actually prevailed against Lithuanian nationalism too. The Lithuanians did not get their own school supervisor. They were allowed just one new parish during the 1920's, and their schools added only 500 new pupils in these ten years.[31]

In fact, by 1930, the tide had turned against all the Eastern Europeans with the possible exception of the Polish, and even for the Poles there were signs that time would eventually run out. The Poles, though probably no more nationalistic than their Eastern European neighbors, had one point in their favor—size. There were four times as many people in the Polish parishes as in all the other Eastern European combined, and five times the school enrollment. Their very numbers constituted a buffer against assimilation. So large were the Polish inner city strongholds that they remained virtually impervious to outside influence. And the expansion of the Polish population out of the ghetto constituted a mass migration in itself. Wherever they settled in Chicago, the Poles moved in groups large enough to constitute new parishes as they went. A report in 1919 indicated that Poles still lived "in clearly defined segregated districts." [32]

From the beginning Mundelein tried in various ways to effect the gradual dissolution of Polish Catholic nationalism in Chicago. In 1917, he assigned several newly ordained Polish priests to non-Polish parishes. Though the Polish congregations were already well staffed with priests of their own nationality, the move drew bitter protests from angered nationalists who had "striven to educate so many of the Polish youth for the priesthood, and now, the fact that these young clergymen are being taken away from them has created a feeling of sorrow and bitterness in their hearts." In 1919, the Archbishop refused permission for a monumental new church in the already existing St. Stanislaus Bishop and Martyr parish on the northwest side. He contended that with immigration cut off during the war, the City's industrial future unsettled, and the movements of the Polish population uncertain, "the time has gone by when a Polish speaking parish could incur with safety a very heavy indebtedness." But it was in the newly developing areas that Mundelein's Polish policies got him into deeper water. He wished to erect only territorial parishes. Yet some areas, especially on the far northwest side, were filling up largely with people of Polish descent who still demanded Polish parishes. Mundelein devised a curious non-solution to this problem. On the one hand, he stuck to his principle: "My position in the formation of these new parishes is to make them largely territorial; i.e., to give them certain limits." On the other hand, he actually bowed to nationalistic pressures and conceded control over these new territorial parishes to the Polish: "At the same time, if the parish is formed near you, it will be predominantly Polish, i.e., although mixed and the people in a certain territory belonging to that parish, yet naturally because of the preponderance of the Polish people the principal language used there will be the Polish language." In all,

Mundelein formed seven such parishes in Chicago during the 1920's—officially territorial, but Polish in reality, complete with Polish priests and the use of Polish language.[33]

This ambiguous solution apparently pleased no one. Non-Poles objected to Polish domination. For example, in 1924, one real estate firm complained to Mundelein of its predicament. It had just completed a large number of bungalows within the limits of one such parish, and the potential purchasers, mostly Catholic but not all Polish, were informed that in the school they "teach English for half a day and Polish for the other half of the day. These people do not want their children to study Polish." [34] The Poles, on the other hand, looked upon Mundelein's refusal to grant them parishes exclusively their own as a hostile act.

It was such allegedly hostile acts that led to widespread allegations among Chicago's Polish population that the Archbishop disliked the Poles and wished to drive their language out of Chicago. In 1925, after almost ten years of such rumors, the Reverend Thomas Bona, Consultor to the Archdiocese and original member of the Catholic school board, himself of Polish descent, wrote a leaflet for distribution in Polish churches, refuting the charges. Bona called the opposition to Mundelein "formal warfare," and dismissed the complaints one by one. He denied the claim rampant since 1916 that Mundelein wished to throw the Polish language out of the schools and quoted a speech made by the Cardinal encouraging the St. Hedwig's orphans to learn Polish. Bona reminded his fellow Poles that, in 1925, there were 51 Polish schools in the Archdiocese and that the chairman of the Catholic school board was a Polish priest, as was one of the school superintendents. At the diocesan-run Quigley Preparatory Seminary, 171 of the 625 high school boys studying for the priesthood were Polish, and "by order of the Cardinal the Polish boys are obliged to study Polish." Four priests and three laymen taught Polish at Quigley. Forty seminarians at St. Mary of the Lake Seminary were Polish. "In this institution the teaching of Polish is obligatory" for Polish priests-to-be. Eighty percent of the revenues collected in Polish parishes by the Chicago Catholic Charities went to Polish charitable institutions and the other twenty percent to Polish needy families. A Polish priest directed the Big Brothers Association for the Archdiocese, and the Vice President and Secretary of the Holy Name Society were Poles. Therefore, argued Bona, if anything Cardinal Mundelein had favored the Poles; yet Polish Catholic papers continued to attack him.[35]

There was some truth in the allegations of both sides. Mundelein did in fact seek to appease the Poles in many ways; but, whenever possible, he also chipped away at the still firm foundation of their national solidarity. With the Poles the situation demanded extreme patience, very difficult for a man who said of himself in another context, "When I want anything, I want it now and I don't want to wait a long time to get it." Yet Mundelein apparently convinced himself that in this sensitive area, too abrupt action could precipitate another ethnic Donnybrook. He saw, too, that time ran in his favor. As early as 1918 he perceived "Polish people or those of Polish descent who did not wish to go to Polish parishes." With each new generation there would be more. And the anti-immigration laws of the 1920's promised to hasten the end. Firm but gentle nudging here and there would hasten its coming.[36]

Meanwhile, as he put it, "the healing influence of time" and "just a little patience" would slay the ethnic dragon.[37]

8

A Minority to Be Counted with

One could hardly contend that, by the 1920's, Chicago's religious wars had subsided. Indeed, if anything, this decade emerged as one of the more religiously turbulent in the City's history.[1] Yet, the heightened agitation itself seemed to mark a turning point in the tide of battle. To that time Catholics had fought as underdogs in the long-drawn religious conflict. Despite substantial victories, they remained the struggling outsider. But by the 1920's, as visiting educator George Counts accurately perceived, a "marked reversal of fortunes which have attended the growth of the city" finally enabled the Church of Rome "to challenge the power of the combined Protestant Churches." "Protestants feel the reins of power already slipping from their hands," said Counts, "and the more imaginative among them have visions of Chicago obeying the will of the Vatican."[2] Protestant hegemony over the City's institutions had been slipping for decades, of course, but not until the 1920's did the actual momentum shift. In part, the reversal of fortunes reflected the progressive assimilation of Catholic immigrants and their movement into the middle class. It also simply resulted from the growth in size of the Catholic bloc, and its increasing importance in Chicago politics. But perhaps more than anything else it was the leadership of

Archbishop Mundelein after 1916 that marshaled all these forces into the instrument that for the first time threw the enemy into a distinctly defensive position. In particular, Mundelein's adroit manipulation of political influence, though probably unperceived by all but a few, resulted in victories that forced the City to realize, in the 1920's, that the religious tide had turned.

The Church's enemies, of course, had long feared the rise of Catholic political power and often accused the Church of its use to further parochial ends. In one sense, their fears were obviously well founded. The City's Catholics, especially the Irish, had entered the political arena early. Even in the 1840's, the Irish controlled enough of the Democratic party "to elect officers for the sole reason that they are Irishmen." In 1846, when the Irish Democrats "believed that party's candidate for the mayoralty held Nativist sympathies," they defected to cause a loss of the election. In following decades, though often opposed by the party's native Americans, the Irish "kept their eyes unswervingly on the goal they had in mind." By the 1880's, they controlled the Democratic party on the ward and precinct levels, and after 1883, city hall closed regularly on St. Patrick's day.[3] When Englishman William Stead visited Chicago in the 1890's, he found that "almost all the offices are held by Catholics," and almost all the Catholic office holders were Irishmen. "The Irish," observed Stead, "being forbidden to rule their own country, have recouped themselves by ruling the great American cities."[4] For the next several decades, Irishmen continually controlled one major faction of the City's Democratic organization, first under Roger Sullivan and then George Brennan, and they were prominent among the Republicans as well.

Yet, despite the sizable slice of the political pie that belonged to Catholics, until well into the twentieth century the Church did not benefit as much as might have been expected in the religio-educational wars. The reasons were several.

For one thing, Stead's judgment that the Irish ruled Chicago missed the true complexity of the City's politics. Though Irish Democrats controlled many heavily Catholic wards and could elect aldermen from these at will, they could not command the city-wide elections without fusing with other interests. To achieve victory for the Democracy they usually supported either a native American or a reform candidate, neither of whom could promise heavy payoffs for Catholic parochial interests. Thus, the two Harrisons rode to ten mayoral victories between 1879 and 1911 with solid Catholic support. Carter Harrison I, though an old-line American business-man, sedulously courted the Catholic vote, and rewarded it at least with such small favors as providing the parochial schools with free city water.[5] His son, educated at St. Ignatius College and married to a devout Catholic, parlayed this advantage into heavy Catholic pluralities of his own. Harrison later admitted that "friendships made during the years at St. Ignatius, plus the standing that taking a degree at a Catholic institution of learning gave me with the Catholics of the community" helped his political career, as did "the further fact of my having married a Catholic wife under whose ministrations two children were baptized and grew up in the ranks of that faith." [6] The Catholics, unable to rule Chicago on their own, in fact recouped themselves by supporting those who at least remained "uninfluenced by anti-Catholic bigotry." [7]

And when a Catholic ran successfully for the mayoralty, he did so only with credentials that at least partially nullified Protestant bigotry and rendered favoritism to the Church's interests highly unlikely. In 57 mayoral campaigns prior to 1930, Catholic candidates won only three. None of the three came from the regular Democratic organization. In 1893, Irishman John Hopkins managed a narrow margin of 1,200 votes in the confusion following the elder Harrison's assassination. He ran as an insurgent Democrat on a pseudo-reform ticket that attracted an estimated 38,000 Protestant votes. But Hopkins' corrupt performance in office served neither Catholic nor City interests, and after a two-year term he escaped for an extended trip to Europe with his two-elevenths share of the infamous Ogden Gas deal.[8] The next Catholic mayor, Edward F. Dunne, a "rigidly honest" judge with reformist leanings, though a convinced Catholic, sent his numerous children to public schools. As Mayor from 1903 to

1905 he "named a Board of Education composed largely of persons representing social ideals," among them Jane Addams of Hull House. A vote for Dunne did not mean a vote for the Pope, and many Chicagoans knew it.[9] William E. Dever, Chicago's third Catholic mayor, served five consecutive terms after 1902 as reform alderman of the 17th ward, sponsored by Graham Taylor of the Chicago Commons, the Civic Federation, and the Municipal Voters League—groups as distant from the regular Democratic organization as Martin Luther from the Pope. After serving with distinction as Judge of the Cook County Supreme Court, he captured the mayor's seat in 1923 with only grudging support of the Brennan–Sullivan faction but "the good wishes of every respectable Chicago citizen." [10] Despite Dever's reputation as a reformer and political idealist, his Catholicity proved a serious liability. In the campaign of 1923, by the "final weeks of electioneering, the religious issue seemed to overshadow all others," and the Ku Klux Klan got credit for an "inundation of scurrilous religious pamphlets against Catholicism." [11] Dever "marred" his record as reform mayor by participation in a Eucharistic Congress held in Chicago, and "a picture freely circulated" taken as he kissed the Cardinal's ring probably contributed to his failure to gain reelection in 1927.[12]

Thus, despite the large bloc of Catholic voters, a politician's image as a Catholic, if not carefully handled, could lose an election. Given the precarious balance of power in the City, the Church could not expect to benefit unduly from the rise of her sons to political prominence.

Only in the Catholic-dominated inner city wards could a politician's Catholicity be heralded with impunity. Yet even here the Church did not reap a rich harvest. Ward heelers like Johnny Powers, Mike McInnerney, "Hot Stove" Jimmy Quinn, Bathhouse John Coughlin, Hinky Dink Kenna, and others, though marching regulars in the St. Patrick's Day parade and even perhaps pew holders at the local parish, no more adhered to Catholic dogma than to political ideology. Boodle and patronage were their creed. Only the wildest dreamer or the most myopic bigot could see in a

Bathhouse John or Hinky Dink agents of the Pope. As Johnny Powers put the matter in 1890, "the people of the 19th ward are a people that is governed by the saloons—not by the church." The "seven hundred and fifty saloons at my back" were all the support Powers needed to rule the notorious 19th. To their patrons he owed favors, not to the Church. If a school board appointment had to be secured, it would go to a trusted laborer in the political vineyard first, to a guardian of the faith only by chance. Indeed, Church spokesmen often complained that Catholic board members would "gladly and greedily sacrifice Catholic principles to their secular interests." Only on the rebound did the Church's educational interests benefit, as when the "Democratic spoilsmen" in the city council cut back public school expenditures to provide more for patronage jobs, according to an accusation leveled by the *Chicago Tribune*. More often than not, Catholics of this ilk in office proved an embarrassment to the Church. The *Tribune* once asked, "of the Aldermen of the City of Chicago, how many owe their instruction in morality to the parochial schools, and how do those there educated compare as to boodling with those who were trained in the public schools?" And whether trained in public or parochial schools, corrupt politicians, argued the Church's adversaries, were consistently returned to office by Catholic voters educated in the parochial schools. The criticisms sometimes extended to the hierarchy itself. Thus, Stead complained in the 1890's that, although "in Chicago the Irishman is everywhere to the front" as an office holder, "the Catholic Archbishop Feehan does not stretch out a finger to keep him in the straight path." [13]

The truth was that, prior to 1916, Church authorities in Chicago seldom stretched out a finger into the political arena at all. Despite frequent Protestant accusations of Church interference in politics, Catholic clerics for the most part stuck to religion in a narrower sense. In the 1880's, Carter Harrison I criticized intrusions of Protestant ministers into politics, and asked "Did you ever hear the priests talk politics? . . . When they get up they preach Jesus Christ and him crucified." Stead himself expressed surprise that the Church "should have so little influence on the civic life of Chicago" despite

the large number of office holders, and castigated Archbishop
Feehan for failure to heed Pope Leo's concern for the social order.
But for over twenty years Feehan had shunned controversy and
usually followed the easier path. Thus, when militant Catholics
demanded the appointment of a priest to balance the Protestant
minister and Jewish rabbi serving on the Board of Education, Carter
Harrison II went to Feehan, who acquiesced in calling them off.
Feehan's successor, James Quigley, too, made his mark as a
"peacemaker" who "knew how to be silent with his tongue." His
reign from 1903 to 1915 was "one long treaty," interrupted by but a
single recorded denunciation of discrimination against Catholic
teachers in the public schools.[14]

Thus, between boodling ward bosses, reform-minded Catholic
mayors, and reluctant ecclesiastical authorities, the Church probably
did not benefit as much from its broad political base as it might have
or as its enemies liked to think.

Yet the potential for exploitation was there and growing by the
decade. No one really knew for sure just how many Chicagoans
professed the Catholic faith. The Church's own parochial census
placed the Catholic population at 18 percent in 1900, 25 percent in
1910, and 26 percent in 1920. But Catholic authorities themselves
discounted the figures as a highly inaccurate estimate. In 1916, an
independent religious census put Catholics at 30 percent. By the
1920's, both Catholics and others generally assumed the Catholic
population to be approaching 50 percent of the total. This figure was
probably bloated by Catholic hopes and Protestant fears. Yet,
judging from the number of Catholic children in parochial schools by
1930, and the number generally assumed to attend public school,
Catholics must have constituted about 40 percent of the population.
Though estimates differed, two facts were clear to all. One was that
Catholics made up a very large portion of Chicago voting strength,
the other that the percent of Catholics in the City, though always
high, grew steadily in the first two decades of the century. In sheer
numbers, Catholics carried ever increasing weight in Chicago
affairs.[15]

What they lacked was a unifying force to capture the vote and marshal the power of Catholic office holders to the Church's advantage. That force they finally found in Archbishop George Mundelein, who arrived in 1916. Mundelein combined a bold optimism with considerable political savvy that helped tip the scales in the Church's favor. His direct entry into politics did not bring dramatic change or ensure against all setbacks, but it did for the first time place the enemy on the defensive. "We are living in an age of bigotry," he declared. "The only thing for us to do is to keep our people united and combat against this all the time." With confidence that "we are going to win out in the end," he did not leave the victory to providence as his predecessors had done. Instead, he intruded directly into the fray.[16]

For example, one issue that had aroused public ire for decades was the State's practice of subsidizing educational programs at private and denominational orphanages. In 1879 and 1883, the State Legislature passed laws enabling a fixed payment each month for every dependent boy and girl committed to private manual training schools in orphanages. In 1888, the State Supreme Court declared the practice unconstitutional in a suit against the Catholic Chicago Industrial School for Girls. But, since Cook County lacked adequate facilities of its own, the funding of Catholic and other private orphanages continued. Catholic institutions in Chicago received a large portion of the state funds. But in 1916, a "mentally afflicted man with a litigious mania," according to Mundelein's account, brought suit against the Catholic orphanages. A decision by a lower court in the plaintiff's favor cut off the state funds, and Mundelein found himself "in a serious quandary to find the means to support these orphaned children for whom the state is no longer paying." [17]

In calculated anger he appealed to the State Supreme Court and set about ensuring a favorable outcome. To create a healthy climate for victory, he wrote a public letter "to the people" depicting the orphans' plight and "placing the state in a defensive position." Within a few weeks, after securing support from the "public at large," some "business and professional people," and the newspapers, Mundelein expressed confidence that "if we can only keep the atmosphere up we might have it penetrate into the Supreme Court and have them throw Judge Baldwin's decision into the junk pile." To help public sentiment "penetrate into the Supreme Court" he enlisted the aid of Cook County Democratic leader Roger Sullivan, in whom he confided that "I know I need not add any suggestions, for in matters of this kind you are probably better versed than I am, after the many years you have spent in public life." Whether or not Sullivan influenced the State Supreme Court, the Court reversed the decision on grounds that no church actually benefited from the state money, since the amount given did not cover the total cost. In truth, said the Court, the church saved the state money.[18]

Meantime, legislation adverse to Catholic orphan schools was introduced into the State Legislature, and Mundelein took action again, this time writing to Speaker of the House, David Shanahan, asking him to "bury these bills in the wastebasket or in a committee where they cannot be resurrected. . . . I know that this matter rests in safe hands while it is with you." [19] The bills were buried.

The orphanage question came up again in 1920, this time at the State Constitutional Convention in a minority report that would have made aid to denominational orphanages unequivocally unconstitutional, with no latitude for interpretation by the courts. Again Mundelein went into action, threatening that "If we don't succeed in killing that minority report . . . then about the only thing that remains for us to do would be to kill the entire Constitution." To kill the report he "got in touch with Senator Shanahan and learned the lay of the land." He then "got Bishop Dunne started and he spoke to the Knights of Columbus at their state convention about the matter and in other places in the diocese urged bringing pressure on the delegates." Mundelein also turned to the Catholic ethnics and "got the Bohemians busy on the representatives from their districts," and "Father Eisenbacker was sent to Quincy where the Staatsverband was in session." The Archbishop personally "reached" Mayor Thompson, "who promised to call off two of his men who had voted against us." And he sent Monsignor Edward Kelly with Senator

Shanahan to "see Governor Lowden and incidentally ask him to reach some of the southern delegates." [20] The motion failed to carry and was not included in the proposed new State Constitution of 1920.

Catholic power had come a long way in the fifty years since an earlier constitutional convention outlawed aid to parochial schools without a single Catholic delegate or any effective Catholic opposition. The Chicago Church had long had loyal sons in positions of influence, but only recently a politically knowledgeable bishop ready to reach out for their help and unafraid to bring pressure on mayors, governors, legislators, and judges alike.

In 1919, when the Smith-Towner bill posed a threat of federal aid to education for the first time, Mundelein swung his influence into the national arena. He urged the Jesuit weekly, *America*, to "maintain a strong position in regard to the educational measures now pending." In a long letter to James Cardinal Gibbons of Baltimore, he outlined the danger to parochial schools inherent in federal aid, and expressed confidence that "united opposition on the part of Catholics" would kill the bill. "We may be a minority, but we are a minority to be counted with," he boasted. Mundelein fought the bill strenuously and again mobilized both public support and aid from Catholics in high places. He wrote to Catholics in the United States Congress and relied upon them as the "safe guardian of our interests." [21]

On the home front, the doughty prelate moved almost immediately on the public school board. Not satisfied with haphazard Catholic representation characteristic of the past, he approached Catholic member Charles Ffrench at a meeting of the Irish Fellowship Club with a request for information. The annotated list of board members Ffrench supplied revealed five Catholics on the twenty-one member board, two of whom constantly warred with one another. Mundelein expressed astonishment that "in a city like this, in which the population is more than one half Catholic, we should have so little or so poor representation on the Board of Education," and concluded that "it is a matter certainly that requires attention."

The matter got immediate attention. A week later he met with Jacob Loeb, Chairman of the Board of Education.[22] He also went directly to the mayor. The following year when school board appointments were due, he wrote to Mayor William Hale Thompson that "In accordance with the request expressed by you in our interview of last Saturday, I herewith submit ·for your approval the names of Mr. Anthony Czarnecki . . . and Mr. Richard Gannon . . . for appointments as members of the Board of Education. I have selected these names with a great deal of care, both as to their personal qualifications and their fitness for the position." Thompson appointed both.[23]

Mundelein's exercise of blatant political power, of course, was not entirely unprecedented. In the early 1890's, Chicago's Catholics had mobilized against the Edwards Law that threatened to put parochial schools under the thumb of public school boards. They had fought successfully first to remove the Bible from the public schools and then to keep it out, and to reduce anti-Catholic bias in textbooks and curricula. But earlier efforts had been sporadic, not particularly well organized, and defensive. The battle against the Edwards Law, for example, was largely organized by the Germans as an ethnic group, not by the hierarchy. It was Mundelein who first carried the battle to the enemy in a spirited, organized, unified effort that marked a new era of confidence and optimism for Catholic educational interests in Chicago.

By the 1920's, there were more reasons for confidence and optimism. Despite opposition, Catholics had for decades been moving into important positions in the public schools themselves. Large numbers of girl graduates of the Catholic high schools were taking and passing the required examination for admission into the Chicago Normal School in the 1890's. In fact, two Irish Catholic teachers, Margaret Haley and Catherine Goggin, organized the Chicago Teachers Federation in 1897.[24] By 1898, the *New World* reported annual reunions at the Normal School, a news service normally reserved for Catholic schools only. By 1902, two-thirds of the class entering the Normal School came from three Irish parochial high schools on the south side, St. James, St. Elizabeth, and St. Gabriel. And by 1911, four hundred graduates of St. James alone were said to be teaching in the Chicago public schools. In addition, schools like St. Mary's on the west side placed many Catholic girls, and some Catholics entered the teaching ranks directly from the Catholic colleges without attendance at the Normal School.[25]

Repeated attempts by authorities during the first two decades of the century to limit the number of Catholics admitted to public school teaching posts either failed or enjoyed only temporary success. By 1908, second-generation Irish girls alone accounted for almost a quarter of all Chicago's teachers.[26] With the addition of third-generation teachers and Catholics of other nationalities, the Catholic proportion of the teacher force must have been at least a third by 1910. By the 1920's, many became convinced that "the Pope is endeavoring to place a Catholic in every classroom in Chicago." [27] Common opinion actually placed the proportion of Catholic teachers in the public schools at from 70 to 90 percent. Even Archbishop Mundelein reported in 1920, "I am told that 70 per cent of the teachers in the public schools are graduates of the Sisters' schools." [28] No one, apparently, knew for sure. In 1926, George Counts examined seven "representative" elementary schools and found 41 percent of the teachers to be Catholic. Whatever the percentage, many found the presence of so many Catholic teachers a cause of deep concern. But Catholics rejoiced that their children attending the public schools had been delivered from the hands of Protestant schoolmarms and that so many Irish girls over the past several decades found decent employment in the classroom. The daughters of more recent Catholic immigrant groups, especially the Polish, were also encouraged to take their share of the public school teaching positions.[29]

At the upper levels, too, many believed that "the Catholics are conspiring to place their own members in the more important administrative and supervisory positions." In 1926, Counts found that though "an intense struggle" was being waged between Protestant and Catholic for administrative positions, only 32 of the

98 principalships studied were held by Catholics, but that "positions in the school system which in the past have always been held by Protestants are now passing into the hands of Catholics." [30] In the 1920's, Protestants tried desperately to hold fast to the last citadel of public school supremacy—the superintendency. In 1924, Mayor Dever wanted to appoint William J. Bogan, principal of Lane Technical High School, an acknowledged leader in education, and a committed Catholic, to the post. He was diverted by "some of the Protestant leaders who had given campaign support to the new mayor . . . declaring that many Protestants who had supported Dever, a Catholic, for mayor would resent it if he gave the important school post to one of his faith." [31] But finally, in 1928, Bogan, after four years as an assistant superintendent, became the first Catholic superintendent of the Chicago public schools. The evidence indicates that Bogan, though intensely active in Catholic affairs, remained above both politics and religion in his administration of the Chicago schools and that he deserved the post.[32] Yet his appointment symbolized for Catholics an achievement of power undreamt of in the Chicago of former years.

Thus, by 1930, Chicago Catholics had in large part accomplished the objectives of protecting their interests in the public schools and establishing at least proportionate representation there. Moreover, the initiative was now theirs, and the Church could count on ever greater influence in the future. Meantime, Catholics had to convince the public—and probably themselves—that their own schools deserved to exist. In this effort, too, they succeeded far beyond any nineteenth-century expectations.

In 1890, the *Chicago Tribune* had asked of the Catholic schools, "How have their pupils compared with those of the American public schools for morality, honesty, truth, and good citizenship? What percentage of criminals and boodlers has been turned out by the Catholic schools and what by the American free schools? . . . What statesmen, what philanthropists, what examples of virtue or morality have come from the parochial schools?" [33]

Challenges such as this could not and did not go unanswered.

Indeed, for decades Catholics struggled to prove first the equality and then the superiority of their schools. A letter signed by the four Catholic bishops of Illinois in the *New World*'s first issue in 1892 assured Catholics that "we do not hesitate to assert that in our parochial schools the various branches of learning are taught as effectively as in the better class of public schools." [34] But it remained for Catholics to prove their assertion. They set about the task with lusty enthusiasm.

Plans for the World's Columbian Exposition of 1893 in Chicago included an educational exhibit, with parochial schools invited to participate. Though the bishops in their letter had dared to assert the high quality of parochial schools, the suspicious public needed convincing, and Catholics saw in the Columbian Exposition the opportunity to lay their schools open before the world. The psychology of a misunderstood minority trying to prove itself probably does more than anything else to explain the exaggerated efforts that went into the Chicago Catholic exhibit. On September 17, 1892, the *New World* announced that the diocesan school board had been "empowered to prepare a plan of work and to supervise the entire exhibit," and on September 24 printed the letter from the board to the schools of the Diocese asking their full cooperation in the preparations. Throughout the coming year, until the exhibit's official opening in July of 1893, the paper carried almost weekly extended reports on developments. The usually dormant school board's activity in organizing the exhibit in itself emphasized the importance attached to the enterprise.

Just as significant, the Exhibition occasioned one of Archbishop Feehan's rare excursions into public view. On September 17, 1892, the *New World* referred to him as feeling "that this diocese having numerically a greater school attendance than any other in the United States and proportionately a decidedly better showing, should at this auspicious time show forth to friends and critics the fruit of the blessed tree of Catholic education." Feehan left the official dedication ceremonies for the National Catholic Exhibit in July of 1893 to the more widely known Bishop of Peoria, John Lancaster Spalding.

But a few days later at the dedication of the Chicago Catholic
Exhibit, standing before a marble statue of himself inscribed "the
protector of our schools," he claimed the Catholic schools of Chicago
as his "greatest pride" and expressed the sentiment that seems to
have motivated all the effort that went into the exhibit: "This work
has gone on silently, and few really know what we are daily
accomplishing in our schools." When the exhibit opened to the
public in September, Feehan again broke his usual silence to
exclaim: "Whoever honestly examines even a part of this can never
again say and never again should be permitted to say that Catholic
schools and Catholic education are inferior to any other to be found
in the whole country." [35]

The vast efforts of the Chicago Catholics received their reward in
the acclamation given the exhibit. The *New World* exulted in a
comment made by the non-Catholic director of the Fair's entire
education department: "Without flattery I can honestly say, and feel
that the compliment is justly given, that the Catholic exhibit is the
gem of my department." [36] And an editorial for August 19, 1893,
proudly quoted a laudatory article from the Chicago *Times* praising
the "method displayed in the schools," the work at all levels, the
"solid knowledge" and the achievements of the convents, which "are
here seen in their real light—homes of culture and nurseries of the
fine arts."

Finally, in an editorial at the opening of the 1893–1894 school
year, the editor felt confident in assuring Catholic parents that "Our
parochial schools are not inferior . . . to the public schools." He
cited the great impact of the Columbian Exposition.[37] This tone
dominated yearly editorials at the opening of school, as well as
frequent comment throughout the year. The new-found note of
confidence in the 1890's perceptibly shifted to one of distinct
triumph over the years as evidence accumulated, at least to Catholic
satisfaction, that parochial schools not only equaled but surpassed
public schools in excellence.

The success of Catholic pupils in competition with the public
schools offered one reason to celebrate. The first success came when

a high percentage of parochial school graduates passed the exams for non-public school pupils seeking admission to the city high schools. In 1893, when 35 of 36 graduates of All Saints passed the exam, the *New World* quoted the statement of the Assistant Superintendent of Schools: "I think it is no more than fair to say that the work of the children on the examination shows that they have had the benefit of excellence in teaching." After similar successes in the next years, the editor reported in 1896: "Through the action of the Board of Education in according to private schools the right to send their graduates to the city high schools without special examinations, the Catholic schools of Chicago, which constitute by far the majority of private educational institutions in the city, are practically conceded to be on the same plane of efficiency with the public schools." [38]

Success of Catholic girls in the Normal School examination also furnished "proof" of Catholic school superiority. Catholic spokesmen ridiculed what they considered to be strategies to exclude Catholic girls from the Normal School as desperate attempts "to cover the incapacity of candidates from the state high schools." In 1915, when superintendent Ella Flagg Young tried to establish a quota system for candidates to the Normal School from each high school, the *New World* printed a feature on page one with the headline: "Mrs. Young Unwittingly Pays High Tribute to Catholic High Schools." The article accused the superintendent of trying to hide the "disgrace" of the public high schools, and reminded her that the Catholic high schools had for years "prepared the greatest per cent of the pupils of the normal school and by the marvelous results of their work have proved the inefficiency in much of the work in the public high schools." [39]

Victories of Catholic school youths in competition with the public schools never went unnoticed. In 1916, a girl from a Catholic academy wrote the prize essay in a contest sponsored by an industrial concern, and the *New World* rejoiced: "The fact remains that in all fair and open tests our schools stand forth as eminently efficient." The same year, four children from two parochial schools won all honors from contestants of thirteen public schools in Cook

County. Finally in 1929 the *New World* boasted that "during the last couple of months Catholic children from Catholic schools have been sweeping all prizes before them when pitted against children from public and private schools." The pinnacle of achievement had been reached. Who could doubt that Catholic schools were best? [40]

The growth of Catholic school enrollment relative to that of the public schools after the turn of the century suggested a further basis for odious comparison. Though the editors of the *New World* could hardly be called systematic statisticians, they did take pride in recording from time to time the sizable increase in Catholic school enrollments and especially delighted in favorable comparisons, when possible, with the public schools. In 1901, the National Teachers Association convention in Detroit discussed the growth of parochial schools, and as a consequence, the Chicago *Record Herald* suggested an inquiry in Chicago to seek the reason. The *New World* volunteered its own explanation: "people know the Catholic schools are better, and besides they want religious education." [41]

A few months later, the *Daily News* pointed out that increase in public school attendance was not keeping pace with the City's population growth. And in 1906, the biennial school census revealed that since 1904 the public schools had grown only 1 percent while the non-public schools had increased 14 percent. The *New World* attributed this to "decline of parental confidence in the public schools," though it implicitly recognized another factor in mentioning the steady influx of Catholic immigrants and their large families.[42] In any event, the proportion of Chicago children attending Catholic elementary schools rose steadily, from 16.8 percent in 1900 to 22.8 percent in 1915 to 28 percent in 1930.

Nor did Catholics simply fabricate the decline of confidence in the public schools. The *New World* carefully documented the rising discontent within the ranks of public education. The paper gave prominent coverage when educational muckraker J. M. Rice exposed a number of skeletons in the public school closet in 1893. At the local level, the *New World* in 1896 accused the school board of mismanagement in its failure to provide adequate facilities for at least 12,000 children and gloated in 1902 when board member Thomas Gallagher, an Irish Catholic, angered at the public school's financial straits, suggested that his confreres "look at the parochial and the private schools. They take care of 100,000 children at only one half the expense the Board incurs. . . . The children get a better education too." The editors suggested that the public schools "trim off the pedagogical barnacles." In 1905, the *New World* carried an article by a Chicago School Board member, Shelley O'Ryan, also an Irish Catholic, charging mismanagement of the Chicago schools, with 11,000 children on double shift, 59,000 kindergarteners without facilities of any kind, and 170 fewer teachers than five years previous. Again in 1906, the *New World* seconded a *Tribune* editorial, "What Ails the School Board," in charging that the people should be getting more for the 13 million dollars spent on the schools annually.[43]

When, in 1903, a group of Chicago pupils burnt down their school, the editor asked: "Who has ever heard of the pupils of a Catholic school willfully setting such an institution afire?" And he commented similarly a year later when a wave of pupil strikes hit the public schools. In 1905, school board member R. A. White criticized the lack of discipline in the public schools, and the editor observed that Catholic schools did not have this problem. Still later, street riots and scandalous parties instigated by public high school pupils and played up in the daily press prompted the reminder: "This much is certain, the discipline of our parochial schools can never be equalled in the public schools." And when a public high schooler in a *Tribune*-sponsored conference on how boys and girls can help one another suggested that girls could "make the boys wait for a kiss," the *New World* pounced again: "It would require considerable imagination to picture a Catholic high school girl lecturing on the theory and practice of kissing." [44]

Finally, one source of discontent within public school circles touched more directly than any other on the basic difference between the public and parochial schools: the question of religion in education. The Illinois bishops in their letter of 1892 had anchored the existence of parochial schools on the necessity of religious education. The *New World* consistently hammered at the same theme, especially in its yearly pre-school editorial. By the late 1890's, Catholics began to find reluctant allies in unexpected places and reported these with obvious self-justification. In 1897, the *Chicago Inter Ocean*, in an article on the increased crime rate, concluded that "these figures are sadly suggestive of a failure in our scheme of education. The spread of mere secular education does not work a diminution of crime." [45] In 1904, the National Education Association's National Council devoted an entire session to the need for religion in the public schools, and the same year saw the founding of the Protestant-inspired Religious Education Association. In 1906, Archdeacon Frederick DeRossel, Rector of the Episcopal Sts. Peter and Paul Church in Chicago, complained that public schools without religion were "only making a more educated or higher class of criminals"; and the *New World* gladly reported similar statements by other Protestant divines as occasion offered.[46] In 1911, a year after the State Supreme Court had banned the Bible from the public schools, the Illinois State Teachers Association at its Chicago convention resolved that the schools needed religion. And Chicago School Superintendent Ella Flagg Young admitted to a gathering of the American Ethical Society: "I know all of you are thinking that the public schools are a failure ethically. . . . We are forced to say that in measure it is true." [47]

In 1914, Mary R. Campbell, a psychologist from the Chicago Municipal Court, threw a "bomb in the NEA convention" when she claimed that the courtrooms were full of boys and girls because the public school failed in moral education. And the next year the NEA offered a $1,000 prize for the best essay on "The Essential Place of Religion in Education, with an outline of a plan for introducing religious teaching into the public schools." The *New World* reacted to the NEA offer as it did to all appeals for religion in the schools, so willingly reported in its pages, with the smug comment: "Catholics solved the problem long ago when they built their parochial schools." In the 1920's, to the promoters of religious education, Catholics laid down the challenge: "We have blazed the way. Let the dissatisfied set up their own schools." [48]

Thus, the combination of successes in direct competition with the public schools, the reported inefficiency and mismanagement of these schools, the growing chorus of voices raised against the absence of religion, plus the apparent increased popularity of the Catholic schools as measured by their rising enrollments, all contributed to the distinct change in the way Catholics felt about their schools.

In 1892, the *New World* had hoped that the World's Columbian Exhibition would convince the dubious of the parochial school's right to exist on an equal footing with the public. A decade later it put the issue quite another way: "The question is not now as in times past 'Is the Catholic school as good as the public school?' but why is it better; wherein does its superiority consist?" And by 1915, the paper, perhaps rhetorically, rejoiced that Catholic schools had developed without public assistance: "It may well be doubted if equal success could have been reached under the trammels of educational bureaucracy." Looking back contentedly in 1924, the *New World* concluded that in Chicago, despite "subterfuges to hinder our progress, we had too much success. . . . In competitive examinations we were phenomenally successful. . . . And now we are accepted by the very force of our schools, their efficiency, and the results, as a recognized system of education. . . . We are even happier at vindication which comes from the religious viewpoint. Other religions are now seeing their mistake in not founding parochial schools." [49]

Indeed, by the end of the 1920's, in their relationship with the public schools and the public generally, Catholics had reached a definite position of strength, at least in the City itself. They enjoyed proportionate representation on the Board of Education, in administrative positions, and in the teaching ranks of the public schools. Though unsuccessful in efforts to attain tax aid for their own schools, they had protected them from restrictive legislation. And, at least in their own eyes, they had improved the competitive position of the parochial schools. The adversary, if not vanquished, had been routed, with the psychological advantage clearly shifted to the Church's side. With good reason could the perceptive Counts conclude that for Catholics "the period of tribulation is over, and the future is bright with promise." [50]

9

Order out of Chaos

In 1907, the editor of the *New World* proudly announced: "The most complete and efficient Catholic school system in the world exists in Chicago." [1] That it boasted the largest enrollment no one could deny. But that it functioned administratively as the "most complete and efficient" could be seriously questioned. In truth, the Chicago Catholic schools remained a hodgepodge of parochial fiefdoms, religious order domains, and ethnic enclaves, all loosely controlled by the bishop. The Chicago public schools had had a uniform curriculum since 1840, and a full-time superintendent since 1853. But not a single person was ever assigned to administer the City's Catholic schools, and the choice of textbooks and curriculum had never been centralized. Even determination of the school's yearly opening date belonged to the local parish.

Part of the reason lay in the absence of Church legislation that governed the conduct of parochial schools. Canon law made minute regulations concerning the authority of the bishop and his priests, and the rights and obligations of local parishes. But only in the United States, with its unique combination of universal education and lack of religious instruction in the public schools, had a vast Catholic educational effort materialized. Nothing in Church law provided for superintendents or school boards to deal with problems that simply could not be handled by bishops and pastors already overburdened with the material needs of an immigrant church. The problem became most acute in the northern urban centers, where Catholics concentrated.

At their periodic meetings, the American bishops attempted to apply Church law to the peculiar problems of Catholic educational organization. The First Provincial Council of Baltimore, in 1829, began the process by ordering the writing of textbooks for use in the parochial schools. The Second Provincial Council, in 1833, appointed a committee for this purpose. But not until the Third Plenary Council, in 1884, did somewhat more extensive legislation come into effect. The Council required that a commission be set up in each diocese to examine prospective lay and religious teachers, a move meant primarily to assure religious orthodoxy in the schools. More important, from an administrative standpoint, the Council of 1884 also ordered the appointment of commissions in every diocese to visit each parochial school at least once a year.[2]

No other clear stipulations existed, either in universal Church law or in the decrees of American bishops. And even the required examination of teachers was commonly conducted, not by a central board, but by the superiors of the religious orders that ran the schools. Even the revised code of Church law in 1918 made no further provision for school system administration. Jurisdiction still resided in the bishop, who had ultimate authority over the choice of religious textbooks, appointment of teachers, and the establishment and inspection of schools. Beyond the requirement of a diocesan school inspection commission, in effect since 1884, no specific legislation regulating the administration of Catholic schools had ever existed.

In Chicago, Archbishop Feehan appointed a board of school examiners in 1887. The board consisted of parish priests, one each for the regular territorial parishes of the north, west, and south sides, respectively, another for the schools outside Chicago, several for the German schools, one for the French, and another for the Polish and

Bohemian. The board helped organize the Catholic school exhibit for the Columbian exhibition in 1892, maintained a Child Labor Bureau, which issued certificates permitting children between fourteen and sixteen to work, and helped plan the meetings of the National Catholic Educational Association when these were held in Chicago. In 1902, the Archdiocesan Synod expanded the board, splitting the Poles and Bohemians into separate groups and adding members for the Italian schools. The 1905 Synod abolished separate national groups, but made provisions for each nationality to be represented on a single fifteen-man board of commissioners. Beyond these incidental activities, there remains no record of any attempt to control the Chicago Catholic schools.[3]

True, the bishops of Chicago enjoyed the same extensive rights over the schools and school affairs as they did over all other aspects of Catholic life. In a sense, they functioned as school superintendents. But this, just one of many episcopal roles, they confined for the most part to activities of a more general nature: encouraging the establishment of a school in each parish, recruiting religious teachers, and exhorting parents to enroll their children.

The actual conduct of the schools the bishops normally left to others. For example, local pastors sometimes made reputations as "superintendents" of virtually independent systems within their own parish. Thus, Jesuit Arnold Damen built Holy Family parish on the west side into a system of parochial elementary and high schools, capped by a select private academy for girls and a college for boys that were considered by Cardinal James Gibbons, in far-off Baltimore, to be "the banner schools of America." And Father Hugh McGuire of St. James parish on the south side gained a name in Catholic circles throughout the country as "the pioneer of free Catholic higher education" at the secondary level.[4] Further, the decentralized economic structure did not lend itself to centralized administrative control. Since each parish financed its own school, the parishioners and their pastors strove mightily to outdo their neighbors in the quest for educational glory. The parish's school plant and its educational program gave testimony to the generosity, prosperity, and interest of its constituents. Thus, each developed, if not in opposition to others, at least in competition with them.

Loose federations of schools did exist, but only as expressions of ethnic affiliation or of bonds between members of religious orders. Each national group built relationships among its parishes and schools, sometimes of mutual aid, always of common interest in promoting ethnic identity. But in constructing little ethnic school systems within the Diocese, national interests tended to exclude the possibility of a central diocesan-wide administration for all the schools. By 1907, the *New World* considered "Prejudices and antagonisms engendered by racial differences" a major obstacle to centralized control of the schools.[5]

It also attributed the lack of unity "to the fact that the communities teaching in the schools are different." [6] Indeed, by 1915, more than forty religious orders operated the Chicago Catholic schools. Though the bishop functioned technically as "superintendent" of schools, and the pastor as a local supervisor, the sisters did the teaching and, for the most part, determined curricula, chose textbooks, and set the policies that most directly affected the children. Each order had its own organization, usually independent of the bishop and extending beyond diocesan borders. Little communication took place between the different religious communities. Language and national origin separated many; rules of the cloister segregated all. Each zealously promoted its own traditions and fostered jealously guarded approaches to pedagogy, propagated through unique teacher training programs.

For example, the Sisters of Charity of the Blessed Virgin Mary, one of the earliest and largest orders of women in Chicago, developed and followed its own curriculum. "Once a good plan was worked out it became the property of the community." Throughout the nineteenth century, in lieu of formal teacher training, the older sisters simply initiated the younger into the order's teaching tradition. By 1902, "the sisters of the congregation assembled at set places during the summer, in order to discuss the most efficient methods of presenting the various school topics." These sisters, probably more advanced than most, also visited the Chicago Normal School and public schools to gather ideas. But they did not communicate with the sisters of other orders teaching in Chicago. Indeed, the evidence more than suggests that each religious order thought of its schools as a system in itself. For example, in 1912, the Sisters of Charity organized an alumnae association for their graduates throughout the Midwest as if these schools constituted a single system.[7] And the Sisters of Mercy wrote of their two private girls' academies and eight parochial schools in Chicago as if these made up a distinct unit.[8] The assumption hardly missed the mark. Certainly more uniformity in textbooks, curriculum, and methods of instruction existed among the schools of a single religious order, even when spread over the entire country, than among the schools of different parishes within Chicago.

Thus, the inbred peculiarities displayed by religious communities, compounded with isolation in the parish unit, ethnic separatism, and the unquestioned prerogatives of local pastors, posed abundant obstacles to centralized control of the schools.

One found these deterrents everywhere in the American church; yet some dioceses made considerably more progress toward unification. New York appointed a part-time superintendent in 1888, and Philadelphia had a full-time one by 1889. In 1905, the Catholic University of America opened a special department to train diocesan superintendents of schools, and by 1907, the National Catholic Educational Association had a Department of Superintendents. By 1908, New York, Philadelphia, Brooklyn, Fort Wayne, Boston, Hartford, Cincinnati, and Green Bay had superintendents.[9]

Chicago Catholics watched the gradual centralization of other diocesan systems with interest but inaction. As early as 1895, the *New World* called attention to Bishop Spalding's institution of a common examination for all parochial schools in Peoria. In 1906, it reported the appointment of a school superintendent in Cincinnati and the adoption of a single set of textbooks there. In 1907, it published the new course of study chosen by Philadelphia's Catholic schools, and the same year reported on the common textbooks adopted by both Pittsburgh and Milwaukee.[10]

Meanwhile, pressure mounted in Chicago for more uniformity. Back in 1894, the *New World* published articles arguing "The Importance of Uniformity in Our Schools" and spelled out a detailed syllabus for each academic subject. In 1895, the editor addressed a letter to a number of unnamed "prominent Catholic educators" asking how parochial schools could best be conducted and maintained and which branches should be taught. He printed two responses. One, as a means of promoting unity, advocated pedagogical courses in the seminaries for future priests and a single normal school for the sisters in each diocese. The other argued in a similar vein: "It is greatly to be deplored that we have not a more uniform system." Two years later an article complained of frequent changes in textbooks because "teacher-so-and-so does not like this arithmetic, or Sister Angela has a prejudice against this geography." [11]

Yet, increasingly, the movement for greater uniformity coincided with more favorable currents within the Chicago Church. For one thing, the "Sister Angelas" began, however hesitantly, to expand their horizons. Whereas, in 1893, each order in Chicago still had its own teacher training institutes, by 1897, the pastor of the influential St. James parish organized "the first general Catholic teachers institute held in Chicago" and attracted 300 sisters. By 1911, fledgling DePaul University offered summer courses to teachers of the Chicago parochial schools as well as extension programs during the year. This helped bring the sisters of different orders together, though isolationism remained strong. Many preferred the shelter of their own cloister, and accordingly DePaul established a branch at the Academy of Our Lady for the School Sisters of Notre Dame and another at Lithuanian St. Casimir's convent. Though these branches did nothing to acquaint the different orders with one another, they at least introduced each to ideas outside their own tradition.[12] Similarly, Loyola University began offering education courses in 1910 and, by 1916, had made "arrangements whereby religious teachers in the parochial and private schools could further their education by an in-service program." [13] This program took the form of lectures at the various convents. The sisters engaged in courses through Loyola

University did not begin to mix with one another until 1918, with the inauguration of summer courses on the main campus. But whether the sisters met or not, their vision began to reach beyond the convent walls.

Other walls, too, had begun to crumble. After 1900, the barriers that separated the influential Irish and Germans were coming down. With assimilation, the barriers that separated other groups would give way as well. If the ethnic entente did not positively promote uniformity in the schools, it at least reduced resistance.

But the real force that made unification not just a possibility but an increasing necessity was the accelerating mobility of the Catholic population. As early as 1902, the editor of the *New World* clearly recognized the phenomenon. "In a large city," he said, "the population is constantly in a state of motion. Every city pastor is aware of this from the continuous incoming and outgoing of his parishioners." He also saw the educational implications of residential movement. "The result is that every year parents find themselves compelled to send their children to new parish schools, and in a great many cases find that they are compelled to buy entirely new sets of textbooks for their children." [14] Subsequent events confirmed the editor's insight. More than anything else the impact of residential mobility overcame isolation in the local parish, the convent, and the ethnic community. A mobile population seemed to demand a centralized system where children could pass from one school to another with minimum friction.

But if the decrease in ethnic divisiveness and the increase in communication among religious sisters made unification more possible; and if the gathering momentum of Catholic residential mobility made it more necessary; the personality of George Mundelein, the new Archbishop of Chicago in 1916, made it a fact. The 43-year-old former auxiliary bishop of Brooklyn arrived in Chicago announcing: "I am different from the late Archbishop. . . . I am likely to act more quickly." [15] If his hearers wondered at the meaning, they had not long to wait.

Within one month Mundelein named three Parish School Supervisors, one Irish, one German, and one Polish, "with the purpose of coordinating the various educational institutions of the Archdiocese into one uniform and efficient system." [16] The supervisors immediately sent letters to every parochial school, asking opinions on the best textbooks and then, in April, summoned two representatives of each school to a meeting at which they adopted the most popular texts for the first four elementary years and appointed an advisory commission of three school principals. By June, it was decided to put the new system into effect in September for the first four grades, and for the upper grades the following year. Further, the unification would include regular teachers' meetings; unified methods of teaching; common exams; standardized promotional cards and diplomas; and the future appointment of school superintendents.[17]

Thus, one bold fiat transformed chaos into order, at least potentially. In reality, the new order had to be of a kind the social situation in the Chicago Church could bear. Partisan interests could not simply be swept away. Indeed, the administrative structure that developed out of Mundelein's decision would reflect the tensions between forces already present for many years; and not until a new equilibrium had been reached would the machinery function smoothly. The process took a decade.

The Archbishop attempted to placate ethnic interests by compromise. Though the national groups had to accept common English language texts for all the basic subjects, Mundelein announced that "Provision will be made to give all nationalities in the Archdiocese opportunity to teach such branches as catechism and reading in their own tongue, but only supplementary to the unified English course." Further, even the supplementary subjects were to be unified within all schools of each ethnic group.[18]

He insisted that residential mobility and not desire to stamp out foreign language prompted the school unification scheme: "The primary motive for the change intended is that of economy, because of the many people moving to and fro from one parish to another and the constant necessity of purchasing new textbooks under the past arrangement." In an attempt to play down the language problem, he insisted that foreign languages had not been outlawed: "The purpose of this committee is simply a unification of the text-books [sic] which are used in all the schools, those of the English language. We are not as yet interfering in any way with catechisms, readers or other books of similar nature that may be used in the foreign languages in our schools." [19]

Oddly enough, the first ethnic broadside against the new program came from Frenchmen residing outside the Diocese. On August 2, 1916, M. L'Abbe V. Germain of L'Action Catholique, Quebec, attempted to intervene in the interest of the French language in Chicago, exclaiming in unbelief: "Je n'ai rien lu a ce suject en ces derniers temps." A French language journal, *La Tribune*, published in Rhode Island, bitterly criticized the Chicago bishop's decision, complaining that Mundelein was trying to out Yankee the Yankees. *La Tribune* offered a brief refresher course in history: The French at great sacrifice had discovered and colonized Chicago. It also tried to renew the Archbishop's theological perspectives: The holy spirit had inspired the Apostles to speak in diverse languages to the people they evangelized. Why, then, did Mundelein, a successor of the Apostles, require a single language? [20]

The answer to Abbe Germain's complaint again stressed the underlying reasons for the Archbishop's move, insisting that "the schools attached to German, Polish, French and other such churches, have not been inconvenienced to the slightest degree," since these could still use "supplementary text-books [sic]" in their own language, approved by the school board. "The action of the Archbishop," read the response, "was really for the purpose of unifying the parochial school system. . . . In a large city like Chicago, a great proportion of the people move from section to section each year. It was found to be a hardship on these to force them to purchase new text-books [sic] for their children each time they moved." [21]

But if Frenchmen elsewhere came to their defense, the Chicago French themselves did not seem to mind the school unification. No opposition is recorded. Indeed, by 1916, the insignificant position held by French Catholics would have rendered opposition meaning-less. The more deep-seated antagonism came from the less assimi-lated and far more populous Eastern Europeans. The Poles, in particular, having by far the largest group of national schools, put up the strongest resistance. In part their obstruction of the law requiring teaching in English could not be avoided. Many Polish sisters spoke English poorly or not at all. To placate the Polish nationalists, Mundelein at first overcompensated by granting a disproportionate voice in the school administrative structure to Polish priests. This in turn led to reaction from other quarters and considerable disquiet.

Another faction that could not be disregarded was the religious orders. Mundelein understood clearly that their diversity had caused a large part of the problem: "There are about fifty different communities of Sisters teaching here in the schools, and as a result, when people move from one parish to another there is considerable confusion and expense attached to the purchase of new textbooks, and for that reason I am trying to bring a unified system of education throughout the diocese." [22]

But in his effort to bring order, the Archbishop did not simply trample on the sisters' sensibilities. Instead, he co-opted them into the diocesan school administration. One sister from each of the major orders operating in the Diocese was appointed as a community supervisor for the schools of that order and as a member of an advisory board that selected textbooks and curricula for the entire Diocese.[23] This, of course, did not eliminate all friction, but it did give the orders a voice in school affairs; and it afforded them a structured means of communicating with one another for the first time. This solution proved an astute compromise that would have a lasting effect on the administration of the Chicago Catholic schools, but not until certain difficulties had been ironed out.

The chief difficulty came in defining the powers and functions of the school superintendents. In essence, its solution rested on the proper balancing of the several diverse and often conflicting power centers that characterized Chicago Catholicism. The complex history of the Chicago Catholic school superintendency through the 1920's dramatically illustrates how precarious was the balance of social realities that had to be harmonized in the new organizational structure.

Mundelein began the process in 1916 by appointing three pastors of parishes as school supervisors. They were to function both as school board and superintendents until a full-time administrator could be selected and trained at the Catholic University of America. But due to "lack of priests," more than a year went by without action. Instead, in February of 1918, Mundelein added two more members to the Board of Supervisors in an effort to spread out the work load, since all five members also served as full-time pastors.[24] By 1919, the Archbishop had decided he needed two men trained for the superintendency, and designated the Reverend John Ford and the Reverend John Kozlowski.[25] Both were sent to Catholic University in Washington for a year's preparation. By the time school opened in 1920, the Diocese had two superintendents of schools, and the five-member board of supervisors became the diocesan school board. The main lines of Mundelein's plan were in operation: "Standardization of the elementary schools is to be effected this year through the work of trained inspectors working in conjunction with or under the direction of the diocesan board of education and aided by an advisory committee of practical educators selected, one each, from the forty-six educational communities of the archdiocese." [26]

Three key elements, then, made up the administrative structure: the diocesan school board, exclusively pastors; the superintendents or inspectors; and the advisory committee of sisters from the various religious orders. But their lines of authority remained nebulous. As a result, between 1923 and 1926 an intense controversy erupted, involving the superintendents, the school board, and the community supervisors. Mundelein set the stage for the conflict and eventually had to resolve it himself.

In 1921, for an undisclosed reason, the president of the school board resigned or was removed, and the Archbishop appointed one of the original members of the board, Monsignor Thomas Bona, a Polish pastor, as the new president. In 1923, co-superintendent

Father John Ford died. To serve with the remaining superintendent, Kozlowski, Mundelein appointed Father Henry Matimore. The new co-superintendent, unlike his predecessor and Kozlowski, had not been sent to Catholic University for training, but as a youth had graduated from the Chicago Normal School and taught in the City's public schools before studying for the priesthood. Matimore and Kozlowski differed radically in their conception of the superintendency.

Matimore immediately attacked his new job with enthusiasm and considerable professionalism. He and Kozlowski divided the Diocese between them, one taking all the schools north of Madison Street, the other those to the south; they later switched territories. Matimore visited the schools under his charge personally and sat in the classrooms. He spoke to individual teachers in each school, to the staff as a group, and organized three centers "for demonstrations and lectures on pedagogical methods," which he gave himself. He spoke on such topics as "school management from the standpoint of the principal and from the standpoint of the teacher; the question as a factor in education; vitalizing our religion; the presentation of arithmetic from a psychological standpoint; the development of the factor of reasoning rather than the faculty of memory, as the aim of education." He promoted the teaching of music, hygiene, and civics in the schools and set up a system whereby the Chicago public library loaned books directly to the parochial schools. He initiated a summer school for parochial school teachers, conducted jointly by himself, a professor from the Chicago Normal College, and a public school teacher. In addition, he wrote articles on education for the *New World* and issued bulletins to the teachers on various aspects of pedagogy. All these activities Matimore reported directly to Mundelein in extensive semi-annual reports.[27]

Kozlowski, on the other hand, rarely visited the schools himself, concentrating instead on setting up a central office in downtown Chicago from which the entire operation could be supervised. He left the actual school visits to the community supervisors of the various religious orders. Further, he worked more closely with the school board than did Matimore, and submitted his reports to them rather than to the Archbishop.

The school board apparently favored Kozlowski's approach. By 1924, it told Matimore to spend at least three days a week at the central office, let the sister-supervisors visit the schools, and submit his reports each month directly to the board. In addition, teachers' meetings could be convened only with the board's approval and only when both superintendents could attend.[28]

The energetic and by now quite frustrated Matimore refused submission to all these regulations, claiming they came from school board president Bona himself and did not represent the entire board's decision. As a result, by 1925 Matimore found himself increasingly on the sidelines. The common examinations for June, 1925, were made out without his knowledge, under Kozlowski's supervision. A new English course was printed without his approval. A new type of uniform report card went into the schools before he had heard of it. By 1926, the school board stopped notifying him of its meetings. And finally, on May 10, 1926, in the midst of an enthusiastic campaign to prepare the children for the World Catholic Eucharistic Congress to be held in Chicago the following year, he received a terse letter from Mundelein stating that after consultation with the school board he had decided to abolish the dual superintendency: "For the present we will retain but one of the two inspectors, and as Father Kozlowski is the senior of you he will continue to work alone with the help the School Board will provide. Your services as School Inspector will be discontinued at the close of this present month." [29]

The Archbishop gave no reason for the dismissal. Matimore himself, always loyal to Mundelein, blamed the chicanery of Father Kozlowski and Monsignor Bona, whom he then attacked. Bona, said the unseated superintendent, had "arrogated to himself all the powers of the board and falsely quoted the board as his authority." Kozlowski, he argued, unable to speak correct English and ignorant of most pedagogic topics, had resented Matimore's success in communicating with the sisters.[30]

More important, both Bona and Kozlowski were Polish, and Matimore had convinced himself of a Polish conspiracy. He complained that Kozlowski had "appointed a Polish Sister to make out the course in English for all our schools." He also accused his co-superintendent of antagonizing "the pastors and sisters of Irish descent by demanding that seven lines praising the Irish be deleted from an American history text before it could be considered for use in our schools. At the same time, however, he requested a paragraph praising the Poles." Finally, the rejected superintendent claimed that "Pastors and Sisters are disgusted with a Polish chairman of the Board, a Polish Superintendent, a Polish secretary in the office, a Polish printing press for educational work—and the Polish domination of the educational work of the diocese." [31]

Thus, Matimore attributed his downfall to Bona's desire for power, Kozlowski's jealousy, and both Bona's and Kozlowski's pro-Polish bias. But the truth appears otherwise. The evidence indicates that Bona may or may not have sought power, Kozlowski had reason for jealousy, and the Polish did have excessive representation in the diocesan school machinery. But Matimore's failure stemmed above all from his inability to understand or cope with the social realities in Chicago. As a result, despite his considerable expertise, he alienated almost everyone—ethnic groups, sisters, school board, and pastors.[32]

For example, no doubt unconsciously and in pursuit of professional objectivity, Matimore offended Polish sensibilities. In reports to the Archbishop, he described the Polish Felician Sisters as "not sufficiently well trained" and their classrooms as "overcrowded to a disgraceful degree." The Polish Sisters of the Resurrection did "poor" work, were "untrained," and "many cannot speak English correctly." In a ranking of the ten largest communities of sisters in the Archdiocese "According to Merit," the Sisters of Nazareth and the Felician Sisters, who each conducted 17 Polish schools, rated ninth and tenth, respectively. In 1925 he reported that "a striking condition prevails in our Polish bi-lingual schools. . . . About one-half of the children drop out of the Catholic school at the end of sixth grade. In the normal schools [non-Polish] there is only a drop out of about one-twelfth." Of high school attendance Matimore reported that "in the English speaking parishes about 65 per cent of the graduates will enter Catholic high schools. In the Slavic bi-lingual schools, Polish, Lithuanian, Slovac, etc., scarcely 35 per cent intend to attend Catholic high schools. The pastors of these places do not encourage it." Matimore found that very few Slavic girls "had any ambition for a high school education." He attributed this to "the tradition of these races not to foster higher education among the girls; or to expend as little money as possible upon it by sending the girls to the public high school for a business course." [33]

Matimore's intentions seemed honest enough, and his facts were probably correct. He tried to use such findings to improve the situation by inviting "these girls to desire something above the factory or the typewriter, stressing especially the teaching profession and the need of Polish Catholic teachers in the public schools located in the thickly settled Polish neighborhoods." [34] But he erred by meddling at all. Polish Catholic Chicago was still too ethnically sensitive to accept this kind of criticism, especially from one of a different nationality.

Matimore just as completely failed to understand the pastors' sensitivities. Thus, in refusing to submit reports to the school board he argued that pastors would resent having the weaknesses of their schools revealed. Better to report them to the Cardinal whose authority they accept. "Imagine where I would find myself," he argued, "were I to report the physical and educational conditions of the schools to the board in a written statement. How would you feel, for instance, if I reported that your school was unsanitary, dirty, overcrowded, ill-taught, without the necessary equipment and you took absolutely no interest in it? Do you think you would welcome a return visit of myself or confrere?" To this position Kozlowski replied simply that the pastors do heed the school board, since it represents them and since it has legal status: "The school board is necessary to back the work of the superintendent," he argued. "They ought to know the conditions existing. They are legally constituted by the Council of Baltimore, whereas the superintendent has no legal

authority except in as far as it is given to him by the Board." [35]
Obviously, Kozlowski's interpretation sat well with the school board,
whose authority it enhanced. But more important, it harmonized
better with the feelings of the pastors who, if their schools had to be
inspected at all, preferred that reports be sent to their own confreres
on the school board and not to their superior, the bishop. Indeed for
all his professionalism, Matimore failed to understand that pastors
simply did not relish being reported to their bishop.

His handling of the sisters revealed the same deficiency. Matimore
had convinced himself that the superintendent must directly oversee
the running of the schools, including the direction of their teachers.
"Our schools need supervision and our sisters need direction," he
argued. In Matimore's view there could be "neither supervision nor
direction without the superintendent's intelligent examination,"
since the community supervisors of the religious orders could not be
trusted. "Loyalty to their community," he contended, took "prece-
dence over loyalty to the School Board." They would hide their
schools' deficiencies unless the superintendent himself did the
inspection. In contrast, his co-superintendent, Kozlowski, relied on
the community supervisors as the only reasonable means of school
inspection. Kozlowski argued that because the superintendent's visit
must of necessity be brief and always creates an unnatural atmosphere in the school, it would give "no indication that the school has a
high educational standard." Similarly, whereas Matimore insisted on
the right to make out questions for the common examinations at the
end of each year, Kozlowski preferred to have community supervisors do the job: "Who can make out better examinations than the
supervisors who are constantly in the school?" [36]

Essentially, Matimore and Kozlowski differed in their understanding of the superintendent's proper function. For Matimore the
superintendent could and should go directly into the schools and
supervise the sisters in every detail. "What our sisters want and need
is intelligent and constant supervision and that can be accomplished
not by sitting in an office but by going the daily grind of school
visitation." [37]

But the very "daily grind of school visitation" ultimately contributed significantly to his downfall. For example, Matimore held a
meeting with the sisters on the conclusion of his visit to each school
"during which the pedagogical defects noticed in the school were
taken up one by one." One can imagine the delight the sisters took in
such sessions. On several occasions he had teachers removed from
the schools. And his habit of ranking the different religious communities according to the merit of their schools could only lead to
dissatisfaction. Significantly, the only community supervisors who
wrote letters of condolence after his removal were those whose
schools he had praised most highly. For the others, their time-hon-
ored traditions could not be criticized without resentment. Matimore
apparently never comprehended this.[38]

Despite the enthusiastic pursuit of his assigned task, Matimore
remained impervious to its political dimensions. His consequent
demise as superintendent simply underlined the persistence of old
loyalties and habits in the face of a newly created machinery for
school administration. Instead of working for a new balance of old
forces, Matimore based his actions solely on educational principles.
Sound as these may have been, their manner of implementation
ignored the entrenched realities inherited from the past.[39]

In dismissing him, Mundelein apparently recognized the nature of
the failure. The Archbishop's next move proved far more astute. A
year after Matimore's removal he appointed Father Daniel Cunningham as Kozlowski's assistant, and the following year promoted him to
the superintendency, reducing Kozlowski to the role of assistant.[40]

The Kozlowski demotion probably resulted in part from a
mediocre performance and in part from the need to limit Polish
power in the school administration. But more important, the
Cunningham appointment put into the superintendency a man
ideally suited both in temperament and philosophy. The new
superintendent was essentially an astute and gregarious Irish politician. He knew well that presence at a parish jubilee could
accomplish more than a directive from the superintendent's office.
He understood that Matimore had met his nemesis through a lack of

diplomacy. It was not his nature to make the same mistake. Indeed, through skillful balancing Cunningham would maintain his position with success for fully thirty years.[41]

Under Cunningham a new equilibrium was reached. He knew where the bishop's authority ended and his began, and never crossed the line. He established personal friendships with the local pastors. His actions quickly convinced the school board, made up of pastors whose preoccupations lay elsewhere, that their interests would never know betrayal. The board willingly receded into the background. Perhaps most significantly, he gave free rein to the sisters' representatives, the community supervisors. Working together, they developed the curricula, chose the textbooks, and inspected the schools. In short, all parties had an ally in Daniel Cunningham.

Thus, by the end of the 1920's, the Chicago Catholic schools did have a fairly smoothly functioning mechanism for dealing with the major problems of a big city school system. In particular, the crisis precipitated by the Catholic population's growing residential mobility had been met. The schools had a uniform curriculum, common textbooks, and even a single testing program to evaluate progress. They had a judicious superintendent who could handle the many factions with a minimum of friction. And possibly most beneficial, the teaching orders now worked with one another and cooperated in inspecting the schools and developing educational materials and procedures.[42] The laity had no voice but apparently still acquiesced in their role of paying for the schools and populating them with children.

In a sense, too, both before and after Cunningham, the whole show was an exercise in puppetry, with Mundelein and then his successors the puppeteers. The bishop appointed both school board and superintendent, without fixed term of office. Legally these offices had only as much authority as he deemed necessary. School board and superintendency functioned as an administrative convenience. In practice, the Archbishop still made major policy decisions. For example, he and not the school board or superintendent handled ethnic school grievances. The perennial difficulties of staffing the schools remained his concern too,[43] as did the question of sisters' salaries. Previously these had been negotiated between the sisters and the pastor of each parish. But this practice led to bickering, injustices, and complaints. By 1919, Mundelein moved to establish more uniform conditions of employment: "The question of the salaries has been taken up by the consultors. A committee has been appointed to investigate conditions in various schools and to examine the contracts that are now in force in order to come to a form that would be uniform and could be accepted by all communities." This committee drew up a uniform contract and fixed the salaries for all sisters at $300.00 a year.[44] Significantly, the Archbishop through his consultors, not the school board or the superintendent, handled the salary issue. The reason was simply that the schools remained an integral part of the parish structure. Diocesan mechanisms set up to regulate parish expenditures remained the logical vehicle for handling problems of school finance. Thus, the Archbishop's building committee and not his superintendent or school board approved plans for the construction of new schools or the expansion of old ones.[45]

In truth, then, the apparatus set up for school administration functioned within rather narrow limits. The Archbishop granted the 1916 school board "authority to enforce regulations . . . which have my approval." [46] He did delegate control over all "questions regarding class matters and school curriculum." Thus, opponents of the first adopted set of textbooks were told that the school board had been responsible. Disappointed textbook publishers received the same treatment: "I had agreed with the Board that I would abide by their decision." [47] By the end of the 1920's, such decisions passed from the school board directly to the superintendent and his community supervisors. But no power had been extended.

Still, whether directly under the Archbishop or indirectly under the superintendent and the Board of Education, the Chicago Catholic schools underwent a profound organizational transformation in the 1920's. The centralization of control signaled a distinct stage of maturation resulting from the assimilation and mobility of the Catholic population. Irrespective of any real pedagogical advantage or disadvantage resulting from creation of a more unified system, consolidation underlined the 1920's as the turning point in Chicago Catholic school history. Again, as with the ethnic question, the forceful personality of Archbishop Mundelein seized the historical trend, giving shape and form to its fulfillment.

10

Consolidation of a Total Effort

The administrative structure of school board and superintendent initiated by Archbishop Mundelein after 1916 extended only to the parochial elementary schools. Though the superintendent's reports, published annually after 1926, included information about the high schools and universities, the Archbishop had insisted that these be left to function independently, without unified curricula or admissions policies. Other aspects of the Catholic educational program, too, including the orphanage schools, settlement houses, adult and continuing education centers, did not come under the school board's jurisdiction. Yet, as with the elementary schools, the 1920's saw greater coordination and centralization of all these activities, which marked a distinct organizational coming of age for the total Catholic educational effort.

By 1930, the idea of a place in a Catholic high school for every Catholic youth had only recently gained acceptance as an essential part of the total effort. When the Catholic bishops at the Third Plenary Council of Baltimore, in 1884, legislated universal parochial elementary education, they dared voice only a hope for Catholic secondary schooling. "Would that even now," said the Council fathers, "as we trust will surely come to pass in the future, the work of education were so ordered and established that Catholic youth might proceed from our Catholic elementary schools to Catholic schools of higher grade and in these attain the object of their desires." [1] But the work of providing sufficient elementary schools had not yet been "so ordered and established" that the next step could be systematically undertaken. Nor at the time was the matter urgent. Few children of any persuasion went to school beyond the eighth grade. Less than 15 percent of the eligible age group attended secondary school. Higher schooling remained a privilege of the few.

Catholics in Chicago provided for these few in rather haphazard fashion. Religious communities, quite independently of the parish structure, founded private academies for girls and colleges for boys. These bore little resemblance to the modern American high school. The girls' academies, private convent schools run by nuns, included both elementary and secondary grades and usually a boarding department. In the days when few young ladies attended college, these schools offered a more exclusive "finishing" for a selected few under the watchful eye of solicitous sisters than did the parochial elementary school. They varied in quality and exclusivity according to the backgrounds and reputations of the religious communities in charge. By 1900, the fifteen Catholic girls' academies in Chicago educated only about 2,600 girls from the elementary grades to the equivalent of high school completion. For boys, after the demise of St. Mary's of the Lake University in 1866, St. Ignatius College led the way in providing a highly academic classical secondary school program. Between 1887 and 1900, four other private Catholic "colleges" came into being, including one for Czech boys and another for Polish. All of these followed the European tradition in admitting youngsters from the upper elementary grades and stressing a highly academic curriculum, though each at least partially acquiesced to the demand for commercial and business programs. Altogether these five schools enrolled only a little over 600 boys by 1900. In addition, the Christian Brothers ran an academy for boys loosely attached to St. Patrick's parish just west of the Loop and the De La Salle Institute on the south side. These two institutions offered commercial subjects mainly, building upon the foundations laid in parochial elementary school, and by 1900, their popular programs had attracted a total of 700 youngsters.

The academies for girls and the colleges for young men, select and beyond the financial reach of many, did not function as natural extensions of the parochial elementary schools. The Christian Brothers schools at St. Patrick's and De La Salle did. By the 1860's, some parishes, too, had begun adding secondary departments, most of them for girls, to their elementary schools. In all, by 1900, fourteen parochial high schools existed in the metropolitan area. These had developed as upward extensions of the parochial elementary school. Where Catholics had expressed the demand for more than a basic education and where the local pastor felt sufficient motivation to provide facilities and recruit sisters as teachers, these units came to be. Often they began as two-year commercial programs, later expanding into four-year high schools. Though not run on a large scale, these schools did help satisfy the growing educational needs of the common man, and some proved phenomenally successful at moving girls into the teaching ranks of the public schools.

Thus, by the end of the century, two quite different types of secondary institutions were available to Chicago Catholics. On the one hand were the private colleges and academies; on the other the parochial high schools. Increasingly, neither really satisfied the need. Usually with an elementary department of their own, the colleges and academies had no organic relationship with the parochial schools, and transfer from one to the other was difficult. And the existence of a local parish high school, depending as it did on the support and stability of a rather small community, proved precarious at best. Most parishes could ill afford their own high school, and those that had one gave preference to their own parishioners. Further, experience proved that changes in the local parish fortunes might quickly eliminate its high school; and this had already happened at Holy Family, where, after three thriving decades the departure of most parishioners from the near west side forced the parish's secondary schools to close.

Dissatisfaction with both the parochial and private institution naturally increased as secondary schooling became more universal. By the early twentieth century in most cities, including Chicago, compulsory education extended only to the fourteenth year. But the needs of the labor market for better educated personnel and the economy's increasing ability to postpone a youth's entry into the work force led inevitably to the expansion of secondary school enrollments. Since they lived in the same society, Catholics also felt the pull toward universal secondary education. By 1902, the *New World* observed that "'formerly the majority of Catholic children left school at the completion of the eighth grade; but now the larger number continue their school course either in the high schools, colleges, or in some one of the business schools downtown." [2] Though the words "larger number" no doubt exaggerated, the trend was unmistakable.

If larger numbers were to go beyond the elementary school, then Catholics felt obliged to provide their own facilities. The small private academy and the local parish high school would hardly suffice. This demand for a more extensive secondary education posed not only a practical problem of providing facilities, but a theoretical one of determining its nature. Should Catholic secondary education continue in the European tradition of the colleges and academies by offering a rather highly academic program articulated with the university, or should it concentrate instead on providing an extension of the elementary school, irrespective of college aspiration, as the parochial high schools did? Or could a dual system solve the problem—the college and academy for the elite university bound, the parochial high school, as a terminal extension of the elementary school, for the masses?

Time and the American egalitarian passion ran against this latter view. Public educators in the 1890's had attempted to straddle the issue. The National Education Association's famous Committee of Ten advocated a highly academic program for the high schools as the best preparation both for college and for life. Thus, by offering the same program to all, regardless of destination, a two-track secondary program could be avoided, and with it, odious judgments about elites and non-elites. This position had many supporters, including the public schools of Chicago. Here the decades from 1890 to 1910 "marked an ascendancy of the college preparatory functions of the public high schools." But in Chicago as elsewhere, "by 1910 the college domination of the high school curriculum began to weaken." By 1918, the National Education Association in its *Cardinal Principles of Secondary Education* almost completely reversed the 1890's position. It opted now for large, comprehensive high schools in which all youth would master not the mysteries of Latin and Greek but the necessary skills for "complete and worthy living." [3]

Catholic educational circles fought essentially the same battle. When the National Catholic Education Association came into being in 1904, formed from the Association of Catholic Colleges and the Association of Catholic Elementary Schools, the issue of Catholic secondary education came immediately to the fore. On the one hand, the representatives of the Catholic academies and college prep schools insisted that secondary education should serve the elite as preparation for college. But the majority at the first meeting thought differently and passed a resolution stating that "while the high school is intended mainly for pupils who do not go to college, it would fail of an essential purpose did it not also provide a suitable preparatory curriculum for those of its students who desired to prepare for college." [4] This resolution did not end the controversy, which continued for at least a decade. But it did show that Catholic educators were moving in the same direction as public school educators. They wanted a secondary institution that would serve both as preparation for college and for life.

But most of all, they wanted an institution that could efficiently handle the large numbers of students continuing their education beyond the elementary school. The existing academies and prep schools were not sufficient. A high school in every parish was unthinkable. Catholic educators began to take their cue from public education in which small elementary school districts had begun banding together to form consolidated or community high schools.

Thus, the Committee on High Schools of the Catholic Education Association in the first meeting of 1904 recommended that "in cities where there are several Catholic parishes there should be a central high school connected with the parochial schools of the several parishes." [5] Representatives of the Catholic academies and prep schools, who saw the development of such institutions as a threat to themselves, bitterly opposed the resolution. But in some dioceses the central high school caught on. Philadelphia had one as early as 1890, and by 1912 fifteen central Catholic high schools existed in the United States.

But the old pattern continued in Chicago through the first two decades of the twentieth century. Between 1900 and 1920, ten new academies for girls and three for boys, as well as fully forty-seven small new parochial high schools were founded, though many of the latter existed for only a year or two. In 1899, the Sisters of Charity did open the large St. Mary's high school for girls on the west side. Though private, this school differed from the girls' academies in having no elementary or boarding department and in serving the graduates of the surrounding parochial schools. De La Salle Institute and St. Patrick's Academy served essentially the same functions for boys. But beyond these, the idea of central Catholic high schools failed to catch on in Chicago during the first two decades of the century. The Diocese itself built none. And the private academies and colleges continued. Under pressure of expanding admissions some did drop boarding departments, and the boys' colleges began to drop their elementary sections and to move closer in organization and curriculum to the typical American high school. But up to 1920, secondary education for Chicago Catholics remained a combination of nonsystematic local parish response and private initiative from the religious communities.

The need for a more organized effort became more apparent. As early as 1904 the editor of the *New World* urged: "Let us build and organize the Catholic high schools we really need, equip them well, make them strong in the character of their work and then we will have nothing to fear for the standard of our schools." By 1909, he warned that "a parochial school education is good, as far as it goes, but it does not go far enough." By 1915, the persuasion had become still more insistent: "This is again the time when Catholic parents must shut their ears to the pleas of the grammar school graduate that he would sooner go to work than to high school. There should not be a question as to what course to follow unless extreme poverty bars the thought of higher education." And in 1917, he looked prophetically into the postwar years: "Keeping the children in school until they are equipped in fullest fashion to meet life's obligations is going to become a more grievous problem than ever." [6]

But if the children were to stay in Catholic schools, space had to be available. Again, as with the organization of the elementary schools, it was George Mundelein who finally stepped into the breach. From the beginning of his administration in 1916, Mundelein had discouraged the perpetuation of small academies. For example, when in 1916 the mother general of the Polish Sisters of Nazareth wrote asking permission to begin an academy adjoining the sisters' novitiate in suburban Des Plaines, Mundelein urged a different plan: "If you can see your way clear to accepting the offer, I am perfectly willing to give you and your community one of the six or seven neighborhood high schools that are to be established here for girls in Chicago in the near future. . . ." The Archbishop proposed location of the school not in sylvan Des Plaines but "in the center of the great Polish district" of the City where it could use the "various large Polish parochial schools in the neighborhood" as feeders of at least 600 students.[7] The Archbishop's intent was clear: to discourage the academies and move the religious orders into large high schools. But the advent of World War I reduced the possibility of new school construction, and high prices afterwards postponed building still more.

Finally, after a five-year delay, Mundelein announced his master plan for central Catholic high schools located strategically, with easy availability to all.

Rather than start anew, he chose to work toward ordering the already existing though diverse structure. Some other dioceses, most notably Philadelphia, had chosen to finance, build, and control a high school system of their own—the central Catholic high school in the strict sense. But Mundelein seemed to care little who owned and operated the institutions, provided Catholic secondary education was made available. He therefore cajoled already existing centrally located private academies to drop elementary and boarding departments and to expand their facilities. He encouraged religious orders of men and women to build new private Catholic high schools wherever needed. And in some instances, he turned to a local parish to provide a large high school for its own and the youth of surrounding congregations. The overriding concern was to provide the schools. Though the method varied, the objective did not. Thus, in accordance with "the plans of the most Reverend Archbishop for such regional institutions," the Sisters of Mercy built Mercy High School in a fast growing Irish district of the south side. To complement the new girls' high school, the energetic pastor of St. Leo's parish opened one for boys. "Though located in and maintained by St. Leo's parish," it was designated as "one of the central high schools" open to students "from all parts of the city." In 1924, "the north side parishes of Chicago, those of Evanston, and five other suburbs in the north shore district were assessed to provide funds" for the new St. George boys' high school in Evanston. Urged on by the Archbishop, in 1929, the Dominican Fathers agreed to build a new private high school for boys in Oak Park that "would provide a unit in the chain of Catholic high schools which we are extending about the city and the diocese." In all, by 1930, four new schools provided facilities for girls on the north, west, and south sides, plus a school for the still heavily ethnic Poles. For boys, the Diocese had its first two large suburban high schools, one in Evanston and another in Oak Park, and a large new school on the south side. These seven new high schools were further complemented by the eighteen already existing institutions that through the Archbishop's urging during the 1920's were either rebuilt totally or added major facilities. Many of these dropped elementary and/or boarding departments in the transition from the small, convent-type academy to the large city high school.[8]

By the end of the 1920's, the Chicago Archdiocese had taken a giant step in the attempt to provide adequate high school facilities for its children. Cardinal Mundelein had made a systematic effort to locate the needed schools in strategic positions. The tradition of the academy had been broken and the transition made to the large, four-year high school. The parochial high school, except for fairly numerous commercial schools and a few four-year institutions that had gained wide appeal beyond parish boundaries, gave way to the private Catholic high school owned by the religious orders. By 1930, these accounted for 80 percent of the Chicago Catholic enrollment. Except for the Quigley Preparatory Seminary, the Diocese itself maintained no high schools at all. For this reason, despite Mundelein's insistence on control over their location, the secondary institutions remained outside the school board's direct jurisdiction. Most functioned as private institutions, owned by the religious orders, not the Diocese.

Further, since most Catholic high schools were not tied into the parish structure, they had no geographical boundaries. Students could and did come from anywhere. St. Patrick's Academy on the old west side, for example, boasted in 1927 that the "world's record mileage for a day school student" belonged to Quinn McGuire who traveled 425 miles each week from his home in Grayslake. In close second was a student who journeyed 77 miles each day from another suburb. Several others commuted 50 miles or more daily from Naperville, Downers Grove, Wheaton, Lombard, Glen Ellyn, Winnetka, Niles Center, Des Plaines, Norwood Park, Deerfield, Morton Grove, and Highwood.[9] The Catholic residential mobility that had prompted the unification of elementary schools with uniform curricula did not affect the high schools. A student could attend the same school regardless of where his family lived.

Because of their largely private ownership and lack of attendance areas, Mundelein did not attempt to unify the high schools. He

simply settled for coordinating their construction on a scale that met
the increased demand.

The industrious Archbishop did much the same for Catholic higher
education. Through the nineteenth century, Church-sponsored university education hardly existed in Chicago. The grand hopes of the
City's first bishop for the University of St. Mary's of the Lake did not
materialize. The boys' "colleges" sometimes had a one- or two-year
program beyond the secondary. But these programs attracted few
students. Yet by the end of the nineteenth century, with a still small
but growing minority of Americans enjoying the advantages of
university education, Catholics increasingly felt both the need for
and the lack of highly educated laymen. In 1899, Chicago hosted the
first meeting of representatives from the nation's Catholic colleges,
and Catholic leaders placed great hope in the organization they
formed—the Association of Catholic Colleges and Universities.
Pressure mounted to build and support Catholic colleges and
universities. If John D. Rockefeller could create a full-blown
University of Chicago, then Catholic leaders were asking, "What are
our Catholic millionaires doing?" [10] But Catholics of wealth were
hard to find.

Against this background of discontent, the news came in December 1907 that St. Vincent's College on the north side had just been
chartered by the State Legislature as DePaul University and would
open a liberal arts program, a school of general science, and a school
of engineering. In 1911, the young university added a summer school
for teachers; in 1912 it became affiliated with the Illinois College of
Law to form the College of Law of DePaul University, and the same
year, opened a college of commerce. By 1915, DePaul had a
downtown campus "convenient for students in every part of
Chicago," and, by 1920, Chicago's first modern Catholic university
had colleges of arts and science, engineering, law, commerce, art and
design, and education.[11]   Meanwhile the college department at St.
Ignatius on the near west side had begun to grow away from the high
school. By 1905, 80 students attended the college, and in 1906, the
Jesuits of St. Ignatius announced plans to build a second institution

in Rogers Park on the north shore which "may in time attain the dignity of a university." By 1908, the north shore branch had a law school, and was establishing a medical school affiliated with the Illinois Medical College. "That Chicago is to have a Jesuit University is now a certainty," exulted the *New World*. By 1910, there were 50 law students, 83 medical students, and 67 collegiate department students in the newly named Loyola University, which Chicago Catholics expected "to occupy a very foremost place among the great Catholic universities of America." In 1912, Loyola began a department of sociology and a "special course of lectures for social workers." In 1914, the university inaugurated a course of extension lectures, which by 1920, counted "over fifteen hundred students, largely drawn from religious communities." And by 1920, with a college of arts and sciences, ánd departments of medicine, law, engineering, sociology and pharmacy, the new university seemed well established.[12]

Thus, the first decades of the century gave the Archdiocese two flourishing universities for men, and none too soon. World War I shocked Chicago Catholic leaders into a deeper realization of the Church's inferior educational position. Statistics showed that Catholics had high representation in the ranks, but not among the officers during the war. Thirty-five percent of United States enlisted men but only five percent of the officers had been Catholic, reported the *New World*. "They lacked the education. . . . Certain educational requirements were necessary. . . . Our boys did not have them. This is the naked truth. . . . Now more than ever Catholic parents should be adamant in their determination that their children, particularly their boys, shall have the fullest measure of education." With the crush on to compete at the college level, Catholics were urged to emulate the Jews, whose "ascendancy" was "accounted for not alone by their financial ability but vastly more by their passion for education and their sacrifices to secure it." The *New World* urged graduates to "apply at either DePaul or Loyola, or at some Catholic college in the vicinity," and Catholics were asked to contribute to the support of the Church's colleges and universities: "The vaunted

protestations of Catholics on education will fall by the way unless
Catholics of wealth come to the support of Catholic institutions of
learning." DePaul and Loyola labored to meet the growing challenge. They hardly qualified as the Yale and Harvard of the Midwest,
nor could they match the wealth of Northwestern and Chicago
universities nearer home. But they at least afforded the sons of
Catholics the chance to move into the medical, legal, and business
professions, and perhaps developed an occasional scholar or two.[13]

By the turn of the century, Catholic authorities in Chicago also
began expressing concern for the higher education of women. They
felt that, though woman belonged in the home, the proper education
of her sons would depend upon her own educational background. "If
we are to have a race of enlightened, noble, and brave men," said the
New World, "we must give to woman the best education that is
possible for her to receive." [14]

In 1901, the Sisters of Mercy moved their St. Xavier Academy to
Cottage Grove Avenue at 49th Street, and in the following year, the
New World announced that "its new curriculum comprehends a full
college course." In fac. the college department did not actually open
until 1914 and, because the sisters deliberately kept it small,
graduated only 18 students in its first eight years. In 1903, the
Religious of the Sacred Heart moved their select girls' academy from
the near west side to the northern suburb of Lake Forest. They
expanded the school to include a junior college department; and by
the time of its incorporation by the State of Illinois as Barat College
in 1918, it had developed into a four-year college empowered to
grant degrees. But Barat was far outside the City, and remained
small and much too exclusive for the average Catholic girl. Meanwhile, the *New World*'s dream of a "strong up-to-date college for
Catholic women" went unfulfilled.[15]

DePaul University had some time earlier opened its extension
courses to women, "thereby enabling nuns, teachers in the public
schools, and young women who would otherwise have been forced to
seek instruction in an atmosphere and in a manner perilous to their
faith, to study branches of higher education for one or two hours

each day." And in 1917, the president of DePaul requested permission of the Archbishop to make the entire liberal arts college coeducational. But Mundelein had other plans. "I do not desire DePaul University to accept any young women as students in your college of Liberal Arts and Sciences," he responded. "Within another year or very little later we will be prepared to take care of all of these applications. For by that time I think that the separate College for women in Chicago will be started and, as I informed you, I do not care to have any other institution detract in any way from the work that I have mapped out for this College." [16]

The separate college for women was to be Rosary College in west suburban River Forest. In the spring of 1917, having heard of his desire for a woman's college, the Dominican Sisters approached Mundelein with the possibility of moving their St. Clara's College from out-of-the-way Sinsinawa, Wisconsin, to Chicago. Mundelein, who already had a high regard for the Dominican Sisters, acted with characteristic speed and decisiveness. By June he was telling the Mother General, "The need is immediate. I expect that a college will begin operation no later than September, 1917. . . . You are sufficiently familiar with my desires to know that when I want anything, I want it now and I don't want to wait a long time to get it." In October, he announced at a gathering of 1,000 members of the Catholic Women's League: "We need certainly one, perhaps two, first class colleges for women, right here in Chicago. . . . One of the two great colleges for women in the United States will move to Chicago!" And the Women's League was "invited" to finance one of the three main buildings of the new college. By the year's end, an architect had been chosen, and Mundelein boasted that "somehow things move very fast here in this big city and there is abundant opportunity here for anyone who has the courage and the quickness to grasp it." [17]

But the Archbishop had not been quite so ebullient about the sisters' choice of a site for the college—River Forest. "The property in River Forest is out of the question," he contended, "it costs $2,000 an acre. Chicago wants a day college for women. That means it must be in close proximity to efficient railroad connections." Yet, the sisters stood up to the powerful Archbishop and had their way in choosing a site more in keeping with the secluded and exclusive tradition of Catholic women's education. The new college would be in exclusive River Forest. Mundelein, though not pleased with the location, supported the fund raising campaign enthusiastically, and argued the importance of Catholic higher education for women: "More and more are women taking places formerly occupied by men, in the professions, in business, in literature, in the shaping of public opinion, even in science." [18]

To enlist the enthusiasm of the common people, Mundelein emphasized that the new institution would be a commuter college "where girls of intellectual promise but limited means" could have the advantage of higher education. The new college would give opportunity "to the rank and file of our girls, to the bright, promising, ambitious daughters of the mechanic, the tradesman, the man who works for his daily bread." He also announced that the sisters had "agreed with me that each year a goodly number of free scholarships will be open for public competition to the graduates of our high schools. . . . There is to be no distinction of class or race." [19] Through the month of February and into March, the *New World* carried articles about the drive to raise funds for the establishment of Rosary College, and the cornerstone was laid on June 25, 1920 on a 35-acre tract in River Forest.

Thus, through Mundelein's efforts another women's college came to be in the Chicago diocese. The choice of River Forest had almost determined that it would not fulfill the dream for a "peoples' college." Many girls from Chicago did attend. Indeed, the College inaugurated a bus service from the City. But Rosary hardly became identified as a college for the "daughters of the mechanic." Mundelein had to look elsewhere for that.

Finally, in 1928 the announcement came that ground would soon be broken on the far north side at Sheridan Road and Devon Avenue for a girls' college to be named after Cardinal Mundelein himself. "As it is intended to administer to the educational needs of Chicago and outlying districts only, it will be a day college, no resident students being received." [20] Conducted by the Sisters of Charity, BVM, it would offer a complete college program in the liberal arts and sciences, comprising departments of philosophy, history, English, ancient and modern languages, mathematics, science, journalism and education, with offerings in fine arts as well as secretarial studies. Mundelein College opened in September, 1930, with 250 students in a 14-story building equipped to handle 1,000.

This new college adjoining Loyola University completed the basic plan. Mundelein had felt that "in a great city like Chicago, with its dense population, its enormous distances and its widely scattered residential districts, it is necessary that educational facilities, to be available at all, should be numerous and judiciously located." [21] The women's colleges, if not located most advantageously for all, at least covered a broad area—St. Xavier's on the south, Rosary on the west, and Mundelein on the north.

But the Archbishop, always the grand planner, had envisioned something more than simply a number of independent Catholic colleges and universities for young men and women. In April, 1920, he called a press conference and revealed to the world his master plan. "Chicago is to have a great Catholic University, one to rank with the best in the country," he announced. "We have many Catholic institutions for higher education . . . but there is no real bond of union between them. . . . Each has its own state charter, and each struggles along as best it can, all alone." In Mundelein's view this was not sufficient. "Almost all the material for a university is already here," he stated, but not the university itself. "What we need is the assembling of it, the addition of new departments, and then the constant effort to perfect the whole, under a plan aiding each financially from a central fund, while binding all together under one scholastic standard, one degree giving board." The scheme was bold indeed, and unique in the United States—to bring all the Catholic colleges of the Diocese under the umbrella of a singly financed, degree-granting institution—a Catholic University of Chicago. "It is a big task," admitted Mundelein, "too big perhaps for one man's lifetime, but yet a task worthwhile. I have dreamed of it and planned for it." [22]

The next step would be to resurrect the University of St. Mary's of the Lake as the great University's theological school where the seminarians of the Diocese, since 1866 farmed out to other diocesan seminaries, would be trained: "The divinity department will be located on a thousand acre tract at Area, Illinois." This part of the plan went into effect almost immediately. The new philosophical and theological seminary at Mundelein, Illinois, though only partially built, opened to its first students in September of 1921. By 1924, the entire plant had been completed, an almost palatial group of 25 structures where all the future priests of the Diocese were to live and receive their higher education. Mundelein induced the highly respected Jesuit order to provide the faculty and tried to persuade both the Jesuits and the equally renowned Dominican Fathers to merge their own seminaries into the University of St. Mary's of the Lake. The latter requests were refused by the two orders, who preferred to preserve their independence. Indeed, it may well have been this desire for independence that ultimately shattered Mundelein's dream of a united Catholic University in Chicago. An earlier caution that the task was "too big, perhaps, for one man's lifetime" proved an underestimate. Neither Mundelein nor any of his successors ever brought it to completion.[23]

Still, as with the elementary and high schools, it was largely Mundelein's forceful seizure of the national trend toward higher education that brought the 1920's to a close with the Diocese well stocked in Catholic colleges and universities for both men and women, and a complete school of philosophy and theology for the education of the City's priests. Though he failed to bring the various branches into an administrative and economic unit, he did succeed in creating a degree of functional cooperation that made the universities living members of the total Catholic educational organism. For instance, in 1920, when the Loyola University medical school ran into financial troubles, Mundelein, "considering it a necessary part of the structure of Catholic education in the Archdiocese," announced that special collections would be taken up in all parishes annually to keep the medical school solvent. In 1920, he also determined that the nine nursing schools in the various Catholic hospitals should be affiliated with Loyola Medical School. Some of these were already affiliated with Northwestern University and other institutions, affiliations they at first refused to abandon. The Archbishop threatened to withdraw all support and recognition and let it be known that "the Cardinal positively forbids any Catholic hospital in Chicago affiliating with any non-sectarian or non-Catholic university." He clearly saw the Catholic universities in the context of the overall Archdiocesan educational effort and sometimes resorted to heavy-handed methods in the process of weaving them into a single fabric.[24]

During the 1920's, Mundelein also gave the came sense of coordinated direction to the various programs that had for many decades satisfied the needs for special and continuing education. In part, this direction consisted simply of stopping up the gaps that still remained. For example, the Archdiocese itself had for years conducted an orphanage, as did the Germans, Bohemians, and Poles. But in 1916, Mundelein purchased property in Oak Park and founded the Bishop Quarter Military School, an elementary institution for motherless boys whose fathers could not afford the high fees of a more exclusive boarding school. Thus, the Church had an institution for the child who could neither qualify for an orphanage nor be cared for at home.[25]

On a somewhat grander scale, Mundelein moved to develop a program to prevent delinquency. From 1859 to 1882, delinquent boys had been remanded to the Christian Brothers Bridgeport Industrial School. After that boys in trouble, after processing through the City Boys' Court, if convicted, went to the House of Correction. Thus, the Church had no direct control over the delinquents themselves. Mundelein determined instead to prevent delinquency among Catholic youth. In 1916, he asked for the establishment of a men's Holy Name Society in every parish, including a Big Brother Committee in each to work with "those wayward boys of our faith, who appear daily in the Boys' Court and who, if left unaided, are in

grave danger of becoming confirmed criminals." He also proposed a
"preventative school," which finally came to fruition in 1928 with
help from Catholic millionaire Frank J. Lewis. The Archbishop
bought 160 acres at Lockport, Illinois, and announced the beginning
of Holy Name Technical School. He had the Holy Name Society
launch fund-raising drives in all the parishes to build this new school
"for under-privileged boys of the Chicago Archdiocese." The
intention was to provide a technical high school and in the future a
college in a boarding school atmosphere for boys unable to finance
their own education and already in danger of delinquency. When the
school finally opened in 1932 with living quarters for 500 boys, the
2,000 applications already on hand forced Mundelein to select a
special committee for screening candidates.[26]

As a more ambitious venture still, in addition to the Big Brothers,
who provided a kind of voluntary Catholic corps of probation
officers, in the late 1920's Mundelein appointed a dynamic young
auxiliary bishop to organize a diocesan-wide Catholic Youth Organization (CYO). One of Bishop Bernard Sheil's first enterprises was to
establish boy scout troops in local parishes. In addition, by 1930, the
CYO began to sponsor vacation schools for elementary school
children and to develop a program of recreation centers, gyms, and
clubhouses that were to play a major part in the Chicago Catholic
battle for youth during the Depression.[27]

All of these programs in some way functioned on a diocesan-wide
basis. Some, like the Holy Name Society, Big Brothers, and CYO,
were meant to reach into every parish of the City. Others, like the
Bishop Quarter School and Holy Name Tech, appealed to qualified
youngsters from any parish. In addition, all were supported on a
diocesan-wide basis that reflected Mundelein's efforts at consolidation and unification.

Indeed, of far more fundamental importance than the actual
institutions and programs that the Archbishop, in the 1920's,
launched to fill the gaps still left was his centralization of control
over the myriad of institutions and activities that already existed. In
the past, the several orphanages, 18 settlement houses, numerous

homes for young working people, schools for the deaf or blind, and the like, had been separately organized and financed by local parishes, ethnic groups, lay societies, or religious communities. As with the parochial schools before their unification, the many disparate efforts led to inconvenience, inefficiency, and waste. As early as 1899 at least one Catholic layman complained that "there seems to be lacking that cooperation and harmony of action necessary for the accomplishment of the best results." With the proliferation of charitable activities the layman in particular came under pressure for donations to the bewildering welter of projects that sprouted everywhere. Special collections and fund drives had him continually dipping into pocket. But Mundelein, in 1917, decided to create a central agency for coordinating all the Catholic charities, including a single collection of funds for distribution to individual agencies. It was hoped that "the promiscuous begging, so annoying to the general public, would be eliminated, and that the duplication, which so frequently follows when there is a lack of coordination and proper supervision, would be avoided." Thus, the Associated Catholic Charities of Chicago came into being, with all Catholics in the Archdiocese invited to participate. In March, 1918, Mundelein created the Central Charity Bureau in charge of distributing the central fund to the various institutions on condition that they submit audited financial reports. The unification, admittedly loose, at least centralized control over the purse strings, gave the Archbishop a handle on policy formation, and a new opportunity, without unduly cramping individual and local initiative, to coordinate the whole for the general good.[28]

Like the unification of the parochial school system and the direction given to high school and university construction, the creation of a centralized Catholic Charities during the 1920's marked the achievement of a certain institutional maturity for Chicago Catholicism that reflected the general improvement of Catholic fortunes in the City as a whole.

III
THE BURDEN
OF SUCCESS—
1930-1965

11

A Golden Age?

By the late 1920's, Catholic efforts across a broad spectrum of educational endeavor gave cause for almost unmitigated hope. The parochial schools were expanding at a rate that more than kept pace with the growth of public elementary schools. The Catholic populace had begun its move to prosperity and the transformation of its schools from a working to a middle class phenomenon. The end of mass immigration and the ineluctable process of assimilation already gave promise of a unified school system for Catholic, unhyphenated Americans. A workable central administration now supervised the school program. The secondary schools had been transformed into large, urban high schools and momentum created to provide universal high school education under Catholic auspices. The Church could offer to young men and women the advantages of higher education in Catholic colleges and universities right here in Chicago. From the orphanage to the settlement house to the adult education class, steps had been taken to provide education at all levels under the protective mantle of Mother Church. And the defenders of Catholic education had successfully learned to cope with those who opposed it.

Yet, just when the enterprise seemed at the threshold of a golden

age, the nation's financial collapse in the years after 1929 threw it
back again on all too familiar hard times. The situation seemed worse
than any in the Church's earlier long period of tribulation. "Never in
the history of our Catholic school system," wrote the superintendent
of schools, "have the pastors of the diocese, the teaching priests,
brothers, and sisters, and the people of the Archdiocese been called
upon to make greater sacrifices, and to display greater loyalty and
zeal for Catholic education, than in the year 1930–31." Reports of
the following years referred constantly to the "heavy burden" and
"unsettled times." [1]

The Archdiocese reacted to the crisis in a variety of ways, all of
them designed to save money without curtailing the educational
program. First, all building activities ceased. "In the days of our
national prosperity," wrote the superintendent, "his Eminence,
Cardinal Mundelein, adopted a plan of wide educational expansion
to meet the needs of the times. In the recent less favorable period, he
wisely advised pastors to curtail their school building programs."
Whereas in 1928 and 1929, 17 new elementary schools opened, the
four years after the stock market crash saw only three more. Second,
the Archdiocese followed a tenacious policy of operating every
already existing institution for the full school year. After four years of
struggle, the superintendent announced in 1934 that "our Archdiocese should feel proud that not a single school has been forced to
close, and that there has been no shortening of the school term." [2]

He made these statements as an explicit comparison with the
public schools of Chicago, in which financial troubles, begun even
before the crash, had forced a curtailment of operations and
shortening of the school year. Indeed, in a sense, the Depression left
the Catholic schools, especially the elementary, with certain advantages over the public. In the parochial school, teachers, almost
exclusively sisters, could work merely for their subsistence. The
voluntary labors of willing parishioners, many out of work anyway,
helped maintain the buildings. With practically free labor, the
schools functioned at minimum cost. Further, the entire congregation, not just the parents, supported the meager expenditures. This

made free tuition possible for children of the unemployed, and the superintendent claimed that "pastors have in innumerable instances and in the face of diminishing revenues, gladly admitted the children of such parents free of charge." The *New World* advertised that "no parochial school will bar a boy or girl because the parents are unable to pay tuition. In fact, there probably is no school in the Archdiocese which does not have its quota of pupils who are enrolled without payment of tuition." Schools like St. Cecelia's on the eastern fringe of the stock yards reported that, though "a large number of children could not pay even a small monthly tuition . . . no child was turned away because of the failure of parents to contribute to the support of the school." [3]

Yet, though the schools remained open, and Church authorities maintained that no child should be turned away for financial reasons, after 1930 parochial school enrollments declined for the first time ever. In 1930, the superintendent commented that "this is the first time we have reported a loss in the number of first grade children in our Catholic schools." In the five years between 1929 and 1933, the parochial school enrollment decreased by 11,000 in the City alone and by another 2,000 in the suburbs. In 1934, the superintendent mused that "during the past four years the falling off in the first grade enrollment has given us much food for thought." [4] Despite a gradual leveling off, the first grade register continued to decline through the 1930's until, by 1939, it was 30 percent lower than a decade earlier. In all, Catholic parochial school enrollment in the entire tricounty area dropped by over 22,000 between 1930 and 1940, 20,424 in the City (14 percent) and 1,859 in the suburbs (7.8 percent).

The superintendent attributed this decline to a single factor: "This general decrease in the elementary enrollment can be explained only by the fact that there has been a nationwide decline in the birth rate during the past ten years." Statistics supported his explanation. The public schools of the City lost 84,192 pupils (22.4 percent) between 1930 and 1940; and those in the suburbs lost 10,724 (9.8 percent). There were simply not as many school-age children in the area as in

1930. The most obvious assumption seemed that both public and Catholic school rolls had decreased for the same reason—a decline in the birth rate. But the editors of the *New World*, associating a declining birth rate with the practice of birth control, could not accept the implication that Catholics were using birth control.[5]

They were probably at least partly correct. Some of the decline in Catholic school enrollments seemed directly related to the strained economic conditions. Despite the offer of free tuition, either some parishes did not support the policy or many parents would not accept this form of charity. Three-quarters of enrollment decline in the crucial Depression years came from the upper grades, which seemed to indicate that Catholic parents had simply removed their children from Catholic schools, probably for financial reasons. In 1930–1931 alone, between one and two thousand children dropped out of every grade. Further, the decline in Catholic enrollment took place only in the City's poverty areas and the industrial suburbs. In the City, Catholic schools in the 24 poorest community areas lost over 23,000 pupils between 1930 and 1940 and the schools in the workingman's suburbs of Cicero, Calumet City, Chicago Heights, and Harvey alone lost 2,600. Other industrial suburbs such as Argo, Blue Island, Midlothian, North Chicago, Posen, Waukegan, and Melrose Park lost another 900 pupils. In contrast, the middle class Catholic schools continued to grow during the Depression. After 1934, the building of elementary schools, all of them in substantial neighborhoods, began anew; these included a second parish and school for upper middle class Beverly "in response to a growing demand made by Catholic families who are moving to the southwest in search of more desirable residential neighborhoods." [6] In the City's 19 highest status community areas, Catholic schools actually gained 5,242 pupils during the 1930's. Whereas the number of public school children decreased by 14 percent in these communities, Catholic school enrollment jumped 25 percent. In the middle class suburbs, they inched ahead by another 1,000 pupils.

Whether influenced by the economic situation or the declining birth rate or both, the Catholic elementary schools, despite their losses, actually did somewhat better than most public schools. They ended the decade with almost 30 percent of the total enrollment in Chicago itself, higher than ever before, and 18.2 percent in the suburbs, also the highest in history. Further, middle class communities registered the greatest gains. Thus, in the highest status areas of the City, Catholic school enrollment jumped from 16.4 percent to 21.4 percent during the decade. And in the suburbs, solidly middle class areas like Evanston moved from 12.2 percent to 14.5 percent and Oak Park from 14.2 percent to 21.3 percent. Surprisingly during the 1930's, the Catholic movement into the middle class, though greatly curtailed, did not abate.

At the high school level somewhat different factors came into play. Elementary pupils, at a record high in the 1920's, had now reached high school age. Further, the ideal of universal secondary education, plus youth's inability to find work during the Depression, threw unprecedented numbers of students into the high schools. Thus, though elementary enrollments plummeted, attendance at secondary schools burgeoned. Because of the financial pinch, the Church could not cope with this phenomenon. Catholic high schools required more money to function, and had always charged significantly higher tuition than the elementary schools.

During the Depression the secondary schools responded as best they could. In 1931, the superintendent reported that "at no other time have they been called upon to carry so many boys and girls on their free lists." The several large new high schools opened in the late 1920's provided some room for more students into the early 1930's, and in fact, enrollment in Catholic high schools between 1930 and 1935 increased by 1,000 students, which delighted Catholic authorities. "Inability to find employment, reduced tuition rates, and the splendid spirit of generosity on the part of sisters, brothers, and priests towards boys and girls unable to pay tuition," claimed the superintendent, "are the factors which have enabled us to show an increase in attendance, where one would naturally expect to find a decrease." Yet, the great expansion of facilities set in motion during the 1920's had to be curtailed. During the worst years, 1930 to 1934, no new high schools opened, and the existing schools could not absorb the increasing number of students seeking secondary education. As a result, a larger percentage than ever entered the public high schools. The superintendent explained that "the pupils who ordinarily would seek employment after graduation from the eighth grade could not find work and therefore continued their education in the public high schools." [7]

Thus, despite the increase in Catholic high school attendance, the schools did not keep pace with the public high schools. Between 1929 and 1934, while the number of Catholic grade school graduates going to high school jumped from about 75 percent to 85 percent, the number going to Catholic high schools dropped from 37.3 percent to 32.5 percent for boys and from 45.5 percent to 38.3 percent for girls. More and more Catholic youth were attending the public high schools.

But by the mid-1930's, as economic pressure began to ease, Catholics moved again to meet "the need of more Catholic high schools." Between 1935 and 1936 four new schools opened, one each on the northwest and southwest sides where Catholics had moved during the 1920's, and others in suburban Elmhurst and Des Plaines. But these, except for the school in Elmhurst, were all private institutions, which necessarily had to charge higher tuitions. For many Catholics, even after the worst Depression years, these schools remained out of reach. To meet the immediate need, Archbishop Mundelein reversed his 1920's policy of promoting large, centrally located high schools that had proven "very expensive." Instead, he reverted to the earlier practice of opening small, two-year institutions wherever space could be found. The decline of elementary schools in the workingman's areas had left vacant classrooms. In these a program for the first two years of high school could be introduced and tuition kept "substantially the same as in the lower grades." In 1937, the *New World* announced that "In accordance with the wishes of his Eminence, the Superintendent arranged for the establishment of six new junior high schools in parishes where shifting populations made vacant classrooms available. A two-year academic curriculum was outlined, and the schools were fully accredited as two-year high schools by the State Board of Examiners." [8] Six more such schools came into existence in 1938, two more in 1939, and another two in 1940.

Though some of these two-year high schools soon added the full four-year program, all classes were conducted on a small scale. By 1940, the 16 institutions thus established enrolled only 2,023 students, an average of 126 per school. But they did provide an inexpensive high school education for the children of at least some workingmen. Significantly, 12 of the schools established between 1937 and 1940 were in ethnic parishes of the inner city.

The several new private schools and the numerous small parochial high schools increased the opportunities for a Catholic high school education. The improved economy in the late 1930's also improved the ability of many Catholics to pay high school tuition. As a result, by 1939, over 41 percent of the Catholic boys graduating from the parochial elementary schools and 48.4 percent of the girls entered Catholic high schools. By 1940, Catholic secondary enrollment in the City had jumped fully 49 percent over 1930, and the number of high school students in Catholic schools rose slightly from 13.8 percent to 14.1 percent. In the suburbs, Catholic high school enrollment increased by one-third, but with only 3,000 students, accounted for just 6.4 percent of all the high school students there.

But all things considered, the Catholic schools did not do too badly during the Depression. No schools closed or shortened their school year. The elementary school enrollment declined less than did the public school; and ended the decade with a higher percentage of the school-age children than ever before. Further, the gains made were in the middle class. The high schools, after a faltering few years, managed to keep up, too, and ended the decade without losing ground to the public schools despite the greatly increased percentage of youngsters attending high school. Catholic education in Chicago had weathered the Depression, and Catholics felt they were sitting once more in the catbird seat.[9]

In 1939, the new archbishop, Samuel Cardinal Stritch, moved

quickly to promote further expansion of school facilities that had already begun in the late 1930's. But the war years made building difficult, despite the inclusion of parochial schools on the list of civilian construction priorities. The end of the war saw an increase of only 6,000 pupils in the elementary schools over 1940, and Catholic authorities worried over the fact that fully one-third of the Catholic children still attended public schools. The superintendent complained that "many thousands of applicants just have to be turned down." But with the release of construction materials for civilian use, the situation changed rapidly. Between 1945 and 1950 the parochial schools added almost 30,000 pupils, and the *New World* reported in 1951 that "eighty percent of the $46,000,000, which the Cardinal labeled for school construction during the last five years, has gone into the erection of new grade schools." In the next fifteen years, expansion occurred with almost monotonous regularity. Between 1950 and 1965 Catholic elementary schools in the tricounty area added over 124,000 pupils to their lists.[10]

The development underlined the movement of the Catholic population into the middle class, so long dammed up after a beginning in the 1920's. Of the 124,000 additional pupils, 112,000 were registered in the middle class areas of the City and suburbs. The greatest development by far took place in the suburbs. Here, in the counties of Cook, Lake, and DuPage, Catholic schools added 92,000 pupils between 1950 and 1965. In 1950, the suburban school enrollment made up just 19 percent of the Catholic total. By 1965, it was 41 percent. Further, most of the expansion took place in middle class suburbs. Indeed, by 1965, only 19,000 of the 127,000 children in suburban parochial schools came from suburbs in the lowest third of the socioeconomic scale.[11] Fully 41 percent of the Catholic suburban enrollment came from suburbs in the highest third. Catholics in the suburbs had also bettered their position vis-à-vis the public schools. In 1940, the Catholic schools accounted for only 18.2 percent of the suburban enrollment. By 1965, they were 26.9 percent. Better than one suburban child in four attended a Catholic school. Catholic schools among the City's middle class prospered too.

They added 26,000 pupils after 1940, almost 20,000 between 1950 and 1960. More significantly, the percentage of children attending Catholic schools in the City's middle class rose from 19 percent in 1930 to almost 35 percent in 1960.

The move of the Catholic population into the middle class stood out as a highly visible fact. Not quite so visible but nonetheless real was the fact that Catholic schools made strong advances on the public schools among the City's other social classes, too, except in the Black ghetto. Thus, in the so-called common man communities, Catholic schools added 25,000 pupils after 1930, 19,000 after 1950. And the proportion of children attending Catholic schools in these areas rose from 25 percent to 34 percent between 1930 and 1960. In the lower class areas, the proportion in Catholic schools declined from 32 percent to 25 percent during these years. But this was due to the tremendous increase in the number of Black children, most of whom attended public school. In the City's predominantly white working class sections, the proportion of children in Catholic schools actually rose from 35 percent in 1930 to 45 percent in 1960. Catholic inner city schools enrolled a steadily increasing proportion of the white remnant. If the actual numbers in Catholic schools here declined, this was only because commerce and industry encroached on these residential areas. Thus, by the 1960's, though by far the greatest increase in numbers had been registered in the middle class sections of the tricounty area, Catholic schools at all the white socioeconomic levels accounted for a higher proportion of the children than ever before.

The Catholic high schools experienced much the same development during these years as the elementary—very slow growth during the 1940's due to the war, and then unprecedented expansion.

During the war years, though the economic situation greatly improved, defense priorities made expansion of facilities impossible. The superintendent announced that "plans for the construction of new buildings and additions to already existing plants have been shelved for the duration." Yet, even without the expansion of physical facilities, between 1940 and 1945 Catholic high school enrollment increased by almost 8,000. Whereas in 1940 only 53 percent of the parochial school graduates in the City went to Catholic high schools, by 1945 72 percent did. The result was severe overcrowding. Further, as the number of parochial school graduates began to increase again during the 1940's, the need for more high schools became pressing. By 1944, the superintendent complained that "high school facilities were taxed to capacity" and that "it was necessary to turn away hundreds of high school applicants because of lack of space." There was pressure "especially on the northwest and southwest sides." [12]

By 1945, archdiocesan authorities announced that "just as soon as building conditions permit" plans for new high schools would be implemented. Two small parochial high schools opened to help relieve the pressure, and seven already existing schools launched fund-raising drives for major expansion. In 1948, the pastors of thirteen parishes in Steger, Homewood, Glenwood, Park Forest, Hazel Crest, and Chicago Heights banded together and began raising funds for the first Catholic high school in the southern suburbs. By 1949, a new girls' high school opened on the northwest side. Still, the growth of facilities up to 1950 was minimal, apparently due to "restrictions on steel and other construction materials." Scarcities during the early postwar years, and the attendant high prices, posed a serious problem. Said Cardinal Stritch, in 1948, "The plain fact is that we simply haven't facilities adequate to our needs. . . . We have some high schools planned but the cost of construction is proving so much higher than our estimates that we are facing difficulties." Many applicants were being turned away, and the Cardinal Archbishop of Chicago had to "assure parents of the Archdiocese that we are working and laboring to increase our Catholic high school facilities and that it is our hope to have in the Archdiocese sufficient high schools to meet the demands of Catholic parents." [13]

By this time Stritch had decided "the only way that we shall get the high schools that we need" would be to launch a fund-raising drive throughout the Diocese by taxing the many parishes for the erection of new schools. Still, as in the past, the Archdiocese did not elect to undertake the schools itself. Instead, throughout the 1950's, the Cardinal negotiated with religious orders over the building of new schools to be partially financed from the archdiocesan fund raised in the parishes. For example, Stritch agreed in 1951 to contribute one-half the cost of constructing a new boys' high school in Niles, to be conducted by the Holy Cross Fathers. When St. Mary's girls' high school on the west side needed more classrooms, the Archbishop gave the sisters $250,000. He also gave funds for the expansion of Madonna High School, and the archdiocesan high school building fund gave $1,000,000 for a new St. Xavier High School on the far southwest side.[14]

With the help of such archdiocesan grants, Catholic high school facilities expanded tremendously during the 1950's and 1960's. In the fifteen years between 1950 and 1965, Catholic high school enrollments more than doubled, going from 38,653 to 80,735. Twenty-nine already existing schools made major additions and added a total of 12,360 places, an average of 426 per school, and 20 of these 29 were in the City itself. Five other already existing schools moved to new locations, and thereby increased their enrollments by 5,900. Four of these moved within the City from the center outward, and one moved from the City into a suburb. In addition, 25 brand new schools were built, and, by 1965, enrolled 26,437 students, an average of 1,057 per school. These new schools were largely in suburban areas, with 17 of the 25 outside the City proper. The rate of expansion picked up momentum, with 7,000 additional students between 1950 and 1955, 15,000 between 1955 and 1960, and 20,000 in the following five years. Whereas during the Depression years expansion had been achieved in the most inexpensive way possible, by establishing small high schools in already existing parochial elementary schools, the 1950's and 1960's saw a return to the large private high school. Only two of the 25 new schools were parochial.

Despite the great demand, expansion kept better pace than in any previous period; and by 1965, 69.5 percent of the boy and 71.3 percent of the girl graduates of Catholic elementary schools entered Catholic high schools. Enrollments had increased over threefold since 1940. In the same period, the number of high schoolers attending Catholic schools rose from 14.2 percent to 28.7 percent in the City, and from 6.4 percent to 14.3 percent in the suburbs.

Meanwhile, Chicago Catholic efforts to provide education for every possible need continued unabated. By 1965, the six Catholic colleges and universities of the area enrolled 24,000 students, an increase of 500 percent over 1930. Though the institutions of higher learning moved toward greater functional independence of the Archbishop, in important ways they remained a part of the total effort. For example, the Diocese continued to help support the Loyola University Medical School by assessing each parish, and later, by sponsoring a fund-raising dinner. The colleges and universities performed numerous special services for segments of the Catholic population. Sisters from the parochial schools attended summer sessions at these institutions. Loyola ran a child guidance center for parochial school children. Rosary College conducted an adult education program and lecture series. St. Xavier College's Mercy Forum offered lectures for adults. The Holy Name Society Lecture Bureau provided speakers from the Loyola and DePaul University faculties for its monthly meetings in the parishes as "an extension of the educational arm of the Catholic universities." [15]

But most of all, the Catholic colleges and universities recruited their students from the high schools of the Archdiocese. The bishops urged that "Wherever possible and whenever possible Catholic parents should send their children to Catholic institutions of higher learning." [16] Many high schools put strong moral pressure on their graduates to attend Catholic universities; and, if the pressure was gradually eased, it was mainly because the universities could not handle the mounting numbers going to college.

In other areas, the decades after 1930 saw a continuation of the movement begun in the 1920's toward more unified activity. Though educational programs often had outlets through the parishes, they now depended less on local organizations and more on diocesan-wide promotion. The men's Holy Name Society Speakers Bureau sponsored lectures for its chapters in the local parishes. The Archdiocesan

Confraternity of Catholic Women had 290 parish discussion clubs by 1957; it ran 118 parish libraries and sponsored 790 girl scout troops. In 1943, the Christian Family Movement began to form discussion groups of men and women. By 1958, there were 140 such units in the Archdiocese. In 1944, Monsignor James Egan founded the Cana Conference to provide lectures and discussion series for engaged and married couples. By 1955, 130 parishes had Cana Conferences. Cardinal Stritch introduced the Confraternity of Christian Doctrine (CCD) into the Archdiocese in 1942, in a belated effort to structure the religious instruction of Catholic children in the public schools. By 1964, over 80,000 youngsters attended CCD-sponsored religion classes, half of them on released time. Another 25,000 high school students participated in afterschool and evening CCD classes.

But possibly the most dramatic of all the movements was the Catholic Youth Organization (CYO). Founded in the late 1920's to deal with the youth problem, and promoted through the charisma of its leader, Auxiliary Bishop Bernard Sheil, the CYO quickly undertook the sponsorship of varied educational activities. In 1930, it opened two vacation schools "for children in crowded areas and the underprivileged districts." [17] These multiplied each year until, by 1936, 24 vacation school centers served 35,000 children and employed 700 teachers. Catholic sisters, brothers, seminarians, college girls, and laymen staffed the centers. These summer sessions were held in parochial school facilities, but the Chicago Park District actively cooperated as well. The program lasted six weeks, and included manual training, sewing, cooking, handicraft, weaving, dramatics, singing, civics, religion, and athletics. As late as 1955, the CYO still maintained 40 vacation school centers, 33 of them in Chicago parks.

In addition to its vacation schools, the CYO sponsored boy scout troops and established recreation centers, gyms, and club houses. It organized a Catholic high school and college student organization (CISCA) and offered scholarships to Catholic high schools for needy students. It ran debating, dramatic, study, and glee clubs; a symphonic orchestra; a band; and classes in public speaking and radio technique. The organization also cooperated with the parochial schools to provide child guidance centers and a reading service. Finally, in 1943, the CYO founded the Sheil School of Social Studies in a downtown center. The Sheil School offered non-credit courses in public speaking, foreign languages, psychology, current events, specializing in various aspects of labor studies.

When Bishop Sheil resigned from the CYO in 1954, its many activities were reorganized. Out of the Sheil School of Social Studies came the Catholic Adult Education Center. The new leadership abandoned the downtown location in favor of more numerous decentralized centers in Catholic high school, college, and parish facilities. By 1965, 12 such centers offered adult, non-credit evening courses in theology, social action, and general culture, including art and film appreciation, politics and foreign affairs, and contemporary literature.

Meanwhile, the Catholic Charities extended its sway over most of the educational enterprise for the dependent, delinquent, and deprived. It supported orphanages, day nurseries, special schools, social centers, settlement houses, and summer camps. In the reorganization of the CYO, after 1954, the Charities took over the reading service for parochial school children. In cooperation with the Catholic School Board, it administered reading tests to all Catholic school pupils, conducted summer remedial reading programs, and financed the training of teachers for the project. By 1958, there were 31 summer remedial centers for 5,000 children. In 1962, the Catholic Charities also began sponsoring a Junior Great Books Program in 77 parochial schools. In 1951, the Catholic Charities had begun to offer hearing tests for all parochial school children and to provide special education for those with impairments. By 1953, it had financed three parochial schools for the deaf, conducted in special classrooms of regular schools where the children could intermingle with other pupils. It also provided similar classes for the blind and trained teachers for both programs. In addition, the Catholic Charities helped finance three resident schools for some 600 mentally retarded, though one of these, the Lt. Joseph P. Kennedy School, owed its existence to a large grant from millionaire Joseph Kennedy.

Thus, the years after 1930 saw a distinct and steady movement toward further unification of the many enterprises that characterized the total effort to provide comprehensive educational coverage. Though none of these activities were directly supervised by the diocesan school board, they were increasingly coordinated by such diocesan-wide organizations as the Catholic Charities, Holy Name Society, Confraternity of Catholic Women, Cana Conference, Christian Family Movement, Confraternity of Christian Doctrine, Catholic Youth Organization, and the Catholic Adult Education Center.

The Catholic school board itself continued to consolidate its administration of the system's nerve center in the elementary schools and the increasingly important high schools. Daniel Cunningham's superintendency, lasting until 1957, proceeded without much innovation, but also without turmoil. His successor, Monsignor William McManus, moved cautiously toward more centralization, though he too recognized the social realities and tried to "co-ordinate the schools' varied activities not by heavy-handed regulation but by the development of a spirit of generous cooperation in working for the good of all schools." [18]

Under both men, the superintendent's staff gradually expanded to eventually include three assistant superintendents, several permanent curriculum experts drawn from the religious orders of sisters, a business manager, and by the early 1960's, a recruitment officer for the hiring of lay teachers. The community supervisors continued to work closely with the superintendents in the supervision and inspection of schools and the development and selection of curricula. The ten religious orders with the largest number of schools in the Archdiocese each supplied one full-time supervisor for this task.

Many religious orders continued to hold summer institutes which helped preserve their educational traditions. But each year found more sisters mixing in the Catholic universities. And in 1940, Cardinal Stritch inaugurated annual teachers' institutes for the entire

Diocese. The increased communication led gradually to the formation of Catholic teachers' and principals' organizations. For example,
in 1946, the music teachers organized; they later sponsored annual
music festivals. The same year, first-grade teachers founded a group
of their own. By the early 1950's, the second-grade teachers held
regular meetings. Finally, under Monsignor McManus, three major
teachers' groups took shape: a primary association for grades 1–3, an
intermediate group for grades 4–6, and one for the junior grades 7–8.
In 1952, the Catholic Elementary School Principals Association held
its first meeting "to seek the most effective means to attain our
spiritual and professional end." [19]

Finally, in 1963, the Archdiocese for the first time admitted sisters
and laymen to school board membership, but the pastors maintained
a clear majority. And still the real authority resided in the Cardinal
Archbishop. The official *Book of Policies* for the school board clearly
stated that "His eminence, the Cardinal Archbishop, is head of our
school system. . . . Ultimate responsibility for educational policies is
his. . . . The Catholic School Board is an advisory board which is
appointed by the Archbishop in the successful execution of the
Archdiocesan educational program." A further clarification noted
that "When the Board and the Superintendent have a difference of
opinion, both points of view are reported to the Archbishop who
then makes his own decision." [20]

The Catholic high schools, most of them private, remained largely
outside the control of the school board and superintendent, and even
in many respects, exempted from the Cardinal's jurisdiction. Yet
practical necessities led to greater coordination. The process began
with the formation of associations among the high schools themselves. For example, in 1937, the science teachers formed an
organization, followed in 1946 by the language teachers. During the
1940's, the Catholic high schools began sponsoring joint music,
speech, and drama festivals and a debating society. In the 1940's,
too, the girls' and boys' high schools formed separate Principals'
Associations "for the purpose of supervising and controlling inter-
scholastic activities and providing a means for united group coopera-

tion with the diocesan authorities." [21] By the 1960's, the presidents of the two high school principals' associations sat as ex-officio members of the Catholic School Board. And one of the three assistant superintendents supervised coordination of high schools.

But still, actual central supervision remained minimal. Each school determined its own curriculum, set admission policies, and functioned without attendance boundaries, though by the late 1950's, diocesan authorities did begin moving against this much freedom. In part, economic necessities gave the Archbishop a stronger hand. Contracts negotiated with religious orders to build high schools partially financed from the archdiocesan fund often contained riders that directly affected the new school's policies. For example, when in 1955 Loyola Academy decided to move from Chicago's Rogers Park to suburban Wilmette, it applied for aid from the fund. But the Cardinal, whose "first consideration has been to meet my pastoral problem of making some provisions for the lesser I.Q.'s who need our care and have not been getting it in high schools which base entrance requirements on ability to do college work," refused assistance until the highly scholastic academy agreed to "provide for the needs of non-college prep students." [22]

Similarly, by the late 1950's, the superintendent's office applied pressure to regularize the high school admissions policies. In 1959, 79 high schools began participating in a common admission examination administered through the school board offices. Individual students could still select their schools, and the schools retained their right to accept or reject students. But the superintendent now coordinated the entire procedure. The new plan met with opposition from the prestige high schools, two of which refused to cooperate.[23] They rightly saw in it the ultimate intention of creating high school attendance areas, which would destroy their ability to draw gifted students from all over the City. Yet, from the superintendent's point of view, adoption of the neighborhood high school concept would make planning for new facilities much more rational. By the mid-1960's, the issue of control over the high schools emerged as a minor crisis in the administration of the Chicago Catholic schools.

Yet this crisis itself simply underscored the fact that Catholic education in Chicago had continued to grow toward a truly comprehensive and all inclusive system.

The continued growth in a sense seemed an anomoly. The religious, ethnic, and socioeconomic alienation that had contributed so much of the original impetus largely dissipated as Catholics moved progressively into the mainstream after the 1920 watershed. Only a small minority of recent immigrants to the City still valued the parochial school as a buffer against the New World. True, ethnic consciousness held on in Chicago much longer than many theorists of the melting pot had anticipated. As late as 1950, over 140 City parishes still listed themselves as national. And far into the 1960's, archdiocesan priests still spoke of the Polish, or Irish, or German circuits, which meant that certain parishes were always assigned priests of a particular nationality. Yet, nationality as a mainspring for the Catholic school had all but disappeared. The teaching of foreign language had become an exception by the 1940's. By 1950, though all but seven of the City's 43 Polish parishes were still located in heavily Polish neighborhoods, enrollment in the Polish schools had in 20 years declined from 49,000 to 25,000. A few national parishes gained new strength from the influx of refugees after World War II, and parish schools for small bodies of more recent immigrants like the Spanish-speaking and Chinese Catholics were founded. But the vast majority of Catholic Chicagoans no longer looked to the parochial school as a refuge from the Anglo-Saxon establishment.[24]

Then, too, the former Protestant and anti-Catholic bias of the public school was now forgotten history. True, sources of conflict over the schools still existed, and old animosities re-emerged on occasion. The *New World* yearly exhorted its readers to send their children to parochial schools at peril to their souls. And bishops often reminded their flock that failure to frequent the Catholic school "places parents in the condition of those who refuse to satisfy a grave obligation." Such admonitions at least implied the imminent danger to faith and morality awaiting the child in public school. Catholic spokesmen, too, continued to emphasize both the injustice of

Catholic school exclusion from tax money and the savings that parochial schools made for the public. Catholic leaders maintained their vigilance in legislative chambers, habitually opposed the many proposals for federal aid to education that excluded parochial schools, and exhorted Catholics to pressure congressmen to kill these bills. Such tactics did not help make friends with the advocates of public education. In 1963–1964, Catholic efforts to establish a shared-time, public–Catholic high school in Chicago was hailed by some as another "denominational power play" that would result in "vast savings by the Catholic school system . . . at the expense of the general tax payers." Controversy over this proposal prompted comment from the New York *Herald Tribune* that "Chicago, second American city but first in religious controversy, is engaged in one of its periodic holy wars." [25]

Yet, over the years, cooperation between the general public and Catholic institutions had grown out of necessity. The shared time plan itself gained approval, with solid backing from such influential non-Catholic leaders as Dr. Edgar Chandler of the Church Federation of Greater Chicago. Long before that, public health agencies extended their services to Catholic schools, and the government milk and hot lunch program found its way into parochial schools. The public library provided sets of books to enhance many school libraries. In the suburbs, many districts transported parochial school pupils free of charge. And during the 1930's, Chicago Catholics finally joined forces with Protestant groups to inaugurate released-time religious instruction for public school children. By 1965, there were 215 Catholic released-time centers in Chicago and another 15 in the suburbs, with a total enrollment of 41,000. Catholic children could now receive religious instruction at least in cooperation with the public schools, an indication that the Church was making its peace with state education.

Then, too, Catholics further enlarged their circle of influence in the public schools. By the late 1950's, for example, it was reported that over 40 percent of the principals in Chicago public schools had graduated from DePaul University alone. After 1930, fully one-third of all school board members appointed were Catholics. Chicago Catholics also enjoyed an unbroken succession of friendly Irish mayors after 1933, and certainly had little to fear any longer from a real or supposed conspiracy to undermine their faith. In many important respects, they ruled the City.[26]

Yet, despite diminution of the religious and ethnic factors, the total effort to perpetuate a Catholic educational ghetto did not abate, with 1965 finding more Catholic children in parochial schools than ever before. The reason may have centered in what the official Church had argued all along—that the public school, even when not openly anti-Catholic, could not infuse religious principles into its educational program. Significantly, the 1929 encyclical of Pope Pius the XI on the *Christian Education of Youth* got wide publicity in Catholic circles as the definitive re-affirmation of the Church's teaching that "education belongs preeminently to the Church" and that "all the teaching and the whole organization of the school and its teachers, syllabus and textbooks in every branch be regulated by the Christian spirit, under the direction and maternal supervision of the Church." [27] This kind of education the public school could never provide. And in Chicago, the parish and its school hammered that fact home. Perhaps Catholic parents of the 1960's had learned the lesson so well that they could countenance nothing for their children but an educational program infused with religion. This characteristic still distinguished the parochial school from the public.

On the other hand, the continuing momentum of the 1960's may have resulted simply from the inertia of unreflective habit. Catholic education had become a way of life for many in Chicago, as natural as the air they breathed. What the parents had done, the children must do, simply because the parents did it. If this were the case, then one had the distinct impression even before the 1960's that momentous problems might soon erode the commitment.

Despite an apparent prosperity, the Chicago Catholic educational program at both the elementary and secondary levels had moved into deep trouble by the late 1950's. In a sense, it suffered from the weight of its own past success. The number seeking admission had grown astronomically. And the continuing exodus into the suburbs taxed the Church's capacity to build new schools. Complaints from Catholic authorities about the shortage of schools during this period became ever more strident.

In 1953, despite an expenditure of $12,000,000 for new elementary schools, the Cardinal reported to his flock that though "at first sight, Catholic schools in the archdiocese are prospering as they never prospered before in all our history . . . despite all our efforts, we have not yet met the demands of our people for adequate Catholic school opportunities." In 1957, the superintendent complained that "we need more classrooms, more teachers, and more money." By the time Cardinal Stritch left Chicago in 1958 for a new assignment in Rome, the Archdiocese had invested $85,000,000 for 75 new elementary schools in the 18 years of his administration. Yet, his successor, Albert Cardinal Meyer, was immediately faced with "the great need for expansion of our educational facilities." [28]

By the mid-1950's, suburban parishes reported overcrowding everywhere, and warned that "conditions will even be worse as the numbers are ever increasing." In Skokie, for example, despite the establishment of two new parishes in 1951, the schools were overcrowded by 1952. St. Peter's parish there reported that "an average of three new families a week call at the rectory and announce themselves as 'new parishioners.' " In Hometown, Our Lady of Loretto had "become a large parish in just a few years," and the school facilities were "fully inadequate to take care of the increasing number of school children." In Westchester, the population more than doubled between 1950 and 1954 to over 10,000; Catholics made up almost one-half the population, and the demand was raised for a second parish. "The immediate need for considering a new parish is caused as usual by the school enrollment," complained the pastor of one overcrowded parish. Many schools went on double session, and finally in 1962, resorted to mobile classrooms to relieve the pressure.[29]

Most alarming, the unprecedented rate of expansion created a severe shortage of teachers from religious orders, because their growth rate by the early 1950's "had not kept pace with the increasing demand for Catholic education for our youth." The *New World* admitted that "never perhaps before did we have as grave a problem in Catholic education as we have today in our shortage of religious teachers." In 1959, one pastor of a new parish reported contacting 170 different communities of sisters in an effort to get teachers for his school, without success.[30] The Archdiocese started a desperate advertising campaign for lay teachers and instituted instant training programs for women college graduates. By 1961, 250 of the 300 new teachers engaged were lay people. Indeed, as late as 1950, lay teachers made up only 4 percent of the elementary school teaching staff. By 1965, they were 38 percent. Lay teachers in the high schools increased from 16 percent to 36 percent over the same period. The dramatic change added a huge financial burden to an effort already staggering from the battle to build new schools.

The sudden advent of the lay teacher also gave pause to some Catholic parents. They had always identified Catholic education with nuns, brothers, and priests. Some began to weigh the ever-spiraling tuitions and diocesan fund drives against what seemed the diminishing Catholicity of the schools themselves. Arguments that the Catholic schools provided academically better education, too, carried less weight as the competition shifted to the well-financed and supervised public school districts of the suburbs. For other Catholics, the windows opened by the Second Vatican Council prompted a questioning of the need for Catholic schooling at all. Some now argued for a re-allocation of funds away from the parochial school to what seemed more urgent religious and social needs. While some questioned the financial viability of such a vast independent system, others denied its necessity. Whatever the outcome, by the mid-1960's, it seemed clear that the issue hung in the balance between the crushing financial challenge and the true depth of Catholic belief in the religious necessity of the parochial school. The intervening years had all but stripped away every other motive, except, perhaps, as some argued, the racial one.

12

The Racial Crisis

By the 1960's, another problem that plagued Catholic Chicago for decades had assumed ominous dimensions, creating a paralyzing crisis of conscience and threatening irreparable loss. No one could have anticipated the eventual dilemma when the City's 23 Black Catholic families began worshiping in separate services at the old Catholic parish of St. Mary's in the 1880's. They were but one-third of one percent of the 30,000 Negroes in Chicago, who were themselves but 3 percent of the total population. At their own request and against the advice of Archbishop Feehan, who reportedly feared the step might lead to permanent segregation, the little group of Black Catholics was given exclusive use of St. Mary's basement in 1888.[1] At least in a figurative sense, their descendents in the faith never quite escaped from that basement.

By 1889 the congregation had its own pastor, a Negro born in slavery in Missouri, converted to Catholicism, educated for the priesthood in Rome, and ordained there in 1886. Under his leadership, the number of Negro Catholics in Chicago grew to over 200 by 1892. Father Augustine Tolton set about gathering money for a separate church, succeeding in obtaining $10,000 from a Catholic lady on condition he could raise a matching sum. In April of 1892 he opened the church of St. Monica's at 36th and Dearborn on the south side; and by 1895 he had "nearly 300" parishioners.[2]

Despite financial difficulties, the future looked bright for this small Negro congregation, reported to be the only one in the United States at the time with a pastor of its own race. But in 1897, Father Tolton died from sunstroke, and St. Monica's became a mission of white St. Elizabeth's parish nearby. Between 1897 and 1909 the Negro mission suffered from inattention, and many parishioners strayed. But in 1909, Father John Morris, a white priest, became the full-time resident pastor. By 1910 there were some 600 in the congregation, many of whom did not live in the immediate vicinity.[3]

The need of a school for the Negro Catholics had been felt in Chicago for some time. In 1904, the editor of the *New World* boldly declared that the "public-schooled Negro, as a rule, is a dangerous Negro." The new pastor of St. Monica's saw a school for his parish as the matter of top priority: "though the colored people have a place of worship, the one thing essential for the permanency of any parish is lacking—a school. This is the one great need, upon the supplying of which, I am going to concentrate my efforts." By 1912 school facilities had been provided, and the Sisters of the Blessed Sacrament, founded for Indian and Negro work, came to Chicago to teach the 150 Black youngsters who attended that first year. Though Church authorities later hailed the founding of this school as "the turning point in the history of the Negro in the Archdiocese," Chicago's Blacks did not all agree. Because St. Monica's accepted only Black children and St. James just four blocks distant only whites, the *Defender* called it "that Jim Crow School." While praising Father Morris' attempt to build a mixed congregation and even acknowledging the Catholic Church's behavior toward Negroes as better than most, the *Defender* came down hard on segregated schooling at St. Monica's: "God pity the simple-minded mother and father who would drag their children down so low as to send them to a Jim Crow school in the heart of this great city. Such Negroes should be deported back to the land of the rapists and the home of the bigamists at the South." Still, despite such protests, the school prospered moderately and by 1917 numbered 250 children, who paid no tuition whatsoever.[4]

But by this time, the Negro presence was being felt in other parishes too. In the decade after 1910, prompted by poor conditions in the South and the need for urban manpower during the war, the Chicago Negro population more than doubled to 109,000. By April of 1917, the diocesan paper ran a front page headline: "Increasing Negro Population New Catholic Problem." The article explained that the single Catholic parish for Negroes "ministers to the Catholic colored in every section of the city. . . . At present there are about 2,000 Negroes who attend its services, though this is by no means the entire Catholic colored population of the city. Many of that race attend services at the churches closest to their homes." The fact that Negroes now attended not only St. Monica's but "the churches closest to their homes" posed a serious color problem for Chicago Catholicism. Most white churches did not welcome the Black man, especially in neighborhoods of shifting population. By October of 1917, Archbishop Mundelein acted to solve the problem by laying down a policy on Negro Catholics. The Archbishop made the terms of his solution very clear, though his motivation remained obscure.[5]

First, he designated St. Monica's an exclusively Negro parish: "All other Catholics of whatever race or color are to be requested not to intrude." Second, Negroes had the right to attend services at any other church: "It is of course understood that I have no intention of excluding colored Catholics from any of the other churches in the diocese, but particularly if they live in another part of the city." But this right did not extend to membership in other parishes. Negroes could attend services, but not enjoy full membership, which meant that baptisms, marriages, etc., must be solemnized at St. Monica's only. It also meant that Negro children had no legal claim on attendance at other parochial schools. Third, the Archbishop recognized the Negro population, over 90 percent Protestant, as mission territory. He asked the Fathers of the Divine Word at Techny, Illinois, a vigorous German missionary order, to take over St. Monica's with a view to proselytizing in the Black Belt.

The evidence suggests that Mundelein's motives were mixed; he acted partly to placate whites opposed to Negroes in their parishes, partly to facilitate what he considered the best means of promoting the growth of Negro Catholicism in Chicago.

St. Monica's had experienced considerable difficulty in achieving financial stability, and in stressing the exclusive character of this parish, Mundelein apparently hoped that Negroes would work for its success out of personal pride. He compared the situation to that of the white ethnic groups who welcomed the responsibility of supporting their own churches and schools. Further, the Archbishop was apparently convinced that, given the existing prejudices, Negroes would feel at home only in their own church. "I am convinced," he said, "that our colored Catholics will feel themselves very much more comfortable, far less inconvenienced and never at all embarrassed if, in a church that is credited to them, they have their own sodalities and societies, their own church and choir, in which they alone will constitute the membership." Indeed, Mundelein was not unaware of the racial situation in Chicago: "It would be puerile for us to ignore the fact that a distinction as to color enters very often into the daily happenings of our city." Refusing to take a stand on "the justice or injustice" of the racial situation, he confessed himself "quite powerless to change it." The sole concern, he contended, was that "my colored children shall not feel uncomfortable in the Catholic Church."

But Mundelein's solution to making the Chicago Catholic Negroes feel comfortable did not make at least some of the City's Blacks very comfortable. The *Defender* lashed out at the order to "Jim Crow" St. Monica's and at "the man behind the gun," claiming the parish, except for its school, had been well integrated. Parishioners, too, protested vigorously. On December 7, 1917, one month after the directive on St. Monica's, a group of Negro Catholics requested an interview with the Archbishop because "they have felt most keenly the anomolous position in which they have been placed by your policy of segregation in relation to the affairs of St. Monica's mission." Mundelein's assistant answered, asking them to mail their complaint and stating that the Archbishop "sees no reason of altering any such disposition." The committee then submitted "An Address to the Archbishop of Chicago Protesting Against a Policy of Segregation in the Administration of the Affairs of St. Monica's Mission." The "Address" bore 81 signatures and claimed "many others who share in and endorse the sentiment and protest of this appeal, but whose signatures are wanting only through lack of time to visit them in their respective parishes." It protested bitterly the new policy: "The children of the bond woman shall no longer kneel at the altar with the heirs of the free. The Holy wafer of the tabernacle shall rest in solemn benediction only on the tongues of Africa's sons and daughters; and proscribed and forbidden they alone shall enter into the sanctuary over whose portals is written in blazing letters of shame 'SEGREGATED.' " The signees declared that they sat in "stupefied wonder that so uncharitable a proposition should emanate from the Chancery office of the great Archdiocese of Chicago." [6]

Again Mundelein chose to take no further personal part in the controversy, and his chancellor answered for him that the directive of October 26 "contains all he desires to say on this matter. In its preparation he sought and obtained the views of ecclesiastics who were engaged in zealous work among the colored people long before many of your signatories were born, as well as of more than one active and even prominent colored Catholic here and elsewhere." The answer stressed the fact that "nothing was further from the Archbishop's mind than to insist or even suggest anything as segregation, that no such idea was conveyed by his letter. . . . He was very careful to emphasize the fact that the doors of every Catholic church of Chicago are open, the pews of all of them ready to receive any colored Catholic who enters, but that St. Monica's is entirely their own to build and furnish and embellish." [7]

Whatever Mundelein's true motives in the St. Monica's affair, and despite his protests that every church would be open to Negroes, in fact for the next two decades or more, Negroes could participate fully only in their own parish, and the Archbishop made no direct interventions in their behalf. His confession in 1917 that "I am quite powerless to change" the line of distinction between black and white in Chicago seems to have determined the policy. And the editor of the *New World* probably expressed the prevailing attitude in 1919 when he advised the Catholic Negro: "Instead of battering against the wall of white determination that the races shall be kept distinct, he should make an earnest endeavor to better his physical and moral surroundings. . . . In Chicago there is a place for the colored man. And in it he can find opportunity, success, and the respect of his white fellow citizens." [8]

Mundelein did, however, take a very active interest in the development of the mission among the Negroes. In 1921, dissatisfied with the performance of the priest assigned to St. Monica's, he asked for "the best man you have in your community," and got a better one. The new pastor, Reverend Joseph S. Eckert, SVD, put St. Monica's on its feet. In one year he doubled the school enrollment to 300, and in two years trebled the number of parishioners. The school in particular proved a strong drawing card, and "professional men and race leaders" were reported to have "many times approached the pastor of St. Monica's to take their children into the parish school." [9]

By 1922, the little parish had outgrown its physical plant; 300 children had to be turned away from the school for lack of space; and a request was made to take over St. Elizabeth parish at 41st and Wabash, a predominantly Black neighborhood. Between 1910 and 1920, the St. Elizabeth school declined from 752 pupils to 218, and continued to lose pupils each year, but remained an all white school. Therefore, the missionaries in charge of St. Monica's proposed closing that institution and transferring the whole parish to the St. Elizabeth facilities, since "to all appearances there are but few white Catholics living in the neighborhood. . . . It has become a black center." This would also provide opportunity to open a high school, badly needed because "Catholic high schools will not accept our colored children, and in the public institutions their faith is undermined." [10]

Mundelein replied to this suggestion that "the time is not ripe as yet for a transfer of St. Elizabeth's parish buildings to another work. . . . There are still 300 families left in the parish, and they vigorously object to being parcelled out to other parishes." Not until 1924 was the larger St. Elizabeth's finally given over, and the entire congregation and staff of St. Monica's moved to the new location. By 1925, there were some 4,000 Catholics in the parish and 800 children in the school. In 1924, St. Elizabeth's also opened a high school. The parish thrived, apparently appealing more to the middle-class Negro. In 1927, a University of Chicago researcher reported a Sunday morning visit to St. Elizabeth, and found that "the people who attended both Masses were undoubtedly representative of the 'better class' of Negroes at least as far as economic prosperity was concerned. . . . The conversation in the vestibule was that of intelligent, serious minded people. . . . There was nothing of the dramatic, highly emotional type which we see in store-front colored churches." [11]

But by 1930, with over 7,000 members, St. Elizabeth's was still the only Negro Catholic church and school in Chicago, despite the fact that several other parishes had come almost entirely within the confines of the Black Belt. True, Negroes did sometimes attend services in other churches, "particularly during inclement weather when St. Elizabeth's might be inconveniently distant from their places of residence." But the numbers who actually attended were small. Corpus Christi, for example, though in the midst of the Black Belt, seldom had "more than twenty Negroes at high Mass," and the white Catholics at such parishes were said to be "not always cordial to Negroes." [12] Further, under the terms of Mundelein's official policy, Negroes could not be afforded full membership in these parishes or given access to their schools.

All through the 1920's, while their enrollments dropped, these schools excluded Negro children. For example, old St. James, one of the outstanding parishes of the City during the 1880's and 1890's, now struggled on with "but a remnant of its former number." Indeed, between 1910 and 1930 the school enrollment dropped from 1,414 to 185. But the parish as late as 1930 still continued to serve "the white population of the district," and the school was "attended in large numbers by the children of non-Catholic families, who wished to avoid the colored invasion of the public schools." At Holy Angels parish, a reporter in 1930 noted that the power of this once influential congregation "is now waning . . . before the encroachment of the colored people who, while they attend St. Elizabeth's church, deplete the numbers of the Holy Angels parishioners." Every effort was made to halt the changeover. In 1930, the chancellor of the Archdiocese wrote to a real estate dealer: "The pastor of Holy Angels church at 605 Oakwood Boulevard, has informed me that your company plans on renting the building directly across from Holy Angels church to colored people. This will undoubtedly result in great harm to Holy Angels parish." He suggested a solution whereby the pastor would make "every effort to assist you in renting these apartments to Catholic people if these improvements are made." But despite the presence of Negroes across the street, not until 1945 did Holy Angels school finally open to Black children.[13]

Corpus Christi, "once a leading parish of the district" and the "pride of the South Side," had been the home of "influential and cultured people." "Then came the war and the importation of Negro laborers. Almost overnight the great parish declined. One by one the families moved away, their homes to be taken by Negroes. In 1927 only thirty-five children were enrolled in the school and at the end of the year it was closed." Studs Lonigan's boyhood parish of St. Anselm, at the southwest corner of Washington Park, by 1930 found itself in streets remembered as "but dusty souvenirs of the days when they were graced by the homes of people of circumstance." The parish was now "ninety per cent colored, although many of its old parishioners still hold allegience here. The enrollment of the school, which is made up of white children only, has decreased in the last five years from 500 pupils to 175, one hundred of whom come from outside the parish."[14]

On the west side, Archbishop Mundelein had made plans as early as 1917 to transfer St. Malachy's parish where the "Negro invasion spelled the doom of the neighborhood." But the pastor successfully

thwarted the effort to convert it into a Negro church, arguing that
among all the Negroes in the neighborhood there were only five or
six Catholics, who could not support such a large church. St.
Malachy's hung on as a white parish, though depleted from its height
of 1,400 families to just 300 in 1930.[15]

Thus, by 1930, at least five white parishes had been engulfed. But
not one of them opened its school to Negroes. Despite the
Archbishop's assertion in 1917 that Blacks would be welcome in any
church of the Archdiocese, in fact the welcome did not extend to full
membership. Negroes did go to church services in parishes other
than St. Elizabeth's. But their children attended only this one school.

At least some Negroes voiced objections, and in 1930 one colored
woman took her grievance to the Apostolic Delegate in Washington.
The Delegate asked Mundelein for an explanation, and the Archbishop replied that "the doors of any church in Chicago are open to
all Catholics." But he did admit the difficulty in the schools: "In
some districts there is no difficulty: in the Cathedral school there
have been colored pupils at various times; but on the south side
where the menace of a colored invasion is a constant economic
danger, against which all property owners organize, I have found it
to the best interests of religion to leave it to the prudent judgment
and priestly zeal of the individual pastors to act in each case."
Mundelein tried to justify the exclusion of Negroes on two grounds.
The first had to do with tuition in the schools: "We have no free
schools here as in the east; the people pay for the children's tuition
individually; in addition they must pay for books; both are free in the
public schools. Their wishes in regard to the schools must be
respected." The second argument reflected Mundelein's thinking
about the welfare of the Negroes themselves: "Nothing will be
accomplished for the evangelization of the colored in Chicago by
scattering them among the whites in our churches and schools, but
rather by keeping them by themselves and concentrating the work
for them in churches and schools restricted to them." [16]

The first argument, of course, hardly stood up against constant
Church practice, which did not give the people who paid tuition the

right to dictate school policies. Mundelein probably meant that "their wishes in regard to the schools must be respected" or they will withdraw their children and the schools will collapse. The second argument, from a narrow religious point of view, made more sense: 60 percent of the colored children entered St. Elizabeth's school as non-Catholics, but 95 percent graduated as Catholics. The all-colored school proved highly successful in making converts, and this apparently sufficed in the Archbishop's view to justify the continued segregation of Negroes.

Ironically, though he discouraged the voluntary segregation of white ethnic groups, the Archbishop forced segregation on the Negroes. White ethnics could always freely pass into the territorial parishes and schools. Blacks could not. The radical distinction between white Catholic and Black had never existed between the national groups.

By the early 1930's, the spread of the Black Belt placed increasing strain on the Catholic schools and caused considerable embarrassment to Church leaders in their attempt to proselytize the Black man without offending the white. The lone Black parish of St. Elizabeth, both because of its growing congregation and its extensive territory, could not contain all the City's Black Catholics. Further, some white parishes in the Black Belt could simply no longer survive. Mundelein then made the only decision possible consonant with his policy of keeping the Negroes segregated. In 1932 he designated St. Anselm's as the parish for all Negro Catholics south of 58th Street, and transferred Father Joseph Eckert, the City's most successful convert maker among the Negroes, from St. Elizabeth's. In the first few months, 50 adults were baptized, and by 1936, 500 children attended the all Black school. In 1933, he made Corpus Christi the parish for all Blacks between 45th and 58th Streets, and the school, which had been closed for two years because of the white parishioners' exodus, reopened "for the colored children of the district." The Franciscan Fathers who now took over the parish baptized 1,200 adults in the first five years. By 1938, there were 2,000 Black parishioners and 800 Black pupils in the school. Meanwhile, throughout the 1930's, all the other beleaguered parishes on the south side held out against the Black invasion.[17]

On the west side, in 1933, Holy Family parish solved the problem of Negroes moving into its territory by converting a long unused branch school on 13th Street into a combination church and school for Black people, keeping the parish's main church and school for whites only. And St. Malachy's parish, surrounded by Blacks since the 1920's, finally succumbed in 1935, and was converted into a Black parish. On the near north side, where a smaller Negro settlement was developing, St. Dominic's church and school, which had been first Irish and then Italian, opened to Negroes in 1935. But it was quickly abandoned by the whites.

Thus, by the death of Cardinal Mundelein in 1939, three all-Negro schools existed on the south side, two on the west and one on the near north, with a combined enrollment of 2,759. A few other schools apparently accepted an occasional Negro child, but in general the color line held firmly. A *New World* article in the late 1930's describing the problems of Negroes in Chicago concluded that "worst of all they are handicapped in the Catholic education of their children. . . . What are they to do when there is no Catholic school within reasonable distance, or when the Catholic school is not available?" "Prejudice," said the *New World*, "is, of course, chiefly accountable for the rejection of colored children from Catholic schools." [18]

Yet, despite segregation, the work in all-Negro schools had gone on successfully. A report in 1938 estimated that "since 1930 the Negro Catholic population of Chicago has doubled. There are now some 16,000 colored Catholics in the Archdiocese." The Catholic schools claimed credit for the growth: "They have proved to be the best convert makers." But it seemed clear to some that, for further progress, "old prejudices which have hung on for many years, even among our Catholics, must be broken down." [19]

Cardinal Stritch, who took over the Diocese on Mundelein's death in 1939, after a very hesitant beginning, moved more strongly than his predecessor to break down these "old prejudices."

At first the new Cardinal wavered. For example, when a Negro mother tried to enter her two children in Holy Angels parish school in 1942, she was told by the pastor that only Negro children "fair enough to pass for whites" were accepted. She indignantly wrote to Stritch: "I have never heard anything to shock or hurt me so much." The Cardinal answered weakly that "it is distressing that in some things we must go slow, being satisfied with a slight advantage here and there and hoping for the fullness of our hopes. . . . We shall pray to our Blessed Lady." The woman shot back that the prelate's letter proved "you are aware of the conditions that exist at Holy Angels school and apparently you approve of it." Of his suggestion to pray to the Blessed Virgin, she queried: "Why ask her? . . . I consider it sacrilegious to ask of God what we ourselves are unwilling to do. I am going to pray," she retorted, "but not as you suggested. I am asking God, and his Blessed Mother, to give me the grace, strength and wisdom to continue to fight this problem. I realize only too well it may be a bitter struggle and that my child may never reap its benefits. If I should succeed, I will be satisfied knowing that I have made the way easier for some other little children." [20] No record exists of an answer from Stritch, but this lady's reprimand must have shaken the Cardinal, whose administration was generally characterized by warmth and sensitivity.

Again in 1943, a Negro father informed Stritch that he had moved into the west side from south side Corpus Christi parish where his three sons had attended the parish school. On trying to enroll them in Holy Family parish school he was told they would have to go to the branch school of St. Joseph's "which was for the colored children" because the white people of Holy Family would not tolerate Blacks. He asked Stritch to intervene: "I am asking this appeal Father in behalf of people who are so unjustly mistreated for no cause of their own." Again, Stritch answered sympathetically, but without taking action: "Much has been done, and if we work with understanding zeal, the whole thing will be done in the not too distant future." While confessing that "I myself am impatient" at this unfortunate social fact, he counseled against "an emotional

question, stronger than much of his white flock and some of his
pastors were ready to accept.[26] But one by one, Catholic schools in
the Negro areas reluctantly opened their doors to the Black child. In
1945, the old Irish parish of St. Anne's on Garfield Boulevard
accepted its first Black pupils, and by 1949 it was three-quarters
Black. In 1947, the south side German parish of St. George opened to
colored children, and in two years the entire school was Black.
Others, like St. Thomas the Apostle in Hyde Park and St. Cecelia at
45th and Wells, long an Irish workingman's stronghold, admitted a
few Negroes during the 1940's, but remained predominantly white.
In Morgan Park on the far southwest side where an isolated colony of
Negroes made up 35 percent of the population before 1930, Holy
Name of Mary parish was founded in 1941 with a school staffed by
Negro sisters.

Thus, during the 1940's, the Archdiocese made considerable
progress in opening the Catholic churches and schools to Negroes,
though no truly integrated parishes developed, and resistance
remained intense. Still, as the authors of *Black Metropolis* observed,
for many Negroes "one of the primary attractions of the Catholic
Church is its educational institutions. . . . Many parents felt that the
parochial school offered a more thorough education in a quieter
atmosphere with adequate discipline and personal attention." [27]

The great growth of Chicago's Negro population during and after
World War II brought more and more Catholic parishes and schools
within the Black Belt. In all, between 1930 and 1960 the proportion
of Negro children in Chicago's elementary-school-aged population
increased from 5.5 percent to 30 percent, concentrated mostly in the
lower class areas where they made up 70 percent of the school-aged
youngsters by 1960. Catholic schools in the path of the expanding
Negro ghetto did not go unaffected. In 1946, 4,602 Negro pupils
attended 16 Catholic schoools. By 1950, there were 5,780, with
Negroes residing within the boundaries of 38 parishes. By 1960,
13,730 Negro pupils attended parochial schools, and by 1965, over
21,000, one-third of them non-Catholics. Fully 61 City parishes had
Negroes within their confines by 1960, with 15 more in the suburbs.

Few if any of these parishes could be called truly integrated. Thus, 23 of the schools in the City were exclusively Negro, and another 23 had just a handful of Negro children. The rest were in transitional areas where the balance between Black and white children promised to be only temporary.[28]

Racial change, therefore, on Chicago's south and west sides, and to a degree on the near north side, had considerable impact on the Catholic schools there. Despite their appeal to many Negroes, changes in racial composition of a neighborhood almost invariably left the Catholic schools with empty classrooms.

The Negro problem also had serious repercussions in the Catholic high schools. Negroes had long found it difficult to enter these. For over 20 years after its founding in 1924, St. Elizabeth High School on the south side had been the only Catholic high school for Negroes in Chicago. Then in 1945, the Archdiocese purchased the former Sinai Temple at 4622 South Parkway and converted it into a Negro, coeducational secondary school attached to Corpus Christi parish. About the same time, St. Malachy's on the west side, which was now all Negro, opened a high school. By 1947, in addition to the 404 students enrolled in these all-Negro schools, 25 Negro boys attended St. Philips High School on the west side, with another 34 distributed among a total of eight Catholic institutions.[29]

For the most part, even the older schools in what had now become the heart of the Black Belt remained almost totally white by drawing their students from outside the neighborhood. For example, De La Salle High School on the south side, though surrounded by Negroes since 1930, had only seven Black boys as late as 1947. St. Xavier Academy at 48th and Cottage Grove where one found "Negroes on every hand" as early as 1930, twenty years later still enrolled only two non-white girls.[30]

As with the elementary schools, the situation often proved difficult. In 1944, the superior of the Dominican Sisters, who ran Trinity High School in the exclusive western suburb of River Forest, wrote to Cardinal Stritch in distress after being asked by a priest if her high school would accept Negro girls: "My spontaneous answer would be yes," she said. "However, the residents of Oak Park and River Forest see objections to having Negroes at Trinity High School, because the parents of these Negro girls would probably wish to move out into these two suburbs. I do not know whether this consideration should influence us in our decision or not." By this time Stritch had made up his mind about the Negro question and answered unequivocally: "I do not know of any other decision that is possible in the case which you present to me except the answer you have already given to it. . . . The problem is very difficult and all that we can do is try to be Christians." [31]

Not all the schools opened their doors as willingly. In 1946, a Negro mother, herself educated in St. Elizabeth High School, appealed to Stritch in the case of her two girls. She had contacted five different high schools, but "they all turn me down saying they don't take Negroes. Father," she asked, "can you help me place my girls in a Catholic High School?" No record indicates that she got help. Indeed, since the religious orders owned most high schools privately, the Archbishop had no direct control over admissions policies as he did over the parochial schools. Also, after the mid-1940's, serious overcrowding in the Catholic high schools rendered admissions highly competitive. Some Negroes failed to gain admission for these reasons, or at least the schools used this as an excuse.[32]

Though during the 1950's the Church officially encouraged Negro enrollment in white high schools, as late as 1960 the Archdiocese cooperated with the Franciscan Fathers in purchasing the old St. Xavier girls' academy at Cottage Grove and 49th Street and opening a high school for boys. This was advertised as "without regard to race, creed or color," but there could be no doubt that the new Hales High School would enroll all Negroes.[33]

Meanwhile, efforts were made, especially by the Catholic Interracial Council (CIC), to draw more Negro students into white schools. The CIC raised money for scholarships and also launched a campaign to persuade individual Catholic high schools to voluntarily grant free tuition to deserving Negro youth. In 1959, for example, 36 scholarships were thus awarded. Beginning in 1953, the CIC also sponsored interracial study days in the high schools.

By 1965, more Negroes were attending a variety of Catholic high schools, though few of these schools could truly be called integrated. Of the 96 high schools in the Chicago Archdiocese, 59 had at least some Negroes. But only nine were more than 10 percent Black, and three of these nine had no whites at all. Only six qualified as integrated according to the accepted definition of not more than 90 percent of one race. Negroes made up 3.5 percent of the Catholic high school enrollment in the tricounty area by 1965. The high schools in predominantly Negro areas of the City had only 20 percent Negro students. The other 80 percent were bussed in from the surrounding white neighborhoods.

Since the Archdiocese itself had little control over the high schools, each institution adapted in its own way to the problem of racial turnover. One school closed because of change. Another moved out of the Black Belt to the far southwest side. Another, in a generous attempt to promote integrated education, opened its doors wide to Negroes and shortly became an all-Negro school. Others attempted to rigidly control the proportion of Negroes admitted in an effort to maintain a solid white majority. A few, because of high admission standards and relatively high tuition, effectively excluded large numbers of Negroes. Most adapted by bussing white students from other areas. Two, St. Elizabeth's for girls, and Hales for boys—both on the south side—catered exclusively to Negroes. None of these schools situated in Negro areas positively excluded Blacks, though some enrolled a very low proportion.[34]

Surprisingly, viewed from the perspective of the entire system, the parochial schools did not suffer as much as might have been expected from the spread of the City's Black Belt. Until the 1960's the areas of Negro expansion were not those of heaviest Catholic concentration. The Black Belt had hardly penetrated the heavily Catholic northwest and southwest inner city workingman's areas. Catholics had been moving out of the near west side since the 1890's, long before the large-scale Negro in-migration. And the Negro areas of the south side, though the site of some of the City's most prosperous parishes, had never been a heavily Catholic area. Indeed, the communities of the west and south sides, which were later to become a part of the Black Ghetto, enrolled only 17 percent of the elementary school-aged children in Catholic schools in 1930, which was far below the City average. In 1960, they still accounted for 14 percent. The high schools located in these areas did not lose students. Though whites moved away, parents took advantage of the traditional absence of attendance areas in the high schools, and sent their children back to their favorite schools. The diocesan-wide shortage of facilities made even institutions in the ghetto attractive.

Yet, by the mid-1960's, indicators pointed to an imminent confrontation as the Black population moved farther south and west into the more densely Catholic parishes and as Black militancy made the existence of predominantly white high schools in the Black Ghetto increasingly difficult and dangerous. The old Catholic inner city strongholds on the near northwest and southwest sides still educated as high a proportion of the white population as ever before. And the people of such communities still reacted to the Black menace as vigorously and sometimes as violently as their fathers had done in the riots of 1919. But the expanding Black population now pressed ever harder against these inner city white workingman's neighborhoods. In middle-class areas, many Catholic families were on the move to escape the Negro invasion. Though the Church's aggressive missionary efforts had increased the Black enrollment in parochial schools to over 20,000, the great majority of Blacks remained Protestant or unchurched and attended the public schools. Their invasion of a Catholic parish left its school largely unfilled. Catholic authorities had to face both the burden of preventing depopulated parishes and schools from going under financially and of providing facilities for displaced white Catholics migrating to the suburbs. They also had to deal with the problem of enforcing the Church's official racial policy on a largely unwilling constituency. By the mid-1960's the racial issue portended a gathering social and economic crisis.

For some Catholics living on the racial frontier, the parochial school no doubt offered asylum from the increasingly Black public school. But what the Church's educational enterprise dubiously gained from these, it lost both from the growing numbers of parishes completely engulfed in the Black Belt and the staggering burden of providing new schools for Catholics fleeing to the suburbs.

13

Epilogue

Recent research on the nineteenth-century evolution of urban school systems in the United States has tended to stress a single theme—that the public school served to control assimilation of the immigrant into the American urban-industrial way of life. With the social power of family, church, and apprenticeship having been weakened in the process of urbanization and industrialization, the school seemed a potential resource of last resort in the face of urban crime, unrest, and general social change attributed to the immigrant influence. Contrary to the myth created by its protagonists' rhetoric, the common school functioned not merely to provide opportunity for the common man but also to teach him his place. Though the common or public school may not have aimed at oppression, as the radical revisionists contend, it did exercise social control. It served at least as the battleground between society's guardians and those against whose contamination they sought to guard themselves. Further, the guardians' attempt to maintain control and exclude the newcomer from anything but participation as a passive consumer in the educational system contributed to the nineteenth-century preoccupation with professionalizing, centralizing, and inevitably bureaucratizing the urban school. Uniform curricula and textbooks, graded schools, the principalship and superintendency, teacher certification, and the move toward either appointed or at-large elected governing boards all tended to insulate the schools from local interference—in effect, from the common man. The more professionally managed were the schools, and the more in tune with American middle class aspiration, the more uniform would be the product. Thus, to a degree, the urban school emerged as a "culture factory" based on industrial models for maximum efficiency and economy of production. It sought to enforce uniform habits of punctuality, neatness, and submission to authority on the future urban worker and to pour the children of the alien, immigrant poor into a common, acceptable mold.[1]

This less flattering theme in the otherwise noble history of public education has no doubt suffered from exaggeration and excessive attention in the heady aftermath of recent discovery. Its recognition in recent educational historiography, nevertheless, admirably underlines the essential cultural difference between public and Catholic schooling in the nineteenth- and early twentieth-century city. As the public school moved toward centralization and bureaucratic control, the Catholic system, despite the Church's reputation for centralized authority and bureaucratic structure, remained singularly untouched. Aside from enforcing religious orthodoxy in its schools, the Catholic Church in Chicago exercised no central control at all. It allowed the maximum possible local diversity and, as it turns out, each ethnic, cultural, and educational group flourished. Thus, the Catholic Church, as expressed in its school system, emerges as a nineteenth-century exemplar of internal social tolerance and permissiveness in a society that condemned it as intolerant and undemocratic. This seeming paradox resolves itself when the reasons that lay behind the public school's quest for centralized bureaucracy on the one hand and the Catholic school's intentional avoidance of it on the other are compared. The public school, as a symbol of established mores—not merely Protestant in original orientation, but Anglo-Saxon and middle class as well—stood to a degree as a truly organized effort by the established to impose their values on those they saw as deviant.

To the established, creation of the "one best system" followed logically from a belief in the one best way of life. But Catholic schools, as expressions of the deviant, originated from and thrived on rejection of that belief, first in its religious dimension, and then in its broader cultural and socioeconomic ramifications. Thus, as public schools centralized to secure cultural homogeneity, Catholic schools, as an early expression of counter-culture rights and beliefs, deliberately reveled in hopeless—or glorious—diversity. Further, in catering to the culturally diverse, the parochial school appears to have functioned in sympathetic vibration with the Catholic, immigrant, alien poor, whereas the public school, as the increasingly bureaucratized agent of a dominant culture, could not. The intense hostility often expressed by public school advocates to parochial education most probably stemmed not merely from its divergent religious orientation but much more from the general threat it posed to their vision of a thoroughly homogeneous society in America. Conversely, the intense devotion to parochial schooling on the part of many Catholics most probably stemmed not merely from religious belief but from the Catholic's recognition of his image as an alien in the city.

Why, then, did the parochial school not decrease in popularity after the 1920's as the degree of religious, cultural, and economic alienation steadily diminished? If the enterprise fed on alienation, it should have declined on assimilation. The Catholic time of tribulation, rooted deeply in economic deprivation, cultural ostracism, and religious rejection, clearly contributed to the evolution of its educational system. The watershed of the 1920's, marked by the dramatic growth of a Catholic middle class, the pronounced de-ethnicization of the Church's dominant groups, the Irish and the Germans, and the increasing ascendency of Catholics in the City's institutional life, including the public schools themselves, *should* have begun the parochial school's gradual demise. Instead, the upward enrollment curve continued through 1965.

Here one must speculate. What a few contemporary observers and the perspective of history clearly discern as a turning point probably had little impact on the popular consciousness. The average Catholic sensed no transition from alienation to control of the City. Heir to decades of antagonism, he needed more powerful signs than subtle statistical shifts to herald the new era—the future bright with promise. Even with Catholics teaching in so many public classrooms, the public school's image as alien and hostile endured. Changes in fundamental attitude lagged far behind changes in fact. Then, too, the generations had produced a strong, positive tradition associated with Catholic schooling. At the very least, for many concerned parents, it offered familiarity—the comfort of the known. On a deeper level, the Catholic school beckoned as a safe harbor, the womb of Mother Church where children might delay their encounter with life's harsher realities while fabled discipline, coupled with the sisters' loving care, worked its wonders in the formation of strong and resolute character. The emotion-laden image borne by that term CATHOLIC SCHOOL supported its enduring popularity during the Church's period of ascendency in the City. Catholic education—revered, familiar, evoking nostalgic memories of childhood—had become a way of life. Then too, Church leaders had always pictured Catholic schools, like the Church itself, as the product of God, not of man. And Catholics generally believed that Divine inspiration had helped their school system flourish. But the possibility that its continued vitality after the 1920's might have resulted from the Deity's intervention, though perhaps legitimately raised by the historian, can best be left at theology's doorstep.

Yet, if Divine action did explain the phenomenon of Catholic education in Chicago, then after 1965 either God changed his mind or Catholics stopped following the signs. By 1975, Catholic elementary school enrollments in the tricounty area had decreased 43.5 percent, reversing every trend since the first school's founding in the 1840's. With one exception, the only pattern was universal decline. Thus, the suburbs lost almost as high a percentage as the City—42.5 versus 44.4 percent—with no significant difference between middle and working class communities. Every one of 75 areas in the City itself decreased, all but five by more than 25 percent. Only eight city schools had an increase in their enrollment and this by a total of just 637 pupils in ten years. Only six suburbs added to their enrollments, by an average of but 100 students in ten years. Schools in every other suburb declined. In these ten years no new elementary schools opened. The high schools, too, lost 17 percent of their students. Thus, for the first time in history, with one exception, the universal trend was a decline unrelated to local social change.

Race emerges as the only specifically discernible social factor within the larger context of general decimation. Though all 75 community areas in the City declined, of the 33 that lost more than the city-wide average, all but two comprised neighborhoods that either changed racially during the decade or were most threatened by racial change in 1975. For example, Austin, on the City's western boundary, lost 59 percent of its elementary parochial school students as Blacks occupied most of that community. Significantly, each of the five areas that lost the least were racially stable neighborhoods, three on the distant northwest side far from the racial frontier and two in the oldest section of the south side's Black Belt. Yet, despite the accelerated enrollment decrease in areas affected by racial change, the number of Black students in the parochial schools actually increased by 14 percent during the decade. By 1975, Black children accounted for over 23 percent of the elementary parochial school enrollment in the City and 16.6 percent of the high school. Thus, though parochial schools in changed neighborhoods now had fewer pupils altogether, they counted more Black youngsters than ever before.[2]

Still, despite its obvious importance in the Catholic system's changing fortunes, race fails to account for the general decline throughout the tricounty area. White Catholics displaced in the central city did not produce a countervailing increase in parochial schools on its fringes or in the suburbs. White Catholics everywhere had abandoned their schools. Catholic education's escalating costs offered an obvious and popular explanation for the new pattern. Yet that explanation fails to withstand even cursory scrutiny. The economic sacrifices required of the affluent Catholic suburbanite in

1975 certainly did not exceed in real terms those of his destitute Bridgeport or Back of the Yards ancestor a hundred years earlier. This suggests that the economic burden may have provided the occasion but not the cause for what happened after 1965.

Certainly profound changes within the Church itself may have contributed to the decline of Catholic education. The mass replacement of nuns, priests, and brothers by lay teachers, together with the more liberalized religious instruction ushered in by the Second Vatican Council, rendered the parochial school hardly recognizable to many traditional Catholics. For these, parochial education no longer offered the attraction of the known. For others, the Church's post-conciliar renewal implied alternate religious priorities that did not include Catholic schooling. Thus, the more conventional began to find the Catholic school too liberal, while the more liberal found it unnecessary. Yet, granting the impact of these internal factors, the social history of Catholic education in Chicago points to a more fundamental cause still.

The Catholic school, whether as an expression of a distinctive counter culture or as a symbol of protest and defiance, or simply as a security blanket, had lost its meaning. By the 1960's the reality that dawned in the 1920's without recognition in the popular consciousness now had amassed the symbolic power that reached into the awareness of Everyman. The symbols included not merely forty years of Catholic mayors, but a Pope John XXIII, universally loved and admired, who somehow made being American and Catholic no longer a sign of subversion; and, perhaps more powerful still, a Catholic president, whose election signaled the ultimate arrival. Though many Catholics would continue to frequent the Church's schools, some perhaps because they believed them better, others possibly to escape racial intermixture, still others out of pure religious conviction, the Catholic school as powerful cultural agent had ceased to exist.

Notes

PREFACE

1. Lawrence A. Cremin, *The Transformation of the School, Progressivism in American Education, 1876–1957* (New York: Knopf, 1961); Karl F. Kaestle, *The Evolution of an Urban School System, New York City, 1750–1850* (Cambridge: Harvard University Press, 1973); Michael B. Katz, *The Irony of Early School Reform, Educational Innovation in Mid-Nineteenth Century Massachusetts* (Boston: Beacon Press, 1968); Marvin Lazerson, *Origins of the Urban School, Public Education in Massachusetts, 1870–1915* (Cambridge: Harvard University Press, 1971); Diane Ravitch, *The Great School Wars, New York City, 1805–1973* (New York: Basic Books, 1974); Stanley K. Schultz, *The Culture Factory: Boston Public Schools, 1789–1860* (New York: Oxford University Press, 1973); David Tyack, *The One Best System, A History of American Urban Education* (Cambridge: Harvard University Press, 1974); Selwyn K. Troen, *The Public and the Schools: Shaping the St. Louis System, 1838–1920* (Columbia, Mo.: University of Missouri Press, 1975).

CHAPTER 1

1. The Catholic schools of New York City actually enrolled more pupils than did those of Chicago. But the New York schools were divided between two dioceses, New York and Brooklyn. Thus, as a single

diocese, Chicago could lay claim to the distinction of being number one.

2. Catholic usage reserves the term "parochial" for schools conducted as part of a parish, "diocesan" for those conducted by the diocese, and "private" for those owned independently of the diocese or its parishes, usually by religious orders.

3. *Western Tablet*, February 21, 1852, p. 5; February 28, 1852, p. 5. Except where noted, statistics for Catholic school enrollments are taken from the *Official Catholic Directory*.

4. Michael Schiltz, *Catholics in the Archdiocese of Chicago*, Vol. I: *1960 Population and Projections*, p. 7. Published by the Chicago Archdiocesan Conservation Council, September, 1962 (Mimeograph).

5. See Neil G. McCluskey, S.J., ed., *Catholic Education in America, A Documentary History* ("Classics in Education," No. 21, Teachers College, Columbia University) (Richmond, Va.: William Byrd Press, Inc., 1964), pp. 80, 85, 94. Plenary councils did not differ appreciably from provincial councils. The change in nomenclature resulted from division of the original single province in the United States into several ecclesiastical provinces. Plenary councils were gatherings of representatives from the various provinces.

6. Joseph J. Thompson, *The Archdiocese of Chicago, Antecedents and Development* (Des Plaines, Ill.: St. Mary's Training School Press, 1920), p. 28.

7. *Synodus Dioecesana Chicagiensis, Mense Augusti 1860 Habita* (Chicago: Tobey Bros., 1860), Decree VI, p. 8 (author's translation).

8. See Thomas T. McAvoy, C.S.C., *The Great Crisis in American Catholic History, 1895–1900* (Chicago: Henry Regnery Co., 1957), p. 79.

9. *New World*, July 19, 1902, p. 13; quoting from the *Chicago Tribune*.

10. *Synodus Dioecesana Chicagiensis Tertia* (Chicago: Cameron, Amberg & Co., 1906), Decrees 31, 34.

11. *New World*, July 9, 1915, p. 5.

12. George S. Counts, *School and Society in Chicago* (New York: Harcourt, Brace & Co., 1928), p. 243.

CHAPTER 2

1. Melvin Steinfeld, ed., *Cracks in the Melting Pot* (Beverly Hills: Glencoe Press, 1970), p. 175, quoting an anonymous author.

2. Lyman Beecher, *Plea for the West* (Cincinnati: Truman & Smith, 1835), p. 12.

3. See Daniel W. Kucera, *Church-State Relationships in Education in Illinois* (Washington, D. C.: Catholic University of America Press, 1955).

4. Bessie Louise Pierce, *A History of Chicago* (New York: Knopf, 1937), Vol. I, p. 232, quoting Jeremiah Porter, "Address on the Earliest Religious History of Chicago," delivered for the Chicago Historical Society, 1859, Autograph Letters, XVII, 353 (Ms. Chicago Historical Society).

5. See Shepherd Johnston, "Historical Sketches of the Public School System," *Twenty-Fifth Annual Report of the Board of Education for the Year Ending July 31, 1879* (Chicago: Clark & Edwards, 1880), Appendix. See also, Keith McClellan, "Educational Change, 1838–1856" (Unpublished paper, Department of History, University of Chicago, 1965).

6. Sister Mary Innocenta Montay, *The History of Catholic Secondary Education in the Archdiocese of Chicago* (Washington, D. C.: Catholic University of America Press, 1953), p. 10, quoting a letter dated November 23, 1833 by Father John Mary Iranaeus St. Cyr to Bishop Joseph Rosati; St. Louis Archdiocesan Archives, Chancery Office, St. Louis, Mo.

7. Neil G. McCluskey, S.J., ed., *Catholic Education in America, A Documentary History* (Richmond, Va.: William Byrd Press, Inc., 1964), p. 63, quoting from American Bishops Pastoral Letter of 1843.

8. Peter Guilday, ed., *The National Pastorals of the Hierarchy, 1792–1919* (Westminster, Md., 1954), p. 28.

9. Bessie Louise Pierce, ed., *As Others See Chicago, Impressions of Visitors, 1673–1933* (Chicago: University of Chicago Press, 1933), p. 137, quoting J. J. Ampere, *Promenade en Amerique*, 1860. Ampere visited Chicago in 1851.

10. *Western Tablet*, April 3, 1852, p. 4.

11. Ibid., March 5, 1853, p. 4.

12. *Chicago Tribune*, June 6, 1854, quoting the *Western Tablet.*

13. *Western Tablet*, March 19, 1853, p. 4.

14. *Chicago Tribune*, February 8, 1854; February 18, 1854; May 12, 1853. On newspaper opposition see the *Chicago Daily Times*, March 31, 1853; *Chicago Tribune*, March 24, April 7, 22, 24, May 12, 1853; *Northwestern Christian Advocate*, January 5, February 16, 1853; *Watchman of the Prairies*, March 23, 1853.

15. *Chicago Tribune*, May 12, 1853; March 7, 1854; June 12, 1854.

16. Alfred T. Andreas, *History of Chicago from the Earliest Period to the Present Time* (Chicago: Andreas, 1884), Vol. I, p. 615. See also Pierce, Vol. II, p. 211.

17. *Chicago Tribune*, April 19, 1859. See also Pierce, Vol. I, p. 380.

18. Ibid., May 12, 1860.

19. Ibid., June 6, 1854.

20. Ibid., November 4, December 5, 1869.

21. *Proceedings of the Board of Education of the City of Chicago*, 1875–1876, pp. 13, 31.

22. *Chicago Tribune*, October 5, 1875.

23. See *Proceedings of the Board of Education of the City of Chicago*, 1890–1891, pp. 206–207, 224; 1895–1896, pp. 178, 197, 226, 238, 261, 282, 314, 345, 378, 393; 1896–1897, p. 53; 1899–1900, pp. 477, 498; 1900–1901, p. 227.

24. *New World*, July 29, 1911, p. 4; January 6, 1912, p. 4.

25. Ibid., January 5, 1923, p. 4.

26. George S. Counts, *School and Society in Chicago* (New York: Harcourt, Brace & Co., 1906), p. 231.

27. *New World*, December 21, 1895, p. 4; February 14, 1903, p. 4; July 14, 1907, pp. 3, 4; see also August 11, 1906, pp. 3, 4.

28. Ibid., February 18, 1912, p. 4; June 28, 1913, p. 4; July 26, 1913, p. 4; November 22, 1913, p. 4.

29. Ibid., January 2, 1904, p. 1; June 4, 1904, p. 17; June 11, 1904, p. 3; June 9, 1906, p. 15; August 13, 1915, p. 1.

30. Letter of Rev. T. V. Shannon to Archbishop George Mundelein, May 24, 1920, with attached report of the Efficiency Committee. (Archives of the Catholic Bishop of Chicago, St. Mary of the Lake Seminary, Mundelein, Ill. Cited hereafter as "Archives.")

31. *New World*, July 27, 1917, p. 4; October 3, 1924, p. 4; May 22, 1925, p. 4. Interestingly, in the 1920's, unlike today, the most sought-after positions were in the city and not the suburbs.

32. These figures are based on the unpublished files of Professor Robert McCaul of the University of Chicago Department of Education who has researched the personal background of each board member. In some cases, an individual's religion cannot be determined with certainty, but the percentages quoted include those who were probably Catholic. Counts claimed on the basis of research done in 1926 that between 1903 and 1926 Catholics made up 34 percent of the board members, Jews 8 percent, and Protestants the rest. See Counts, p. 50. Whichever figures are correct, Catholics clearly did not control the board.

33. *New World*, June 30, 1906, p. 15; March 2, 1901, p. 8; June 30, 1906, p. 15; October 19, 1907, p. 16; July 20, 1912, p. 4; December 10, 1915, p. 4.

34. *New World*, February 14, 1903, p. 16; November 28, 1908, p. 4; see also January 16, 1897, p. 8; May 18, 1901, p. 1; May 21, 1921, p. 4; see also March 26, 1920, p. 4; April 28, 1922, p. 4.

35. Ibid., January 25, 1902, p. 1; December 31, 1892, p. 4; March 4, 1893, p. 4; March 11, 1893, p. 4; April 6, 1901, p. 14; February 23, 1907, p. 15; February 19, 1910, p. 4; October 24, 1924, p. 4.

36. *Chicago Tribune*, January 14, 1890.

37. Archbishop George Mundelein to James Cardinal Gibbons, Baltimore, July 14, 1919 (Archives). On the same issue, see *New World*, January 16, 1920, p. 4.

38. Kucera, p. 75.

39. *Debates and Proceedings of the Constitutional Convention of the State of Illinois* (Springfield, Ill.: E. L. Merrit & Bro., 1870), p. 1760.

40. Ibid., pp. 1743–1744.

41. *Chicago Tribune*, February 4, 7, 14, 18, 1875; Pierce, Vol. III, p. 389. See also the *Chicago Tribune*, September 13, 1892.

42. *New World*, September 10, 1892, p. 1.

43. See *Abendpost*, June 10, 1892; *Illinois Staats Zeitung*, June 25, 1892, in the Chicago Foreign Language Press Survey, Works Project Administration, 1942 (Microfilms of translations from Chicago foreign language newspapers. Hereafter cited as Foreign Language Press Survey). The Germans found the Edwards Law doubly oppressive because it also banned the use of foreign languages as a medium of instruction in the schools.

44. *New World*, November 26, 1892, p. 4; November 5, 1904, p. 24.

45. Ibid., September 7, 1895, p. 1; February 25, 1899, p. 14; October 3, 1924, p. 4.

46. *Chicago Tribune*, February 18, 1875; September 2, 1890; September 17, 1889; September 2, 1890.

47. Counts, p. 335.

48. *Chicago Tribune*, April 4, 1890; April 30, 1890; November 20, 1892; March 17, 1889; September 15, 1895.

49. Pierce, Vol. III, p. 453, referring to various sources in the religious and secular press.

50. *New World*, March 15, 1896, p. 4.

51. Ibid., August 25, 1920, p. 1; October 7, 1911, p. 4; May 1, 1909, p. 1; July 22, 1911, p. 4; November 18, 1911, p. 4; February 17, 1912, p. 1; July 20, 1912, p. 4; October 24, 1930, p. 8.

52. Ibid., January 25, 1914, p. 4; November 13, 1897, p. 3; September 11, 1931, p. 7.

53. Letter of Cardinal Mundelein to Rev. Herbert C. Noonan, S.J., St. Ignatius College, January 13, 1926 (Archives).

CHAPTER 3

1. Hannah B. Clark, *The Public Schools of Chicago* (Chicago: University of Chicago Press, 1897), p. 109.

2. *Report of the Education Commission of the City of Chicago* (Chicago: Lakeside Press, 1899), p. 65. (Also, University of Chicago Press, 1900.) This commission was better known as the Harper Commission after its chairman, William Rainey Harper, President of the University of Chicago.

3. Sophonisba P. Breckenridge and Edith Abbott, *The Delinquent Child and the Home, A Study of the Delinquent Wards of the City of Chicago* (New York: Russell Sage Foundation, 1912), p. 56.

4. Ella Flagg Young, *Isolation in the School* (Chicago: University of Chicago Press, 1901), pp. 91–92.

5. Op. cit., p. 131.

6. *New World*, January 13, 1900, p. 16; June 25, 1904, p. 4.

7. Op. cit., p. 132.

8. *New World*, October 17, 1896, p. 4; January 20, 1906, p. 12.

9. For a discussion of this issue, see Coleman J. Barry, *The Catholic Church and German Americans* (Milwaukee: Bruce Publishing Co., 1953).

10. See Gilbert J. Garraghan, S.J., *The Catholic Church in Chicago, 1673–1871* (Chicago: Loyola University Press, 1921).

11. See letter of Bishop William J. Quarter to Archbishop John Hughes, February 28, 1845 (Archives: 1-1845, H-1).

12. Letter of Bishop Quarter to President of the Leopoldine Society, December 20, 1845, quoted in Marie Catherine Tangney, "The Development of Catholic Institutions in Chicago during the Incumbencies of Bishop Quarter and Bishop Van de Velde, 1844–1853" (unpublished Master's dissertation, Department of History, Loyola University, Chicago, 1935), p. 37. The Leopoldine Society was a Catholic group in Germany founded to aid German emigrants.

13. See Sister of Mercy, "The Sisters of Mercy, Chicago's Pioneer Nurses and Teachers, 1846–1921," *Illinois Catholic Historical Review*, II (April, 1921); Sister Lucille Wargin, C.R., "The Polish Immigrant in the American Community, 1880–1930" (unpublished Master's dissertation, Department of History, De Paul University, Chicago, 1948); Joseph Krisciunas, "Lithuanians in Chicago" (unpublished Master's dissertation, Department of History, De Paul University, Chicago, 1935).

14. *New World*, June 11, 1898, p. 4.

15. Ibid.

16. *Chicago Arbeiter Zeitung*, December 24, 1879, in the Foreign Language Press Survey.

17. See, for example, *Dziennik Cicogoski*, January 19, 1891; *Dziennik Zwiazkowy*, November 4, 1911, in the Foreign Language Press Survey. See also, *New World*, March 4, 1893, p. 4.

18. *New World*, December 5, 1930, p. 6.

19. Reverend Thomas L. Harmon, *Fifty Years of Parish History: Church of the Annunciation, 1886–1916* (Chicago: Privately printed, 1916), pp. 12–13, 15.

20. *Annals of St. Boniface Parish*, pp. 83, 109–110. See also *New World*, May 22, 1936, p. 6.

21. Barry, p. 289, quoting a petition sent to Rome by German-American Catholics in 1886 asking for separate German bishoprics in the United States.

22. *New World*, November 13, 1897, p. 4.

23. *Dziennik Zwiazkowy*, December 12, 1911, in the Foreign Language Press Survey.

24. Petition of Lithuanian parishioners of St. George Lithuanian Church to Auxiliary Bishop McGavick, 1899 (Archives); letter of Mother Lauretta Lubowidska, Superior General of the Sisters of the Holy Family of Nazareth, Rome, to Archbishop Mundelein, May 5, 1922 (Archives). See also *New World*, January 6, 1933, p. 3; May 3, 1940, p. 11.

25. *New World*, February 24, 1922, p. 8; August 24, 1951, p. 9; correspondence and memos in file for St. Michael's parish, 1957 (Archives).

26. See Report of Archbishop James E. Quigley to Cardinal de Lai, Rome, March 21, 1913 (Archives: 1-1913, L-1). See also Joseph J. Thompson, *The Archdiocese of Chicago, Antecedents and Development* (Des Plaines, Ill.: St. Mary's Training School Press, 1920), p. 660.

27. *Weekly Chicago Democrat*, September 7, 1847, quoted in Bessie Louise Pierce, *A History of Chicago* (New York: Knopf, 1937), Vol. I, p. 242.

28. Barry, pp. 254, 275.

29. Mundelein to Most Rev. P. Fumasoni-Biondi, Apostolic Delegate, Washington, D. C., March 7, 1927 (Archives).

30. Joseph Cada, *Czech-American Catholics, 1850–1920* (Lisle, Ill.: Benedictine Abbey Press, 1964), pp. 44–48; also, *New World*, Centennial Edition, 1900, p. 135.

31. *New World*, July 9, 1892, p. 9; September 19, 1908, p. 1; October 17, 1908, p. 1.

32. Mundelein to Rev. Maurice McKenna, Mary Queen of Heaven parish, November 17, 1920 (Archives). For a general background to Czech nationalism in Chicago, see Jakub Horak, "Assimilation of Czechs in Chicago" (unpublished Doctoral dissertation, Department of Sociology, University of Chicago, 1920); Eugene R. McCarthy, "The Bohemians in Chicago and Their Benevolent Societies: 1875–1946" (unpublished Master's dissertation, Department of History, University of Chicago, 1950).

33. Chancellor Edward F. Hoban to Most Rev. John Bonzano, D.D., Washington, D. C., June 3, 1919 (Archives).
34. Typewritten translation in Archives, January 25, 1925.
35. *Draugas*, February 6, 1925, translation in Archives. *Draugas* was a Lithuanian Catholic newspaper published in Chicago. It championed the attack on "Americanizing priests," calling them "fear stricken rabbits who are raving today in America, prophesying near death to the Lithuanian Nationality." (January 31, 1925, translation in Archives.)
36. *New World*, July 19, 1902, p. 2, quoting an unspecified article in the *Chicago Tribune*.
37. *New World*, April 6, 1895, p. 4; December 18, 1909, p. 1.
38. Letter of Archbishop Mundelein to Mr. Louis J. Bachand-Vertefeuille, managing editor, *Le Courrier Franco-Americain*, Chicago, April 30, 1917 (Archives: 3-1919, B-4).

CHAPTER 4

1. *Western Tablet*, February 21, 1852, p. 5; February 28, 1852, p. 5; *New World*, April 14, 1900.
2. Gilbert J. Garraghan, S.J., *The Catholic Church in Chicago, 1673–1871* (Chicago: Loyola University Press, 1921), p. 16, quoting a letter by a Father St. Cosme from Arkansas, January 2, 1699.
3. Ibid., p. 153. For a more thorough treatment of early French Catholicism in Chicago see *Notre Dame de Chicago, 1887–1937* (Chicago: Privately printed, 1937). See also *New World*, July 11, 1896, p. 6. The name of this parish was St. Louis. It was not rebuilt after the fire of 1871. See Joseph J. Thompson, *The Archdiocese of Chicago, Antecedents and Development* (Des Plaines, Ill.: St. Mary's Training School Press, 1920), p. 271.
4. *Notre Dame de Chicago*, p. 59 (author's translation).
5. Thompson, p. 536. See also *New World*, April 24, 1931, p. 6; August 28, 1936, p. 3.
6. *100 Years, The History of the Church of the Holy Name* (Chicago: Privately printed, 1949), unpaged. For early German Catholic history in Chicago, see F. C. Bürgler, *Geschicte der Katholische Kirche Chicago's* (Chicago: Wilhelm Kuhlmann, 1889). German Catholics were estimated to constitute close to one-half of the total German population in Chicago.
7. *New World*, November 7, 1930, p. 6; Bürgler, pp. 56–57; *St. Michael's Diamentes Jubilaeum 1852–1927* (Chicago: Privately printed, 1927).

8. Thompson, p. 503.

9. Ibid., p. 301.

10. Ibid., pp. 387–389.

11. Letter of an attorney at law, Chicago, to Archbishop Mundelein, March 28, 1916 (Archives: 3-1916, O-21).

12. This was Angel Guardian Orphanage in Rose Hill, along what is now Devon Avenue in the Rogers Park section of north side Chicago. It was then far north of the city limits. See Thompson, pp. 747–751.

13. *New World*, Centennial Edition, April 14, 1900, p. 140; Thompson, p. 383; Sister Mary Inviolata Ficht, S.S.J., "Noble Street in Chicago— Socio-Cultural Study of Polish Residents Within Ten Blocks" (unpublished Master's dissertation, Department of Polish, De Paul University, Chicago, 1952), p. 16.

14. Report of Co-Superintendent of Schools, Rev. Henry Matimore, to Archbishop Mundelein, June 22, 1923 (Archives).

15. *New World*, May 30, 1903, p. 11, quoting article by John R. Ratham in the Chicago *Record Herald*.

16. *New World*, January 19, 1917, p. 1, reporting debate between University of Chicago and Northwestern University.

17. *Narod Polski*, Vol. XVI, No. 25, June 19, 1912, in Foreign Language Press Survey; Ficht, p. 104; *Narod Polski*, Vol. XVI, No. 33, August 15, 1917, in Foreign Language Press Survey; *New World*, October 9, 1925, p. 3; April 20, 1923, p. 2.

18. See *Dziennik Ziednoczenia*, June 24, 1927, in Foreign Language Press Survey; letter of Samuel Cardinal Stritch to Rev. Samuel K. Wilson, S.J., President of Loyola University, September 9, 1941 (Archives); *New World*, March 26, 1904, p. 3; December 12, 1908, p. 1; *Diamond Jubilee, Immaculate Conception BVM Parish, 1882–1957* (Chicago: Privately printed, 1957), unpaged.

19. Eugene R. McCarthy, "The Bohemians in Chicago and Their Benevolent Societies: 1875–1946" (unpublished Master's dissertation, Department of History, University of Chicago, 1950), p. 16; Jakub Horak, "The Assimilation of Czechs in Chicago" (unpublished Doctoral dissertation, Department of Sociology, University of Chicago, 1920), pp. 22–29; Joseph Cada, *Czech-American Catholics, 1850–1920* (Lisle, Ill.: Benedictine Abbey Press, 1964), pp. 44–48; Thompson, p. 355; *New World*, Centennial Edition, April 14, 1900, p. 135; *Chicago Daily News Almanac and Year Book for 1915*, p. 549.

20. McCarthy, p. 69; *New World*, September 29, 1933, p. 7; Horak, p. 85; Cada, pp. 57–61, 77.

21. Joseph Krisciunas, "Lithuanians in Chicago" (unpublished Master's

dissertation, Department of History, De Paul University, Chicago, 1935), pp. 4–5; *New World*, January 6, 1933, p. 3; May 3, 1940, p. 11; August 13, 1943, p. 34; *Draugas*, February 6, 1925, translation in Archives.

22. *New World*, December 5, 1910, p. 6; February 24, 1922, p. 8. About 70 percent of the Slovaks in the United States were estimated to be Roman Catholics. In Chicago, there were also many Lutheran Slovaks who settled in the same areas as the Catholics, and, in some cases, opened parochial schools. See Mary Lydia Zahrobsky, "The Slovaks in Chicago" (unpublished Master's dissertation, Graduate School of Social Service Administration, University of Chicago, 1924).

23. *New World*, August 22, 1941, p. 23.

24. Ibid., June 1, 1923, p. 2. See also Centennial Edition, April 14, 1900, p. 144; Thompson, pp. 590, 602–603, 658, 660; Report of Archbishop Quigley to Cardinal de Lai, Rome, March 21, 1913 (Archives: 1-1913, L-1).

25. Thompson, p. 600. See also *New World*, August 25, 1906, p. 23.

26. *New World*, April 24, 1931, p. 6. See also Thompson, p. 584.

27. Thompson, p. 619.

28. Ibid., p. 646. See also Abdul Ali al-Tahïr, "The Arab Community in the Chicago Area, A Comparative Study of the Christian Syrians and the Muslim-Palestinians" (unpublished Doctoral dissertation, Department of Sociology, University of Chicago, 1952); *New World*, August 5, 1893, p. 1; Centennial Edition, April 14, 1900, p. 143; December 11, 1936, p. 9; Chancellor of the Archdiocese to Most Rev. P. Fumasoni-Biondi, Apostolic Delegate, Washington, D. C., December 13, 1930 (Archives).

29. Thompson, pp. 650–651; *New World*, March 13, 1936, p. 1.

30. Letters of Diomede Falconio, Apostolic Delegate, to Archbishop Quigley, June 30, 1908; and Quigley to Bishop Soter Ortynsky, August 3, 1908 (Archives 1-1908, O-1). The Ukranian parishes were to develop and multiply later, especially as a result of the Stalinist era in Russia, and World War II. By 1960, there were 15,000 Ukranians in five Chicago parishes. See *New World*, August 18, 1961, p. 1. Despite the independence of the Ukranian parishes from the jurisdiction of the Catholic Bishop of Chicago, they were to place their schools under the jurisdiction of the Archdiocesan School Board. See *St. Nicholas Ukranian Catholic School Dedication Book* (Chicago: Privately printed, 1954).

31. Thompson, p. 437. The Servites, themselves a cosmopolitan order, instead founded the Church of Our Lady of Sorrows on the west side near Garfield Park, which became heavily Irish. Later, however, they were instrumental in helping Italian parishes get started.

32. *New World*, March 25, 1898, p. 11; May 7, 1899, p. 14; May 21, 1898, p.

12; December 23, 1899, p. 9; July 2, 1898, p. 11; October 15, 1898, p. 4; March 18, 1899, pp. 8–9; June 17, 1899, p. 4; Centennial Edition, April 14, 1900, p. 144; July 4, 1903, p. 12; November 6, 1909, p. 2.

33. Ibid., June 17, 1899, p. 4.

34. There was also an Italian parish in suburban Melrose Park founded in 1894. See *New World*, October 18, 1940, p. 14.

35. For the number of Italians in Chicago, see Virgil Peter Puzzo, "The Italians in Chicago" (unpublished Master's dissertation, Department of History, University of Chicago, 1937), p. 25, in which he cites the U. S. Bureau of the Census, *Thirteenth Census of the United States: 1910, Population*, Vol. I (Washington: U. S. Government Printing Office, 1913), p. 834.

36. Archbishop Quigley to Cardinal de Lai, March 21, 1913 (Archives: 1-1913, L-1). (Author's translation from the Latin.)

37. Sister Mary Cecilia, B.V.M., to Archbishop Mundelein, May 17, 1917 (Archives: 4-1917, M-58), referring to Mundelein's request.

38. Rev. Louis Giambastiani to Chancellor Hoban, July 30, 1918; June 24, 1919 (Archives). See also *New World*, November 8, 1919, p. 2; October 17, 1930, p. 6. For a vivid description of conditions in the neighborhood, see Harvey Zorbaugh, *The Gold Coast and the Slum, A Sociological Study of Chicago's Near North Side* (Chicago: University of Chicago Press, 1929).

39. Chancellor Edward F. Hoban to Most Rev. John Bonzano, D.D., Washington, D. C., June 3, 1919 (Archives). See also *New World*, June 4, 1920, p. 2.

40. Mundelein to Most Rev. Henry Moeller, Archbishop of Cincinnati, March 13, 1919 (Archives); Mundelein to a parishioner, Chicago, March 12, 1919 (Archives); Rev. Horace D'Andrea, St. Anthony's parish, to Chancellor Hoban, December 6, 1921 (Archives).

41. *New World*, November 21, 1930, p. 6.

42. There were about 74,000 Italians of foreign birth and 149,000 Polish. There were also over 120,000 foreign-born Germans, but at least half of these were not Catholic.

43. Sister Mary Cecilia, B.V.M., to Archbishop Mundelein, May 17, 1917 (Archives: 4-1917, M-58).

44. Thompson, p. 311.

CHAPTER 5

1. Bessie Louise Pierce, *A History of Chicago* (New York: Knopf, 1937), Vol. 1, p. 239; see also Joseph J. Thompson, *The Archdiocese of Chicago*,

Antecedents and Development (Des Plaines, Ill.: St. Mary's Training School Press, 1920), pp. 22, 163.

2. Bishop Quarter to Rev. D. McCloskey, New York, November 23, 1844; Bishop Quarter to President of the Association for the Propagation of the Faith, France, December 19, 1845 (Archives).

3. Bishop Quarter to President of the Association for the Propagation of the Faith, France, December 12, 1844 (Archives: 1-1844, S-1).

4. *Metropolitan Catholic Almanac and Laity's Directory for the Year 1849* (Baltimore: Fielding Lucas, Jr., 1849), p. 135.

5. Marie Catherine Tangney, "The Development of Catholic Institutions in Chicago during the Incumbencies of Bishop Quarter and Bishop Van de Velde, 1844–1853" (unpublished Master's dissertation, Department of History, Loyola University, Chicago, 1935), p. 37, quoting a letter of Bishop Quarter to President of the Leopoldine Society, December 20, 1845.

6. *Western Tablet*, March 5, 1853, p. 4.

7. *100 Years, The History of the Church of the Holy Name* (Chicago: The Cathedral of the Holy Name, 1949), unpaged.

8. Thompson, p. 341; *100 Years, The History of the Church of the Holy Name.*

9. Gilbert J. Garraghan, S.J., *The Catholic Church in Chicago, 1673–1871* (Chicago: Loyola University Press, 1921), p. 115, quoting Saint Louis *News Letter*, August 1, 1846.

10. The resignees were James Van de Velde and Anthony O'Regan. See letters of Bishop Van de Velde to the Catholics of Chicago, October 30, 1853 (Archives); Van de Velde to the Most Reverend Archbishops of the United States, March 1, 1852 (Archives); Van de Velde to Archbishop Francis P. Kenrick, St. Louis, April 9, 1852, and January 8, 1853 (Archives); Bishop Anthony O'Regan to Archbishop John B. Purcell, Cincinnati, January 20, 1855 (Archives); and memorandum of Bishop O'Regan, May 28, 1856 (Archives). The third casualty was Bishop James Duggan, whose erratic behavior seems to have begun with troubles over the university and finally led to his removal from office in 1870. See letter of Bishop Peter Kenrick to Prefect of the Sacred Congregation De Propaganda Fide, Rome, August 10, 1861 (Archives); also Sister Mary Innocenta Montay, *The History of Catholic Secondary Education in the Archdiocese of Chicago* (Washington, D. C.: Catholic University of America Press, 1953), pp. 126–131.

11. *New World*, May 6, 1938, p. 7, quoting the *Chicago Times*, June 19, 1858.

12. Carter H. Harrison, *Stormy Years* (Indianapolis: Bobbs Merrill, 1935), p. 30.

13. Archdiocese of Chicago, *Annual Report of the Catholic Schools, 1929–30*, a report prepared by the Superintendent of Catholic Schools (Chicago: Archdiocese of Chicago, 1930). Hereafter referred to as *Annual School Report*. These reports began in the mid-1920's. See also, *Annual School Report*, 1926–1927, p. 9; *New World*, July 26, 1926, p. 4.

14. Pierce, Vol. 1, p. 179; p. 180, referring to the *Daily Chicago American*, December 28, 1840; Vol. II, p. 13; Vol. I, p. 266, quoting the *Watchman of the Prairies*, December 14, 1847.

15. Lloyd Lewis and Henry Justin Smith, *Chicago: The History of Its Reputation, 1833–1933* (New York: Blue Ribbon Books, Inc., 1929), pp. 74, 79, quoting *London Times*, 1860.

16. *New World*, October 10, 1930, p. 6.

17. Brother Thomas M. Mulkerins, S.J., *Holy Family Parish, Chicago: Priests and People* (Chicago: Universal Press, 1923), p. 719; Pierce, Vol. II, p. 362; Harrison, p. 26; Lloyd Wendt and Herman Kogan, *Big Bill of Chicago* (New York: Bobbs Merrill, 1953), p. 18.

18. Bishop James Duggan to Archbishop of Baltimore, February 25, 1869 (Archives: 1-1869, D-1).

19. Garraghan, p. 221.

20. Alfred T. Andreas, *History of Chicago from the Earliest Period to the Present Time* (Chicago: Andreas, 1884), Vol. III, p. 763.

21. Pierce, Vol. II, pp. 359, 356.

22. Robert Hunter, *Tenement Conditions in Chicago* (Chicago: City Homes Assoc., 1901), p. 12.

23. William T. Stead, *If Christ Came to Chicago* (London: The Review of Reviews, Temple House, 1895), p. 119, quoting Mr. F. W. Parker of the Baptist City Mission. Statistics for school enrollments by wards are taken from the Chicago School Census printed in *The Chicago Daily News Almanac and Year Book* (Chicago: The Chicago Daily News Co., 1891).

24. Descriptions of the various wards are taken from a Report of the Department of Health, City of Chicago, 1891, pp. 19–30.

25. Hunter, p. 58. New ward boundaries went into effect in 1911. Therefore, exact comparisons in school enrollments by wards cannot be made between 1890 and 1915.

26. John M. Gillette, *Culture Agencies of a Typical Manufacturing Group: South Chicago* (Chicago: University of Chicago Press, 1901), pp. 9, 23–24.

27. *Immaculate Conception B.V.M. Parish, South Chicago, 1882–1957* (Chicago: Privately printed, 1957), pp. 26–27; Thompson, p. 491; *Saint Francis De Sales Parish, Chicago, 75th Anniversary, 1889–1964* (Chicago: Privately printed, 1964).

28. These statistics are based on the number of 5- to 14-year olds reported in the United States Census for 1930.

29. "Relatio Archdioecesis Chicagiensis," 1883 (Archives: 1-1883, S-1). (Author's translation.) This was an official report from Archbishop Feehan to the Sacred Congregation for the Propagation of the Faith.

30. Louise Montgomery, *The American Girl in the Stockyards District* (Chicago: University of Chicago Press, 1913), p. 5.

31. Ibid., p. 6; Thompson, p. 433.

32. Pierce, Vol. III, p. 440.

33. *Saint Gabriel Church Diamond Jubilee Souvenir Program, 1880–1955* (Chicago: Privately printed, n.d.), p. 6; Thompson, p. 503, referring to Annunciation Church on the near northwest side; *Reverend Hugh McGuire, A Memorial* (Chicago: Privately printed, n.d.), referring to St. James parish on the near south side; Thompson, p. 493, referring to SS. Peter and Paul parish in South Chicago; Pierce, Vol. III, p. 440.

34. *New World*, December 7, 1897, p. 4; May 1, 1897, p. 8.

35. Ray Ginger, *Altgeld's America: The Lincoln Ideal versus Changing Realities* (Chicago: Quadrangle Books, 1965), p. 235.

36. Charles E. Merriam, *Chicago, A More Intimate View of Urban Politics* (New York: Macmillan, 1929), p. 130.

37. Thompson, p. 62, quoting address of Judge Thomas A. Moran.

CHAPTER 6

1. *New World*, January 2, 1931, p. 6. See also Howard J. Doherty, *The History of Visitation Parish, 1886–1936* (Chicago: Privately printed, 1936); *New World*, January 2, 1931, p. 6; June 28, 1935, p. 6; February 20, 1931, p. 6. St. Anselm's was called St. Patrick's in James T. Farrell's classic about Chicago's south side Irish.

2. Joseph J. Thompson, *The Archdiocese of Chicago, Antecedents and Development* (Des Plaines, Ill.: St. Mary's Training School Press, 1920), pp. 784–785, 789, 781, 795.

3. See Appendix C.

4. *New World*, October 10, 1930, p. 6.

5. Ibid. See also *Reverend Hugh McGuire, A Memorial* (Chicago: Privately printed, n.d.), and *100th Anniversary of St. James Parish, 1855–1955* (Chicago: Privately printed, 1955). Reverend McGuire was pastor of St. James during its heyday and was nationally known in Catholic circles for his promotion of Catholic schools, especially high schools.

6. Rev. James E. McGavick, *A History of Holy Angels Parish, 1880–1920* (Chicago: Privately printed, 1920), pp. 12–13, 33.

7. *New World*, October 31, 1930, p. 6; December 26, 1930, p. 6.

8. Evelyn M. Kitagawa and Karl E. Taeuber, *Local Community Fact Book, Chicago Metropolitan Area, 1960* (Chicago: Chicago Community Inventory, University of Chicago, 1963), p. 92.

9. *New World*, January 9, 1931, p. 6; January 9, 1931, p. 6. See also, Marvin R. Schafer, "The Catholic Church in Chicago, Its Growth and Administration" (unpublished Doctoral dissertation, Department of Christian Theology and Ethics, University of Chicago, 1929), p. 91.

10. Ibid., February 6, 1931, p. 6.

11. Thompson, p. 219.

12. *New World*, December 19, 1930, p. 6; January 13, 1931, p. 6.

13. Ibid., March 27, 1931, p. 6; December 10, 1937, p. 8; April 17, 1931, p. 5; January 25, 1935, p. 2.

14. Kitagawa and Taeuber, pp. 32, 34.

15. *New World*, June 3, 1932, p. 3. Some Oak Park children previously attended St. Catherine of Siena school just over the border in Chicago. St. Catherine later moved into Oak Park.

16. Ibid., April 9, 1926, p. 5, advertisement; June 4, 1926, p. 3, advertisement; April 9, 1926, p. 3, advertisement; May 6, 1927, p. 7, advertisement; April 9, 1926, p. 7, advertisement; October 30, 1925, p. 5, advertisement.

17. Ibid., February 26, 1937, p. 7.

18. Ibid., April 15, 1899, p. 8; October 4, 1899, address printed in full, pp. 4–7; p. 8, editorial.

19. Ibid.

CHAPTER 7

1. *New World*, July 16, 1904, p. 11.

2. *Notre Dame de Chicago, 1887–1937* (Chicago: Privately printed, 1937), p. 67 (author's translation).

3. *New World*, October 31, 1930, p. 6; letter of Archbishop George Mundelein to Rev. Achille L. Bergeron, Notre Dame de Chicago, May 8, 1918 (Archives).

4. *New World*, March 15, 1935, p. 6; Centennial Edition, April 14, 1900, p. 6; May 10, 1902, p. 29; April 24, 1931, p. 6; August 28, 1936, p. 3; Joseph J. Thompson, *The Archdiocese of Chicago, Antecedents and Development* (Des Plaines, Ill.: St. Mary's Training School Press, 1920), p. 536; *New World*, August 20, 1937, p. 6; Marvin R. Schafer, "The Catholic Church in Chicago, Its Growth and Administration" (unpublished Doctoral dissertation, Department of Christian Theology and Ethics, University of Chicago, 1929), p. 50.

5. Thompson, p. 600. See also *New World*, March 3, 1939, p. 9; letter of Julius de Vos to Mundelein, September 28, 1918 (Archives).

6. *New World*, April 24, 1931, p. 6; Thompson, p. 584.

7. Bessie Louise Pierce, *A History of Chicago* (New York: Knopf, 1957), Vol. III, p. 344; *New World*, March 26, 1904, p. 8; June 11, 1898, p. 4; May 3, 1913, p. 1; July 30, 1910, p. 4.

8. *The St. Gregory Story, 1904–1954* (Chicago: Privately printed, 1954), p. 38; *A Historical Sketch of St. Clement's Church, Chicago, 1905–1930* (Chicago: Privately printed, 1930), pp. 9–11.

9. Schafer, p. 20.

10. Letter of Archbishop Mundelein to Rev. George Eisenbacker, December 29, 1917 (Archives); Letter of a parishioner, Chicago, to Archbishop Mundelein, September 21, 1916 (Archives: 2-1916, B-64).

11. Letter of Cardinal Mundelein to Rev. George Eisenbacker, December 2, 1927 (Archives). Mundelein was made a cardinal in 1924. The change in title had no practical effect on the internal affairs of the Archdiocese other than the added prestige.

12. Letter of Archdiocesan Chancellor to Msgr. P. L. Bierman, December 3, 1927 (Archives); Rev. George Blatter to Archbishop Mundelein, June 8, 1918 (Archives); Schafer, pp. 20–21; Letter of Cardinal Mundelein to the German parishes of Chicago, August 23, 1937 (Archives). The letter itself is not preserved, only a memo with the names of the parishes: St. Michael's, St. Alphonsus, St. Augustine, St. Benedict, St. Martin, St. Theresa, St. Mathias, St. Philomena.

13. "Relatio Archdioecesis Chicagiensis," Report of Archbishop Patrick Feehan to the Sacred Congregation for the Propagation of the Faith, 1883 (Archives: 1-1883, S-1) (author's translation).

14. *New World*, January 16, 1931, p. 6. See also Thompson, p. 556.

15. Thompson, pp. 582, 655.

16. *New World*, November 1, 1940, p. 19; March 27, 1931, p. 6; February 4, 1927, p. 1. See also Sister Mary Innocenta Montay, *The History of Catholic Secondary Education in the Archdiocese of Chicago* (Washington, D. C.: Catholic University of America Press, 1953), p. 170.

17. *The St. Gregory Story*, p. 62.

18. Letter of an attorney at law, Chicago, to Archbishop Mundelein, March 28, 1916 (Archives: 3-1916, O-21).

19. F. C. Bürgler, *Geschicte der Katholische Kirche Chicago's* (Chicago: Wilhelm Kuhlmann, 1889), p. 31 (author's translation); *New World*, April 18, 1896, p. 3; *New World*, June 4, 1898, p. 5.

20. Thompson, pp. 307–311. This parish later passed from the Italians to the Mexicans.

21. *New World*, October 17, 1930, p. 6; Thompson, p. 621.

22. Ibid., p. 337.

23. Letter of Sister Agnes Gonzaga Ryan to Archbishop James Quigley, July 15, 1910 (Archives); *New World*, December 29, 1916, p. 1; January 23, 1931, p. 6. In 1952 the parish closed altogether after commerical expansion had forced out most of the area's inhabitants.

24. *New World*, December 4, 1931, p. 2; October 10, 1930, p. 6; May 7, 1915, p. 4.

25. Ibid., June 23, 1916, p. 1. In 1919, the State of Illinois finally made English obligatory as the medium of instruction in all major elementary branches of all schools.

26. Letter of Archbishop Mundelein to Rev. Maurice McKenna, Mary Queen of Heaven parish, November 16, 1920 (Archives).

27. Petition, 1925, with 153 signatures, to Cardinal Mundelein (Archives).

28. By the 1920's, in addition to Bohemians, "Poles, Hungarians, Irish, Germans and other races" attended St. Wenceslaus. *New World*, May 13, 1932, p. 2. The parish buildings were finally destroyed in 1955 to make way for the Dan Ryan Expressway, but the area had long been all but depopulated by commerical expansion.

29. *New World*, July 5, 1935, p. 6. This was St. Simon's parish at 2734 West 52nd Street.

30. Mary Lydia Zahrobsky, "The Slovaks in Chicago" (unpublished Master's dissertation, Graduate School of Social Service Administration, University of Chicago, 1924), pp. 43–53.

31. Letter of Lithuanian priests to Archbishop Mundelein, September 20, 1916 (Archives); Rev. Thomas Bona to Archbishop Mundelein, September 13, 1917 (Archives); Joseph Krisciunas, "Lithuanians in Chicago" (unpublished Master's dissertation, Department of History, De Paul University, Chicago, 1935), p. 35.

32. "Americanization in Chicago," Report of a survey (Chicago: Chicago Community Trust, 1919), p. 11. See also, Julius John Ozog, "A Study of Polish Home Ownership in Chicago" (unpublished Master's dissertation, Department of Sociology, University of Chicago, 1942), p. 71.

33. Letter of Polish priests to Chancellor Hoban, June 26, 1917 (Archives); also letter of Polish lay people to Archbishop Mundelein, June 26, 1917 (Archives); Letter of Archbishop Mundelein to Rev. Stanislaus Swierczek, C.R., December 10, 1919 (Archives); Letter of Archbishop Mundelein to Rev. Francis Cichotzki, Church of Our Lady of Victory, July 10, 1918 (Archives).

34. Letter of Harvey M. Doyle for Martin J. Healy Real Estate Company, to the Catholic Bishop of Chicago, August 23, 1924 (Archives).

35. An English translation of Msgr. Bona's leaflet is preserved in the Archives, September, 1925.

36. Letter of Archbishop Mundelein to Mother M. Samuel, June 2, 1916 (Archives: 3-1916, S-73); Letter of Archbishop Mundelein to Rev. Francis Cichotzki, Church of Our Lady of Victory, July 10, 1918 (Archives).

37. Letter of Archbishop Mundelein to Mr. Louis J. Bachand-Vertefeuille, managing editor, *Le Courrier Franco-Americain*, April 30, 1919 (Archives: 3-1919, B-4).

CHAPTER 8

1. See, for example, Kenneth T. Jackson, *The Ku Klux Klan in the City, 1915–1930* (New York: Oxford University Press, 1967).

2. George S. Counts, *School and Society in Chicago* (New York: Harcourt, Brace & Co., 1928), pp. 236–237.

3. Bessie Louise Pierce, *A History of Chicago* (New York: Knopf, 1937), Vol. I, p. 377, quoting *Chicago Daily American*, August 5, 1840; p. 398; Vol. III, p. 25. See also Edward M. Levine, *The Irish and Irish Politicians* (Notre Dame: University of Notre Dame Press, 1966), p. 145.

4. William T. Stead, *Chicago Today; the Labour War in America* (New York: Arno Press, 1969, reprint of 1894 edition), pp. 107–108.

5. *Chicago Tribune*, January 16, January 21, 1884.

6. Carter H. Harrison, *Stormy Years* (Indianapolis: Bobbs Merrill, 1935), p. 31.

7. *New World*, March 30, 1901, p. 1, speaking of Carter Harrison II.

8. William T. Stead, *If Christ Came to Chicago* (London: The Review of Reviews, Temple House, 1895), pp. 255, 282; Pierce, Vol. III, p. 375; Lloyd Wendt and Herman Kogan, *Bosses in Lusty Chicago, the Story of Bathhouse John and Hinky Dink* (Bloomington: Indiana University Press, 1967; first published, 1943), pp. 88–120. Stead, who visited Chicago during Hopkin's first year in office, mistakenly perceived the new mayor as "heroically fighting against immense odds the battle of municipal honesty." Stead, *Chicago Today*, p. 107.

9. Lloyd Lewis and Henry Justin Smith, *Chicago: the History of Its Reputation, 1833–1933* (New York: Blue Ribbon Books, 1929), p. 302; Wendt and Kogan, p. 68.

10. Wendt and Kogan, p. 234.

11. Jackson, p. 111.

12. Charles E. Merriam, *Chicago: A More Intimate View of Urban Politics* (New York: Macmillan, 1929), p. 288. See also Louise C. Wade, *Graham Taylor, Pioneer for Social Justice, 1851–1938* (Chicago: University of Chicago Press, 1964), pp. 132–133; Lewis and Smith, p. 443.

13. *Chicago Tribune*, April 4, 1890; *New World*, June 30, 1906, p. 15; *Chicago Tribune*, January 11, January 14, 1890; April 30, 1890; Stead, *Chicago Today*, p. 108.

14. *Chicago Tribune*, April 3, 1883, p. 2; Stead, *If Christ Came to Chicago*, p. 254; Carter H. Harrison, *Growing Up With Chicago* (Chicago: Ralph Fletcher Seymour, 1944), p. 239; Joseph J. Thompson, *The Archdiocese of Chicago, Antecedents and Development* (Des Plaines, Ill.: St. Mary's Training School Press, 1920), p. 85; *New World*, January 2, 1904, p. 1.

15. See Marvin R. Schafer, "The Catholic Church in Chicago, Its Growth and Administration" (unpublished Doctoral dissertation, Department of Christian Theology and Ethics, University of Chicago, 1929), pp. 50-55. Inaccuracies in the Catholic census resulted from the fact that each parish submitted a report of its membership to the Archdiocesan Chancery (administration) office. These reports were often subject to considerable manipulation, for example by pastors who deflated parish membership to discourage a possible subdivision or those who inflated to make a better case for an additional assistant priest. In addition, since Catholic parishes did not have a formal membership but simply claimed all Catholics living within a certain area, the census had to rely on an estimate, often based on a count of those attending Sunday Mass. Counts estimated the Catholic population at 45 percent of the total. Counts, p. 230. Archbishop Mundelein apparently thought Chicago was "more than one-half Catholic." See letter to Charles Ffrench, March 24, 1916 (Archives: 2-1916, F-4).

16. Letter of Archbishop Mundelein to Rev. William F. McGinnis, D.D., St. Bridget's Church, Westbury, Nassau County, New York, March 27, 1917 (Archives).

17. Ibid.; Letter of Archbishop Mundelein to Dr. Bernard M. Quinn, Chicago, February 8, 1917 (Archives).

18. Letter of Archbishop Mundelein to Mary Onahan Gallery, March 17, 1917 (Archives); Letter of Archbishop Mundelein to Hon. Roger C. Sullivan, April 6, 1917 (Archives).

19. Letter of Archbishop Mundelein to Hon. David Shanahan, Speaker, House of Representatives, Springfield, Ill., March 3, 1917 (Archives).

20. Letter of Archbishop Mundelein to Rt. Rev. Peter J. Muldoon, D.D., Bishop of Rockford, Ill., May 22, 1920 (Archives).

21. Letter of Archbishop Mundelein to R. H. Tierney, S.J., ed., *America*, June 7, 1919 (Archives); Letter of Archbishop Mundelein to James Cardinal Gibbons, Baltimore, July 14, 1919 (Archives); Letter of Archbishop Mundelein to Hon. David J. Walsh, U. S. Senate, February 4, 1921 (Archives).

22. Letter of Archbishop Mundelein to Charles Ffrench, March 24, 1916 (Archives: 2-1916, F-4). See also letter of Charles Ffrench to Mundelein, March 21, 1916, on Board of Education stationery (Archives: 2-1916, F-4).

23. Letter of Archbishop Mundelein to Hon. William Hale Thompson, Mayor, April 25, 1917 (Archives).

24. John M. Beck, "Chicago Newspapers and the Public Schools, 1890–1920" (unpublished Doctoral dissertation, Department of Education, University of Chicago, 1953), p. 181.

25. See *New World*, July 4, 1896, p. 1; June 18, 1898, p. 4; July 2, 1898, p. 1; July 12, 1902, p. 4.

26. U. S. Congress, Senate Reports of the Immigration Commission, S. Doc. 749, 61st Cong., 2nd Sess., 1911, *The Children of Immigrants in Schools*, Vol. II, p. 558.

27. Reported by Counts, p. 239.

28. *New World*, June 25, 1920, p. 1.

29. Report of Co-superintendent of Catholic Schools, Rev. Henry Matimore to Cardinal Mundelein, December 18, 1924 (Archives). Also, letter of Archbishop Mundelein to Rev. Mother Laureta, Sisters of the Holy Family of Nazareth, Rome, January 29, 1917 (Archives: 4-17, L-17).

30. Reported by Counts, pp. 238, 242.

31. William H. Stuart, *The Twenty Incredible Years* (Chicago: Donahue & Co., 1935), p. 189.

32. See Elizabeth L. Murray, "William J. Bogan as Superintendent of Chicago Public Schools" (unpublished report for the Havighurst-McCaul Project: Society and Education in Chicago, University of Chicago, March 28, 1966).

33. *Chicago Tribune*, April 30, 1890.

34. *New World*, September 10, 1892, p. 1.

35. Ibid., July 8, 1893, p. 5; September 9, 1893, p. 1.

36. Ibid., July 8, 1893, p. 5.

37. Ibid., September 2, 1893, p. 4.

38. Ibid., July 29, 1893, p. 4; June 27, 1896, p. 4. See also June 3, 1894, p. 8; November 24, 1894, p. 4.

39. Ibid., June 9, 1906, p. 15; August 13, 1915, p. 1.

40. Ibid., December 15, 1916, p. 4; March 24, 1922, p. 3; July 19, 1929, p. 4.

41. Ibid., July 20, 1901, p. 8.

42. Ibid., September 15, 1906, p. 15; September 22, 1906, p. 14.

43. Ibid., October 5, 1896, p. 4; January 18, 1902, p. 25; June 10, 1905, p. 13; October 27, 1906, p. 14.

44. Ibid., June 20, 1903, p. 16; October 8, 1904, p. 16; November 18, 1905, p. 14; April 2, 1915, p. 4; November 11, 1932, p. 4.

Matimore to Mundelein entitled, "Father Kozlowski and the School Question," August 17, 1926 (Archives).

31. Ibid.; memorandum of Matimore to Mundelein entitled, "Monsignor Bona and the School Board," August 17, 1926 (Archives).

32. The exposure of Matimore's lack of diplomacy is meant only to illustrate the socially sensitive situation in Chicago Catholicism of the 1920's.

33. See report of Matimore to Mundelein, June 22, 1923 (Archives); report of Matimore to Mundelein, August 4, 1926 (Archives); report of Matimore to Mundelein, June 24, 1925 (Archives); report of Matimore to Mundelein, December 18, 1924 (Archives). Matimore also pointed out that a smaller percentage of Slavic children went to any high school at all: 75 percent of graduates from Slavic parochial schools, 85 percent from English-speaking ones.

34. Ibid., December 18, 1924.

35. Letter of Matimore to Msgr. Thomas Bona, October 1, 1925 (Archives). Apparently Bona showed Matimore's letter to Kozlowski, who wrote comments in rebuttal. These are preserved with the letter.

36. Ibid.

37. Matimore to Bona, April 9, 1926 (Archives).

38. Report of Matimore to Mundelein, June 22, 1923 (Archives). Letters from the Superiors of the Sisters of Charity, Dominican Sisters, Sisters of Providence, Sisters of Mercy of the South Side, and Adrian Dominicans were submitted by Matimore to Mundelein as proof of his success. They are preserved in Matimore's file, 1926 (Archives).

39. This was the view of Matimore's successor, Rev. Daniel Cunningham. Interview, April 16, 1966.

40. New World, June 17, 1927, p. 1. Possibly to soften the blow, Kozlowski was simultaneously made pastor of a Polish parish. New World, September 28, 1927.

41. This description of Cunningham's approach to the superintendency is based on conversations with pastors, sisters, and officials of the school board and on Cunningham's own expressed analysis of his years in office, during an interview with the author, April 16, 1966.

42. By the mid-1920's, as a result of the teachers' meetings called by the superintendents, a Catholic Teachers Association had also begun to take shape. See New World, January 2, 1925, p. 1; January 9, 1925, p. 1.

43. See, for example, letter of Chancellor Edward Hoban to Mother M. Samuel, O.P., Sinsinawa, Wisc., August 17, 1917 (Archives); Chancellor Hoban to Mother M. Camillo, Superior, St. Joseph Convent, Adrian, Mich., September 17, 1917 (Archives: 3-1917, C-31); Rev. Thomas F. Quinn to Mundelein, February 17, 1919 (Archives).

44. See letter of Mundelein to Mother M. Marcella, Superior General, St. Agnes Convent, Fond du Lac, Wisc., November 17, 1917 (Archives). Mother Marcella had complained that her sisters teaching in Chicago were paid only $200 a year. Mundelein considered that "rather low." See also Chancellor Hoban to Reverend Mother M. Cleophas, Superior General, Provident Convent, St. Mary of the Woods, Ind., April 7, 1919 (Archives); Chancellor Hoban to Sister Superiors, July 15, 1920; and to all pastors, July 13, 1920 (Archives).

45. The Archdiocesan Archives contain much correspondence dealing with questions of building schools. In every case, approval of the Archbishop's consultors, with his confirmation, was required. In addition, a building committee considered bids from contractors and approved architects' plans.

46. Mundelein to Rev. J. J. Jennings, June 12, 1919 (Archives).

47. Mundelein to Brother Edmund, La Salle Bureau, New York City, August 22, 1919 (Archives). See also, Mundelein to Mr. Fred Hansen, June 28, 1916; Mundelein to Rev. William Sheran, October 2, 1916 (Archives).

CHAPTER 10

1. Quoted in Neil G. McCluskey, S.J., ed. *Catholic Education in America, A Documentary History* (Richmond, Va.: William Byrd Press, Inc., 1964), p. 180.

2. *New World*, January 25, 1902, p. 4.

3. John M. Beck, "Chicago Newspapers and the Public Schools, 1890–1920" (unpublished Doctoral dissertation, Department of Education, University of Chicago, 1953), pp. 237–238; National Education Association, Commission on the Reorganization of Secondary Education, *Cardinal Principles of Secondary Education. Bulletin*, 1918, No. 35, U. S. Bureau of Education (Washington: U. S. Government Printing Office, 1918). For a full discussion of this issue, see Edward A. Krug, *The Shaping of the American High School* (New York: Harper & Row, 1964).

4. James T. O'Dowd, *Standardization and Its Influence on Catholic Secondary Education in the United States* (Washington: Catholic University of America Press, 1935), p. 28, quoting *Proceedings of the Catholic Education Association*, 1904, p. 41.

5. Edward F. Spiers, *The Central Catholic High School. A Survey of Their History and Status in the United States* (Washington: Catholic University of America Press, 1951), p. 11.

6. *New World*, February 24, 1904, p. 4; September 4, 1909, p. 4; June 4, 1915, p. 4; June 22, 1917, p. 4.

7. Letter of Archbishop Mundelein to Rev. Mother Laureta, Sisters of the Holy Family of Nazareth, Rome, January 29, 1917 (Archives: 4-17, L-17).

8. *New World*, November 16, 1923, p. 3; August 20, 1926, p. 3; Sister Mary Innocenta Montay, *The History of Catholic Secondary Education in the Archdiocese of Chicago* (Washington, D. C.: The Catholic University of America Press, 1953), p. 170; Letter of Cardinal Mundelein to Very Rev. Raymond Meagher, O.P., Provincial, New York, November 14, 1927 (Archives).

9. *New World*, February 25, 1927, p. 1.

10. Ibid., December 16, 1898, p. 11. See also March 18, 1899, p. 1.

11. See *New World*, January 4, 1908, p. 22; Joseph J. Thompson, *The Archdiocese of Chicago, Antecedents and Development* (Des Plaines, Ill.: St. Mary's Training School Press, 1920), p. 689.

12. *New World*, March 17, 1906, p. 26; August 21, 1909, p. 5; October 23, 1909, p. 5; November 30, 1912, p. 2; October 18, 1913, p. 1; Thompson, p. 677.

13. *New World*, August 16, 1918, p. 4; September 13, 1918, p. 1; November 16, 1920, p. 4; September 13, 1918, p. 1; May 19, 1921, p. 4.

14. Ibid., August 25, 1900, p. 8.

15. Ibid., April 12, 1902, p. 4; August 18, 1922, p. 5; Montay, p. 44; *New World*, July 4, 1908, p. 15.

16. Letter of a parishioner to Rev. Dennis J. Dunne, September 11, 1917 (Archives: 3-1917, D-41); Letter of Archbishop Mundelein to Very Rev. F. X. McCabe, C.M., President, De Paul University, September 25, 1917 (Archives).

17. Letter of Archbishop Mundelein to Mother M. Samuel, June 2, 1916 (Archives: 3-1916, S-73); *New World*, October 3, 1916, p. 1; Mundelein to Mother M. Samuel, October 10, 1916 (Archives: 3-1916, S-70); Mundelein to Mother M. Samuel, December 29, 1916 (Archives: 3-1916, S-69).

18. Mundelein to Mother M. Samuel, June 2, 1916 (Archives: 3-1916, S-73); *New World*, January 2, 1920, p. 1.

19. Ibid., February 6, 1920, p. 1.

20. Ibid., December 14, 1928, p. 1.

21. Ibid.

22. Ibid., April 30, 1920, p. 1.

23. See memorandum of Mundelein, 1920, referring to an offer of 100 acres of the University property to the Jesuits for their seminary. See also letter of Rev. Raymond Meagher, O.P., to Mundelein, September 28, 1920, referring to the Archbishop's invitation to the Dominicans

(Archives). In addition to the difficulty of getting the religious orders to cooperate, Mundelein's plan was also apparently resented by proponents among the hierarchy of the Catholic University of America in Washington, D. C. They saw Mundelein's university as a threat to making Catholic University the center of the Church's intellectual life in the United States.

24. Letter of Archbishop Mundelein to Sister M. De Pazzi, Mercy Hospital, November 14, 1922 (Archives); Archdiocesan Chancellor to Rev. Mother Stanislaus, Little Company of Mary Sisters, April 8, 1930 (Archives).

25. Thompson, p. 767.

26. Paul R. Martin, *The First Cardinal of the West* (Chicago: New World Publishing Co., 1934), pp. 21–23. See *New World*, January 6, 1928, p. 1; January 13, 1928, p. 1; January 20, 1928, p. 1; January 27, 1928, p. 1.

27. *New World*, October 24, 1930, p. 8; May 19, 1933, p. 10.

28. *New World*, April 15, 1899, p. 14, quoting a Mr. Bernard McHugh; Thompson, pp. 765–766. See also *New World*, June 4, 1920, Part I, p. 1.

CHAPTER 11

1. *Annual School Report, 1930–1931*, p. 5; *1931–1932*, p. 5; *1933–1934*, p. 5.

2. Ibid., *1933–1934*, p. 5.

3. Ibid., *1930–1931*, p. 5; *New World*, August 21, 1931, p. 12; May 26, 1933, p. 6.

4. *Annual School Report, 1930–1931*, p. 6; *1933–1934*, p. 5.

5. Ibid., *1937–1938*, p. 4; *New World*, November 14, 1930, p. 4; March 13, 1936, p. 4; September 15, 1938, p. 4.

6. Ibid., July 10, 1936, p. 1.

7. *Annual School Report, 1930–1931*, p. 5; *1931–1932*, p. 6; *1930–1931*, p. 7.

8. Address of Cardinal Mundelein at Archdiocesan Priests' Retreat, June 20, 1937 (Archives); *New World*, November 21, 1937, p. 1.

9. According to a confidential report on the state of the Archdiocese at the death of Cardinal Mundelein in 1939, the Chicago church enjoyed a very sound financial position despite the depression years (Archives, 1939).

10. *New World*, September 6, 1946, p. 1; December 28, 1951, p. 1.

11. Based on a socioeconomic analysis in *Suburban Factbook*, published by the Northeastern Illinois Metropolitan Area Planning Commission, revised edition, 1964, Table No. 8.

12. *Annual School Report, 1942–1943*, p. 4; *1944–1945*, p. 3.

13. Ibid., *1945–1946*, p. 6; *1950–1951*, p. 7; Cardinal Stritch to Rev. Gordon Walter, O.P., April 23, 1948 (Archives); *New World*, August 11, 1950, p. 13.

14. Cardinal Stritch to Msgr. Joseph Morrison, July 5, 1950 (Archives). On these negotiations, see memorandum for consultors' meeting, 1950, undated and unsigned; Rev. Theodore Mehling to Stritch, November 29, 1951; Mother Mary Jerome to Stritch, April 27, 1955, May 3, 1955, June 14, 1955; Stritch to Msgr. Thomas Meehan, October 22, 1955 (Archives).

15. *New World*, April 11, 1958, p. 48.

16. Ibid., June 27, 1952, p. 1.

17. *New World*, July 3, 1931, p. 1.

18. Quoted in *New World*, April 11, 1958, p. 29. McManus had been Assistant Director of the Educational Department of the National Catholic Welfare Conference in Washington, D. C.

19. Ibid., February 5, 1954, p. 11.

20. *Book of Policies: Archdiocese of Chicago School Board* (Chicago: privately printed, 1961), p. 8.

21. *New World*, November 25, 1949, p. 1. See also February 16, 1951, p. 9.

22. Memorandum from Cardinal Stritch to Chancellor Casey, 1955, undated (Archives). See also Rev. Robert J. Willmes, S.J., to Stritch, May 25, 1955; July 19, 1955 (Archives).

23. St. Ignatius and Fenwick high schools.

24. See Rev. Francis Houtart and Rev. Norbert Lacoste, "The Parishes of Chicago, 1843–1953, Historical Evolution, Geography, Population, Ecology" (Mimeograph, 1953); Eunice Felten, "The Social Adaptations of the Mexican Churches in the Chicago Area" (unpublished Master's dissertation, Divinity School, University of Chicago, 1941); Elena Padilla, "Puerto Rican Immigrants in New York and Chicago: A Study in Comparative Assimilation" (unpublished Master's dissertation, Department of Anthropology, University of Chicago, 1947); *New World*, January 10, 1941, p. 12 and August 22, 1941, p. 1.

25. *New World*, August 16, 1946, School Supplement, p. 13; May 7, 1948, p. 1; August 16, 1957, p. 4; March 20, 1964, p. 8, quoting Rev. Robert Bond, Chicago Disciples Union; June 5, 1964, referring to a suit filed against the legality of the shared time plan; *New World*, March 27, 1964, p. 1.

26. *New World*, May 1, 1959, p. 13.

27. Pope Pius XI, *Christian Education of Youth* (New York: The America Press, 1936), pp. 4, 26.

28. *New World*, August 21, 1953, p. 1, quoting a letter from Cardinal Stritch; August 16, 1957, p. 21, quoting Superintendent McManus; February 27, 1959, p. 3, quoting Meyer.

29. See Reports on Building Operations, Archdiocesan Consultors, December 1, 1954, December 9, 1954, December 12, 1955, and many others (Archives); *New World*, June 25, 1954, p. 10; Cardinal Stritch to Rev. P. J. Ronagne, March 24, 1955 (Archives); Report of Father Longan to Stritch, March 11, 1955 (Archives).

30. *New World*, August 21, 1953, pp. 2, 12, report of Superintendent Cunningham; February 27, 1959, p. 3.

CHAPTER 12

1. Sister Mary Robert Dennis, S.B.S., "St. Elizabeth's Parish and the Negro" (unpublished Master's dissertation, Department of Education, Catholic University of America, Washington, D. C., 1948). See also Cornelius J. Kirkfleet, *The Life of Patrick Augustine Feehan* (Chicago: Matre & Co., 1922), p. 214. The Third Plenary Council of Baltimore (1884) had urged the setting up of separate Negro churches and schools, but also insisted on the right of Negroes to attend any Catholic church or school. See Thomas T. McAvoy, C.S.C., *The Crisis in American Catholic History, 1895–1900* (Chicago: Henry Regnery Co., 1957), p. 32.

2. *New World*, October 1, 1892, p. 8; May 6, 1938, p. 5. Father Tolton, as the only Negro priest in the United States at the time, also assumed leadership on a wider scale. In 1896, he organized the St. Peter Claver Union on a national basis "to establish orphanages and schools for colored Catholic children and homes for aged colored Catholics." *New World*, February 22, 1896, p. 2.

3. Ibid., September 10, 1893, p. 4; April 16, 1910, p. 1.

4. Ibid., November 26, 1904, p. 17; April 16, 1910, p. 1; May 6, 1938, p. 5; *Defender*, March 22, 1913; March 29, 1913.

5. *New World*, April 20, 1917, p. 1; Mundelein to Very Rev. J. A. Burgmer, S.V.D., Provincial, St. Mary's Mission House, Techny, Ill., October 26, 1917 (Archives: 3–17, B-17); also reprinted in *New World*, November 2, 1917, p. 1.

6. *Defender*, November 17, 1917; James S. Madden and others, to Mundelein, December 7, 1917 (Archives); Chancellor Hoban to James S. Madden, December 11, 1917 (Archives). Copy of Address in Archives, December 20, 1917.

7. Chancellor Hoban to James Madden, December 26, 1917 (Archives).

8. *New World*, December 12, 1919, p. 4, editorial.

9. Mundelein to Very Rev. Peter Jansen, S.V.D., Techny, Ill., July 14, 1921 (Archives); *New World*, May 26, 1922, p. 6.

10. Jansen to Mundelein, March 13, 1922 (Archives).

11. Mundelein to Jansen, March 23, 1922 (Archives); Marvin R. Schafer "The Catholic Church in Chicago: Its Growth and Administration" (unpublished Doctoral dissertation, Department of Christian Theology and Ethics, University of Chicago, 1929), pp. 116–117.

12. Robert L. Sutherland, "An Analysis of Negro Churches In Chicago" (unpublished Doctoral dissertation, Department of Christian Theology and Ethics, University of Chicago, 1930).

13. Ibid.; *New World*, November 14, 1930, p. 6; Archdiocesan Chancellor to Mr. Milton Yandorf, a real estate dealer, August 21, 1930 (Archives). See also, Sister Mary Clarice Sobczyk, O.S.F., "A Survey of Catholic Education for the Negro in Five Parishes in Chicago" (unpublished Master's dissertation, Department of Education, De Paul University, Chicago, 1954), p. 13; Estella Anderson Faulk, "A Study of Catholic Education for Negroes in the Archdiocese of Chicago" (unpublished Master's dissertation, Department of Education, De Paul University, Chicago, 1948), p. 6.

14. *New World*, January 9, 1931, p. 6; February 20, 1931, p. 6.

15. Ibid., December 26, 1930, p. 6; Rev. J. F. Callaghan, St. Malachy's parish, to Archbishop Mundelein, November 29, 1917 (Archives).

16. Mundelein to Most Rev. P. Fumasoni-Biondi, Apostolic Delegate, Washington, D. C., November 20, 1930 (Archives).

17. *New World*, October 2, 1936, p. 8; Dennis, p. 15; *New World*, August 25, 1933, p. 1; June 4, 1937, p. 8; June 17, 1938, p. 5.

18. *New World*, November 5, 1937, p. 7, by Ruth S. Kerr.

19. Ibid., June 17, 1938, p. 5.

20. Letter of a parishioner to Stritch, September 7, 1942; Stritch's reply, September 9, 1942; parishioner to Stritch, September 20, 1942 (Archives).

21. Negro father to Stritch, August 23, 1943; Stritch's reply, August 28, 1943 (Archives). The Holy Family school, predominantly Italian by this time, was not opened to Negroes until after 1960.

22. State senator to Stritch, January 5, 1944 (Archives).

23. St. Clair Drake and Horace R. Cayton, *Black Metropolis: A Study of Negro Life in a Northern City*, 2 Vols. (New York: Harper & Row, 1962), pp. 196–97, footnote; *Defender*, March 9, 1946.

24. Parishioner to Stritch, September 24, 1950; Stritch's reply, September 28, 1950 (Archives).

25. See letters in Archives to Stritch from parishioners, June 27, 1950; July 1, 1950; July 8, 1950; Memorandum of Stritch to Chancellor Casey, 1950; pastor to Stritch, July 10, 1950 (Archives); parishioner to Stritch, September 12, 1950 (Archives); Stritch to pastor, September 15, 1950; pastor to Stritch, October 10, 1950 (Archives).

26. Auxiliary Bishop Bernard Sheil took a much stronger stand, and made an extremely favorable impact on the Negro community. See Drake and Cayton, op. cit., pp. 413–414, footnote; *Defender*, February 24, 1945.

27. Drake and Cayton, pp. 413–14.

28. See Faulk, p. 5; Archdiocese of Chicago Clergy Conference: *The Catholic Church and the Negro in the Archdiocese of Chicago*. Report prepared for the Clergy Conference of September 20–21, 1960 (Chicago: Archdiocese of Chicago, 1960), p. 15; School Board Files; Anthony J. Vader, "Racial Segregation Within Catholic Institutions in Chicago: A Study in Behavior and Attitudes" (unpublished Master's dissertation, Department of Sociology, University of Chicago, 1962), pp. 66–68.

29. *New World*, August 31, 1945, p. 1; see also Drake and Cayton, pp. 413–15; Faulk, pp. 6–7.

30. *New World*, November 14, 1930, p. 6; January 9, 1931, p. 6; Sister Mary Paula to Msgr. Casey, Chancellor, July 31, 1950 (Archives).

31. Sister Mary Samuel, O.P., Sinsinawa, Wisc., to Stritch, August 4, 1944; Stritch to Sister Mary Samuel, O.P., August 17, 1944 (Archives).

32. Parishioner to Stritch, September 11, 1946 (Archives); Letter of a parishioner to Stritch, September 12, 1957; and Stritch's reply, September 18, 1957 (Archives).

33. *New World*, June 17, 1960, p. 14; August 16, 1963, p. 2.

34. Nor did the schools seem to be a major refuge for non-Catholic whites. A study in 1962 found that no Catholic high school in changing neighborhoods had more than six non-Catholic white students. Vader, p. 75.

CHAPTER 13

1. This generalization about recent research in the history of American urban education has been drawn in particular from the works cited earlier by Kaestle, Katz, Ravitch, Schultz, and Tyack. Though these authors differ considerably in their interpretations, from Katz who openly criticizes so-called nineteenth-century educational reform to Ravitch who appears to endorse it, all nevertheless document the connection between growth of a centralized school bureaucracy and the effort to use the schools as an instrument of social control.

2. The parochial schools remained highly segregated, with 87 percent of the City schools 90 percent or more white or Black and 46 percent with no Blacks at all. Only 6.5 percent of the suburban schools had more than 10 percent Black. Spanish-speaking children accounted for another 11.2 percent of the City enrollment by 1975.

A Note on Sources

Of the primary sources used in this study, the Archives of the Catholic Bishop of Chicago, St. Mary's of the Lake Seminary, Mundelein, Illinois, 1833–1959, offered a large room full of letters, reports, and memoranda, most of which were still unindexed when this research was done. The material in these archives was used extensively, as the book's footnotes indicate. Newspapers provided much valuable material, especially the weekly diocesan newspaper, published from 1852 to 1854 as the *Western Tablet* and continuously after 1892 as the *New World.* They offer an invaluable factual record of Chicago Catholic affairs, and for some periods, especially from 1892 to 1917, perceptive social commentary and analysis. During the 1930's, the *New World* published an extended series of articles on the histories of local parishes and other Catholic institutions based both on available records and interviews with old-time parishioners. These afforded an eye witness glimpse into the past. Other Chicago newspapers were also used extensively, in particular the *Chicago Tribune* whose treatment of educational issues in Chicago has been indexed privately by Professor Robert McCaul of the University of Chicago and has now been published in the *History of Education Quarterly,* XIII (1973), pp. 97–107; 201–214. The Chicago Foreign

Language Press Survey, Chicago Public Library Omnibus Project, Works Project Administration, 1942, provided access to a large number of foreign language newspapers in translation. The Office of the Superintendent, Archdiocese of Chicago, holds annual school reports dating back to 1926, and more extensive files since the 1950's. Finally, the *Official Catholic Directory*, published annually since 1817 under a variety of titles and publishers, lists the name, location, ethnic affiliation, and enrollment of every Catholic educational institution in the United States by diocese; it was used as a primary source of such factual information.

The St. Mary's of the Lake Seminary library contains many shelves of local parish histories, memorials, annals, souvenirs, and biographies, most of them privately printed and uncritical, but of great value when used with care. Joseph J. Thompson's *The Archdiocese of Chicago, Antecedents and Development* (Des Plaines, Ill., 1920) contains a brief history of every Catholic institution in Chicago to 1920; F. C. Bürgler's *Geschicte der Katholische Kirche Chicago's* (Chicago, 1889) traces the development of nineteenth-century German Catholicism in Chicago; and Gilbert J. Garraghan, S.J.'s, *The Catholic Church in Chicago, 1673–1871* (Chicago, 1921) is the only published scholarly history of Catholic Chicago, but it ends with the great fire of 1871. A helpful source for Catholic secondary education in Chicago, especially for basic information regarding individual schools, is Sister Mary Innocenta Montay, *The History of Catholic Secondary Education in the Archdiocese of Chicago* (Washington, D. C., 1953). Also helpful is Daniel W. Kucera, *Church-State Relationships in Education in Illinois* (Washington, D. C., 1955). For the Church's approach to general social problems in Chicago, John P. Walsh, "The Catholic Church in Chicago and Problems of an Urban Society, 1893–1915" (unpublished Doctoral dissertation, History Department, University of Chicago, 1948) provided much insight, as did Marvin R. Schafer, "The Catholic Church in Chicago, Its Growth and Administration" (unpublished Doctoral dissertation, Department of Christian Theology and Ethics, University of Chicago, 1929). Numerous other dissertations, especially from the

University of Chicago and De Paul and Loyola universities, dealing
with specific institutions, Catholic religious orders, racial and ethnic
groups, are cited in the notes.

On Chicago public school affairs, in addition to the newspapers,
the *Proceedings of the Board of Education of the City of Chicago*
were used extensively. Among the most useful published and
unpublished works were John M. Beck's "Chicago Newspapers and
the Public Schools, 1890–1920" (unpublished Doctoral dissertation,
Department of Education, University of Chicago, 1953); numerous
papers in the files of the Havighurst-McCaul project, school and
Society in Chicago, University of Chicago; and George S. Counts'
School and Society in Chicago (New York, 1928).

For the general social, economic, and political background in
Chicago, Bessie Louise Pierce, *A History of Chicago*, 3 vols. (New
York, 1937, 1940, 1957) was probably the single most extensive
source. A wealth of other material is cited in the notes.

For the general background to educational developments in the
United States during this period, in addition to the annual proceedings of the National Education Association and the annual
reports of the United States Commissioner of Education, two books
were especially helpful: Lawrence A. Cremin, *The Transformation of
the School* (New York, 1961) and Edward A. Krug, *The Shaping of
the American High School* (New York: Harper & Row, 1964).

There is no definitive history of the Catholic Church in the United
States during this period. Probably the best source for the major
developments is John Tracy Ellis, *The Life of James Cardinal
Gibbons, Archbishop of Baltimore, 1834–1921* (Milwaukee, 1952).
On the problem of the Church's adaptation to American life, Thomas
T. McAvoy, C.S.C., *The Great Crisis in American Catholic History,
1895–1900* (Chicago, 1957) is helpful. For the Church's ethnic
problem in America, especially as it touched on the question of
assimilation to the American way of life, see Coleman J. Barry, *The
Catholic Church and German Americans* (Milwaukee, 1953). On the
specifically educational aspects of assimilation, which involved the
question of the Church's attitude to the public schools and to

building a separate school system, see Daniel F. Reilly, *The School Controversy, 1891–1893* (Washington, D. C., 1943).

The best source for developments within Catholic education nationally is the annual proceedings of the National Catholic Educational Association. There are also a number of published doctoral dissertations dealing with specific issues: on administration and organization, John M. Voelker, *The Diocesan Superintendent of Schools, A Study of the Historical Development and Functional Status of His Office* (Washington, D. C., 1935); on teacher training, Sylvester Schmitz, *The Adjustment of Teacher Training to Modern Educational Needs* (Atchison, Kansas, 1932), and John R. Hagan, *The Diocesan Teachers College* (Washington, D. C., 1932); on Catholic secondary education, Sister Mary Janet Miller, *General Education in the American Catholic Secondary School* (Washington, D. C., 1952), Edward F. Spiers, *The Central Catholic High School, A Survey of Their History and Status in the United States* (Washington, D. C., 1951), and James T. O'Dowd, *Standardization and Its Influence on Catholic Secondary Education in the United States* (Washington, D. C., 1935).

A more complete bibliography of the sources used in this study can be found in my dissertation, "The Education of Chicago Catholics, an Urban History," University of Chicago, 1970, also available on microfilm from the University of Chicago library. Many of these sources are cited in the footnotes.

Appendix A
Territorial History of
the Catholic Diocese of Chicago

1. To 1784: All of Illinois under jurisdiction of bishop of Quebec, Canada.
2. 1784–1808: The entire United States under Bishop John Carroll of Baltimore.
3. 1808–1827: Illinois under jurisdiction of the bishop of Bardstown.
4. 1827–1834: The Diocese of St. Louis, created in 1827, has de facto jurisdiction over northern and western Illinois, including Chicago area.
5. 1834–1843: The new Diocese of Vincennes administers all of eastern Illinois, including Chicago.
6. November 28, 1843: The Diocese of Chicago created, with jurisdiction over entire state of Illinois.
7. 1853: The Diocese of Quincy (changed to Alton in 1857) takes the southern tip of Illinois.
8. 1877: The new Diocese of Peoria created, leaving Chicago Diocese with all of Illinois north of the south line of Whiteside, Lee, DeKalb, Grundy, and Kankakee counties.
9. 1908: The new Rockford Diocese leaves Chicago with Cook, Lake, DuPage, Kankakee, Will, and Grundy counties.
10. 1948: The Diocese of Joliet, created from parts of Peoria and Chicago Dioceses, leaves Chicago with Cook and Lake counties.

Appendix B
Bishops of Chicago

1. William Quarter: March 10, 1844–April 10, 1848.
2. James O. Van de Velde: February 11, 1849–July 29, 1853.
3. Anthony O'Regan: July 25, 1854–June 25, 1858.
4. James Duggan: January 21, 1859–1870.
5. Thomas Foley: February 27, 1870–February 19, 1879.
6. Patrick A. Feehan: September 10, 1880–July 12, 1902.
7. James E. Quigley: January 8, 1903–July 10, 1915.
8. George Mundelein: December 9, 1915–October 2, 1939, made Cardinal, December 4, 1924.
9. Samuel Stritch: December 27, 1939–May 27, 1958, made Cardinal, February 18, 1946.
10. Albert Meyer: November 16, 1958–1965, made Cardinal December 14, 1959.
11. John Cody: August 24, 1965–

/

Appendix C
Editors of the *New World*

Though the *New World*'s policies on the major educational issues remained remarkably consistent under the several editors from 1892 to 1917, variations in treatment are discernible. The personalities of all editors, except the last, tended to dominate the entire paper.

1. James Hyde (September, 1892–March, 1894): The *New World* under its first editor was rather direct, unsophisticated, and focused more on specifically Catholic matters than on the broader issues of the day.

2. William Dillon (March, 1894–August, 1902): Under Dillon the paper may have achieved its peak of excellence. He was a lawyer, deeply concerned about public affairs, civic, national, and international, and commented on these with remarkable perceptivity, clarity of thought, and direct vigor of style combined with a nice touch of humor. He defined his aim as "to help our readers think for themselves, and to reach conclusions of their own" (*New World*, March 10, 1894, p. 6), and for the most part stuck to that intent. He came to the paper in 1893 without journalistic experience, and retired in 1902 to attend to a growing law practice. He later became the first dean of the Loyola University Law School.

3. Charles O'Malley (October, 1902–October, 1905; February,

1908–April 1910): This man came to the *New World* after 10 years of Catholic journalism elsewhere, announcing of himself: "Those who know him best scarcely accuse him of lacking courage" (ibid., October 22, 1902). He hardly underestimated. O'Malley nourished three intense dislikes: Protestantism, Socialism, and the public schools; and his attacks on each were often marked by distasteful and intemperate invective. His prejudices frequently prevented serious analysis of complex issues, and made his coverage of events highly selective and often erratic. He made enemies even within Catholic circles (ibid., January 17, 1903, p. 17; September 10, 1904, p. 16; October 22, 1904, p. 16), and there are suggestions in a farewell editorial of 1905 that his resignation may have been forced (ibid., October 21, 1905, p. 17). When rehired in 1908 after the sudden death of his successor, O'Malley promised that his policy would be "vigorous and aggressive but not unnecessarily abusive" (ibid., March 31, 1908); and one suspects that this was a condition placed on his return. He tried hard to adhere to it until his untimely death at 52 in 1910.

4. Reverend Thomas E. Judge (October, 1905–December, 1907): Judge had been a young Chicago pastor and a man renowned in the Chicago Catholic Church for his intellectual attainments, especially in philosophy and theology. He had edited the *Catholic Review of Reviews* and also founded the *Catholic Review of Pedagogy* in Chicago. The *New World* under Judge probably suffered from too much philosophy and too little journalism. One never feels close to events in reading his paper. He died suddenly in 1907 at the age of 43.

5. Thomas O'Hagan (April, 1910–February, 1913): O'Hagan, Canadian by birth, had been educated at the University of Ottawa, did graduate study at the Universities of Chicago, Wisconsin, Cornell, Columbia, and for a year in European universities (ibid., April 30, 1910, p. 4). He had teaching experience and lectured frequently on history and literature. Under his editorship the literary quality of the paper may have risen. He filled its pages with special features: book reviews, and some of his own poetry. Current affairs,

though not excluded, did not receive the thorough coverage one might have expected of the newspaper.

6. James Conwell (February, 1913–1917): Conwell had worked for several years on Chicago daily papers, then moved into Catholic journalism in Indianapolis seven years before coming to the *New World*. He announced "important changes in the reading matter, style, and make-up of the paper" (ibid., February 22, 1913), and that editorials would "have reference to current public questions and subjects of a practical nature and present importance from the Catholic viewpoint." Conwell approached the *New World* as a professional journalist; and, if he lacked Dillon's personal charm, he, at least helped regain the comprehensive and perceptive coverage of events that had been lost to a degree in the intervening years.

7. Reverend T. V. Shannon (1917–1936): Shannon's editorship marked the beginning of a strong clerical domination of the *New World*. From this period, the paper became mainly a vehicle for diocesan news, with little editorial comment other than reiteration of standard Catholic positions. Both Shannon and his clerical successors receded into virtual anonymity, not even listing themselves as editors.

Index